Instant Answers! AutoCAD 14

To Do This	Choose	Toolbar Button	Command Name or Typed Entry
Start a new drawing	File	New		NEW
Open an existing drawing	File	Open	Choose drawing		OPEN
Save a drawing	File	Save		QSAVE
Print or plot	File	Print	Set parameters		PLOT
Check spelling	Tools	Spelling		SPELL
Match properties	Modify	Match Properties	Select objects		MATCHPROP
Undo last command	Edit	Undo		U or UNDO
Launch your Internet browser	Help	Connect to Internet		BROWSER
Track a point	Cursor menu (SHIFT+right click)	Tracking		TK or TRACKING
Locate an endpoint	Cursor menu (SHIFT+right click)	Endpoint		END
Create a user coordinate system	Tools	UCS		UCS
Measure distance	Tools	Inquiry	Distance		DIST
List object properties	Tools	Inquiry	List		LIST
Save a view	View	Named Views	New		DDVIEW
Change the viewpoint to top view	View	3D Viewpoint	Top		DDVPOINT
Pan	View	Pan		PAN
Zoom	View	Zoom		ZOOM
Zoom to window	View	Zoom	Window		ZOOM W
Zoom to previous view	View	Zoom	Previous		OM P
Set object's layer current			MOLC
Create or edit a layer	Format	Layer		YER
Change the current layer	Format	Layer		LAYER
Change a layer's state	Format	Layer		LAYER
Change object properties	Modify	Properties	Select object or objects		DDMODIFY or DDCHPROP

Instant Answers! AutoCAD 14

To Do This	Choose	Toolbar Button	Command Name or Typed Entry
Draw a line	Draw | Line | Specify start point		LINE
Draw a polyline	Draw | Polyline | Specify start point		PLINE
Draw an arc	Draw | Arc | Follow prompts		ARC
Draw a circle	Draw | Circle | Follow prompts		CIRCLE
Draw a surface 3-D box	Draw | Surfaces | Box		3D
Draw a solid 3-D box	Draw | Solids | Box		BOX
Create a block	Draw | Block | Make		BMAKE
Insert a block	Insert | Block		DDINSERT
Hatch or fill an area	Draw | Hatch		BHATCH
Create multiline text	Draw | Text | Multiline Text		MTEXT
Creating single-line text	Draw | Text | Single Line Text		DTEXT
Erase	Modify | Erase | Select object or objects		ERASE
Copy an object	Modify | Copy | Select object or objects		COPY
Mirror	Modify | Mirror | Select object or objects		MIRROR
Move an object	Modify | Move | Select object or objects		MOVE
Rotate	Modify | Rotate | Select object or objects		ROTATE
Stretch	Modify | Stretch | Select object or objects		STRETCH
Trim	Modify | Trim | Select object or objects		TRIM
Extend	Modify | Extend | Select object or objects		EXTEND
Break	Modify | Break | Select object or objects		BREAK
Fillet	Modify | Fillet | Follow prompts		FILLET
Dimension a line	Dimension | Linear		DIMLINEAR
Insert a raster image	Insert | Raster Image | Click Attach		IMAGE

AutoCAD 14

Answers!
Certified Tech Support

Ellen Finkelstein

Osborne **McGraw-Hill**

Berkeley • New York • St. Louis • San Francisco
Auckland • Bogotá • Hamburg • London
Madrid • Mexico City • Milan • Montreal
New Delhi • Panama City • Paris • São Paulo
Singapore • Sydney • Tokyo • Toronto

Osborne **McGraw-Hill**
2600 Tenth Street
Berkeley, California 94710
U.S.A.

For information on translations or book distributors outside the U.S.A., or to arrange bulk purchase discounts for sales promotions, premiums, or fund-raisers, please contact Osborne/**McGraw-Hill** at the above address.

AutoCAD 14 Answers! Certified Tech Support

1234567890 AGM AGM 901987654321098

ISBN 0-07-882515-6

Publisher
Brandon A. Nordin

Editor-in-Chief
Scott Rogers

Acquisitions Editor
Joanne Cuthbertson

Project Editor
Emily Rader

Editorial Assistant
Stephane Thomas

Technical Editor
Christal Elliott

Copy Editor
Andy Carroll

Proofreaders
Linda Medoff
Paul Medoff

Indexer
David Heiret

Computer Designer
Michelle Galicia

Series Design
Michelle Galicia

Cover Design
Matthew Nielsen

To MMY, for teaching me that all creativity and intelligence come from within.

ABOUT THE AUTHOR...

Ellen Finkelstein has written several books on
AutoCAD and other computer topics. She has
been teaching and consulting on AutoCAD
since 1988.

Contents

Acknowledgments

This book would not have been nearly as complete or useful without the contribution of questions that I received from people who provide technical support on AutoCAD daily. The main body of questions (and answers) came from Technical Software, Inc. (TSI), probably the largest provider of AutoCAD support in the United States. TSI's expertise and experience were invaluable for this book. Thanks, too, to Matthew Kell, Autodesk's Product Support Manager, who gave me Autodesk's top five frequently asked questions (FAQs). These appear in the first chapter.

The great folks at Osborne were instrumental in bring this book to fruition. Joanne Cuthbertson, thanks for that initial phone call and for expertly presiding over the birth of this book. Stephane Thomas kept track of everything and was always supportive and cheerful. Emily Rader was a true professional, controlling every detail of the process. I don't know how she did it! Thanks also to the production people who work behind the scenes.

Andy Carroll was a great copy editor—his logical mind clarified a number of fuzzy paragraphs. Christal Elliott, who answers online questions about AutoCAD for Autodesk, was the technical editor. Her extensive knowledge of the arcane world of AutoCAD and her helpful suggestions greatly improved the book.

Finally, great thanks are due to my husband and kids, who helped out with the chores and put up with me while I was writing.

Introduction

AutoCAD is the most widely used technical drawing program in the world. The AutoCAD DWG file format has become the standard for architects, engineers, and designers everywhere. The reason is that AutoCAD is the most flexible, complete CAD program available. AutoCAD can meet any challenge. The nature of technical drawing and AutoCAD's vast store of capabilities have always made AutoCAD a very complex program.

AutoCAD Release 14 introduced many new features designed to make AutoCAD easier and faster to use. In addition, there are a number of completely new capabilities—for example, all the rendering features, previously sold as a separate product called AutoVision, are now an integral part of AutoCAD.

AutoCAD's interface with your computer system is more complex than that of most computer programs. You may have both a mouse and a digitizer, and you almost certainly have a printer and a plotter. Because most drawings go through several revisions and are often collaborative projects, managing drawings can be a time-consuming task in itself. Questions relating to peripherals and using AutoCAD on a network are often more involved than with most off-the-shelf software. As a result, you should expect that you will have many questions about how to use AutoCAD. Where should you go for answers?

Until recently, Autodesk, unlike most other software companies, didn't provide technical support for AutoCAD. Although Autodesk's Safety Net program now provides support, it does so at a cost of $65 per question. The Help menu within AutoCAD offers an extensive body of information, but it is often hard to locate the answer to your specific question; and search as you might, the answer may simply not be there.

Ideally, you should get support from your dealer. While some dealers include free support, others do not. Therefore,

you may have to purchase a support contract, either immediately or after the initial period of free support. And when you do call your dealer, he or she may not be available to answer your question immediately. (Of course, your deadline was yesterday.)

AutoCAD 14 Answers! is specifically designed to answer the real-life questions actual AutoCAD users ask. Many of these questions have been culled from Technical Software, Inc., probably the largest provider of AutoCAD technical support in the United States, as well as from user groups, the Internet, and Autodesk itself. Some questions also come from my own experience using AutoCAD and encountering its quirks and inconsistencies first hand. The book therefore makes the experience of multiple users available to you in an easy-to-access, question-and-answer format.

AutoCAD 14 Answers! is divided into eight chapters, each covering a distinct topic. Each chapter is further divided into sections organized by subtopics. Look in the table of contents to find the chapter and section that relates to your question. Near your question, you will find other related questions that will supplement your understanding of the topic. Each chapter also starts with "Answer Topics," a helpful listing of sections and questions. Finally, use the index to alphabetically locate a topic that you can't easily find using the table of contents or the "Answer Topics" sections.

In addition to the questions and answers, you will find tips to help you get your work done more quickly and easily, notes that provide supplemental information to help round out your knowledge of AutoCAD, and cautions to let you know when you should be careful to avoid problems. Boxed sections add helpful detail and background on the current topic.

Each chapter has an introductory section called "@ a Glance." This section gives you an overview of the chapter's topic. Taken together, all the "@ a Glance" sections provide a handy summary of AutoCAD 14's features.

CONVENTIONS USED IN THIS BOOK

AutoCAD 14 Answers! uses certain conventions designed to make the book easy to follow, the most important of which are these:

- **Bold** type is used for text that you need to type from the keyboard.

- *Italic* type is used for some labels and names, and for new terms and phrases.

- Small capital letters are used for keys on the keyboard such as ENTER and SHIFT. When you need to hold one key while pressing another, the two keys are connected with a plus sign, as in CTRL+T.

- "Right-click" means you should click something with the right (also called Return) button of the mouse.

- The word "press" is used when you press a key or keys on the keyboard.

- The word "select" is used when you select objects in a drawing. You may do this by clicking them with the pick button of the mouse or by using an enclosing or crossing window.

- The word "pick" is used when you should click an object using the pick button of the mouse.

Chapter 1

Top Ten Frequently Asked Questions

Answer Topics!

Top Ten Frequently Asked Questions @ a Glance

- You may have difficulty pasting a large spreadsheet into AutoCAD. This chapter explains several workarounds.

- Often more than one person shares an AutoCAD workstation. This chapter explains how to create a customized profile for each person.

- OLE objects, which are objects that you paste into your drawing from another application, can be tricky when you plot your drawing. You may need to check the nature of the OLE object, your printer driver, or your printer/plotter settings to resolve the problem.

- When you customize a toolbar button, you may occasionally lose the button image. In its place you will see a smiley face. Here's how to get back your original image.

- Using AutoCAD on a network brings its own set of considerations, including how to work on a drawing that is being used by someone else on the network.

- Another issue that arises on a network is how to restrict access to your drawings.

- An important issue for AutoCAD users is the maintenance of a parts or symbols library. This chapter discusses two methods.

- You may want to use your laser printer to print out drawings. Here's how to get your laser printer to use black-only printing so it looks more like a plotter.

- You can insert an AutoCAD drawing into a word processing document, to create a report or a manual. This chapter explains the best options.

- Find out how to use the many AutoLISP routines that are available to help you work faster and more efficiently.

 1. I pasted a big Excel spreadsheet into my drawing, but part of the spreadsheet was cut off. How can I get the entire spreadsheet into my drawing?

When you copy an Excel spreadsheet to the clipboard and then paste it into your drawing, Excel uses a Metafile, or Picture, format. Microsoft Excel restricts the size of its metafiles to 12½ inches across and down.

 Note: *The measurement of 12½ inches relates to the size of the spreadsheet when you print it from Excel. When you paste the spreadsheet into AutoCAD, it appears much larger. You can resize the spreadsheet in your drawing by clicking it and dragging the handles (small boxes) that appear.*

There are three ways to get around this limitation.

The simplest way is to reduce the height of the rows and/or the width of the columns so the range of cells will fit within the 12½-inch limitation. You can also try using a smaller font size.

Another option is to use the PASTESPEC command (choose Edit | Paste Special) and paste the Excel worksheet as an Image Entity. However, the quality is poorer than with the Picture format. The Image Entity is a one-unit image of the spreadsheet, which means that you will have to enlarge it greatly when you paste it into your drawing. To paste the spreadsheet as an Image Entity, follow these steps:

1. Copy the Excel spreadsheet to the clipboard and return to your drawing in AutoCAD.

2. Choose Edit | Paste Special.

3. In the Paste Special dialog box, choose Image Entity from the list, as shown in Figure 1-1.

4. Click OK.

5. At the "Insertion point <0,0>:" prompt, choose an insertion point.

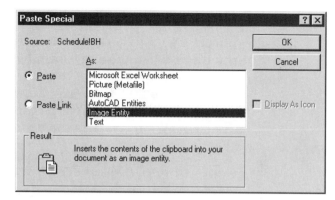

Figure 1-1   Choosing Image Entity in the Paste Special dialog box

6. At the "Scale factor <1>:" prompt, type or pick a scale factor. A scale factor of 1 will give you a tiny, stamp-size spreadsheet.

7. At the "Rotation angle <0>:" prompt, type the rotation angle you want or press ENTER to accept the default.

The third way to get your large spreadsheet into AutoCAD is undocumented and is the most complex of the three methods, but it may provide the results you require. It depends on the fact that Microsoft Word does not have the same 12½-inch limit that Excel does. Follow these steps:

1. In Excel, choose File | Save As.

2. In the Save As dialog box, choose Text (Tab delimited) (*.TXT) from the Save as type drop-down box.

3. Click Save.

4. Open Microsoft Word and start a new document.

5. Choose Insert | File.

6. In the Insert File dialog box, make sure that the Files of type drop-down box reads Text Files (*.TXT). Navigate your folders, if necessary, to find the text file you saved from Excel. Click OK. Don't worry if the text looks unorganized.

7. Choose Edit | Select All (or press CTRL+A).

8. Choose Table | Convert Text to Table. The dialog box should look like the one shown here. Word automatically calculates the number of columns, based on the number of tabs in the text document. Set the Separate Text At section of the Convert Text to Table dialog box to Tabs. Click OK. Word converts the text to a table.

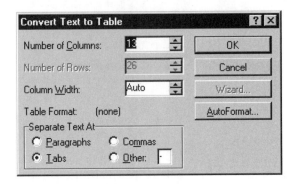

9. If necessary, choose File | Page Setup to format the page. Click the Paper Size tab and in the Paper Size drop-down list, choose Custom. Type in a width and height that will accommodate the entire table. You don't plan to print it, so the exact figures are not important. Click OK.

10. If you get a message, "One or more margins are set outside the printable area of the page," click Ignore.

11. Format the table appropriately, adjusting the column widths and row heights as necessary. You can also create borders.

12. If you want to be sure you'll have this document again as formatted, save it.

13. Press CTRL+A to select the entire table. Copy the table to the clipboard.

14. Open or switch to AutoCAD. Click Paste on the Standard toolbar to get the entire table.

Note: *Windows also has a Metafile limit that will affect any copying to the clipboard. According to Microsoft, this limit is 32,000 twips (1 twip = 1/20 point, 1 point = 1/72 inch).*

2. My coworker and I use AutoCAD on the same computer. One of us wants a black screen, the other wants a white screen, and we have several other varying preferences. How can we set up AutoCAD so we don't have to change all the settings each time we sit down to work?

AutoCAD offers three ways to customize your work environment: profiles, configuration files, and command-line switches. You can use one, two, or all three methods to make it easy for two or more users to share AutoCAD on one computer system. One person can also use these methods to create varying work environments for different projects.

Profiles

Choose Tools | Preferences to open the Preferences dialog box, and then use the Profiles tab, shown in Figure 1-2, to create user profiles. A profile is a collection of preference settings that you create using all the tabs in the Preferences dialog box. You can name your profile and make it current when you open AutoCAD.

Follow these steps to create a new profile:

1. Start by copying the current profile and then modifying the copy as needed. Choose Copy to open the Copy Profile dialog box. Type a name and description for your new profile and click OK. If you have never created a profile, this action copies the current settings in all the tabs of the Preferences dialog box.

2. Click Set Current.

3. Go through the other tabs in the Preferences dialog box and make the changes you want. For example, you might want a black screen, no scroll bars, full screen crosshairs, and no start-up dialog box.

Chapter 1   Top Ten Frequently Asked Questions

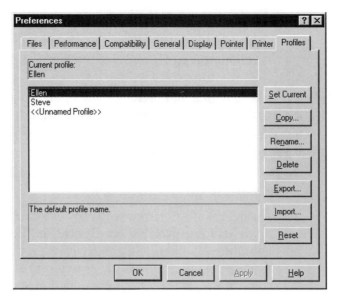

Figure 1-2   Using the Profiles tab to create profiles in AutoCAD

    4. Click Apply.

    The Profile tab also lets you edit a profile name or description, delete a profile, export or import a profile, and reset a profile to the default settings.

Tip: *To open AutoCAD automatically with your profile, use a profile command-line switch, as explained later in this answer.*

Configuration Files

Configuration files are text (ASCII) files that contain hardware configuration information—the computer platform, the configured plotters and digitizers, the plot drivers, pen color assignments, and so on. A configuration file is created automatically each time you open AutoCAD, with a default name of ACAD14.CFG. You may want to create additional configuration files if you often switch hardware configurations.

    To create a new file, follow these steps:

    1. Use Windows Explorer to make a backup copy of the configuration file. Rename the copy, for example, ACAD14-STD.CFG. If you wish to restore the original

configuration settings at a later time, you can change this filename back to ACAD14.CFG.

2. Open AutoCAD. Use the Preferences dialog box to make the hardware configuration changes you want.

3. Close AutoCAD.

4. Open Explorer, locate the updated ACAD14.CFG, and rename it, for example, HPPLOTTER.CFG.

To use a configuration file, you need to change the command-line switch that launches AutoCAD. Command-line switches are discussed next.

Command-Line Switches

When you open AutoCAD by choosing it from your Start menu or double-clicking a shortcut on your desktop, Windows executes a command-line statement. It might look like the following, depending on where you installed AutoCAD:

```
C:\Program Files\AutoCAD R14\acad.exe
```

By adding parameters, or *switches,* to this command line you can control how AutoCAD opens. You add a space after the ACAD.EXE command and add the switch at the end of the command. See Table 1-1 for a complete listing of command-line switches that you can use.

You can use several switches in one command-line statement. For example, the following command opens the drawing "bhousing" in the southwest view and runs the "setup" script file.

```
C:\Program Files\AutoCAD R14\acad.exe bhousing /v
southwest /b setup
```

Note: *Drawing and folder names in the command-line switches that contain spaces must have quotation marks around them.*

To change your command-line statement, the easiest method is to create a shortcut to AutoCAD on your desktop. To do this, use Explorer to find ACAD.EXE. Right-click it and choose Create Shortcut. Drag the shortcut, which is named

Example	Function
/c c:\acadr14\jennie.cfg (syntax: /c *config filename*)	Specifies a configuration file to use. Include the path if the file is not in AutoCAD's support file search path, as set in the Preferences dialog box.
/s c:\fonts	Specifies a folder for fonts, menus, AutoLISP files, linetypes, and hatch patterns when you want to use support files that are not in AutoCAD's support file search path.
/d c:\drivers	Specifies the location for ADI (AutoCAD Device Interface) drivers if you created or bought ADI device drivers or if you keep them in a separate folder.
Bhousing /b setup (syntax: *drawing name* /b *scriptfile*	Opens a drawing and runs a script file. (You can omit the drawing name if you want to run the script file with a new drawing.) "Bhousing /b setup" opens a drawing named "Bhousing" and then runs a script called "setup."
/t A-arch (syntax: /t *template filename*)	Opens a new drawing based on the specified template file.
/nologo	Starts AutoCAD without displaying the AutoCAD logo.
Bhousing /v southeast (syntax: *drawing name* /v *view name*)	Opens a drawing with the specified view.
/r	Resets AutoCAD to the default configuration.
/p jennie (syntax: /p *profile name*)	Specifies an existing profile to use for the current session. Note: The /p parameter does not use a path. In order to specify a profile, the profile must have already been created in or imported into AutoCAD. In other words, it must show up in the Profiles tab in the Preferences dialog box.

Table 1-1 Command-Line Switches

SHORTCUT TO ACAD.EXE, to your desktop. Click it once and rename it as you wish. Then follow these steps:

1. Right-click the shortcut.
2. Choose Properties.
3. Choose the Shortcut tab.
4. Use the Target text box to add your switches to the end of the command-line statement.
5. Click OK.

> ***Tip:*** *If you have customized ACAD.DWT, be sure to use the /t switch to add that template to your command-line statement.*

Multiple Configurations

To put profiles, configuration files, and command-line switches to best use, create as many desktop shortcuts as you need. Use the steps just listed to customize the command-line statements of the shortcuts with profiles and configuration files that you have created. You could name the shortcuts Joe's AutoCAD and Jennie's AutoCAD. Then Joe double-clicks his icon to get his configuration, and Jennie does the same with hers. This method takes some time to set up, but once done, customizing AutoCAD for individual users is a snap.

3. When I paste an image, an Excel spreadsheet, or another object into AutoCAD, it shows up fine onscreen, but doesn't plot or print. Why?

There could be several reasons, including the nature of the object, your choice of printer or plotter, or the capabilities of the selected printer or plotter driver. An object that you insert with the INSERTOBJ command (by choosing Insert | OLE Object), or paste from the clipboard into AutoCAD, is called an *OLE object*. (OLE stands for Object Linking and Embedding.)

Setting Your Plotter as the Windows System Printer

One solution is to use your Windows system printer, or to configure your plotter as the Windows system printer. To set your plotter as the Windows system printer, you need a printer driver for your version of Windows (Windows 95, Windows NT 4.0, or Windows NT 3.51). You can usually get this driver from the manufacturer of the printer or plotter, or from Microsoft. Then follow these steps:

1. Choose Start | Settings | Control Panel and double-click Printers.

2. Double-click Add Printer.

3. Follow the instructions to install the driver. (For example, in Windows NT 3.51, double-click Printers in the Control Panel, choose Create Printer from the

Printer menu, and follow the instructions to install the driver.)

4. In AutoCAD, choose Tools | Preferences and choose the Printer tab.

5. Click New.

6. In the Add a Printer dialog box, choose System Printer. Click OK.

Using OLE/ADI

If you have an older plotter, you may not be able to obtain a Windows driver for it. ADI (AutoCAD Device Interface) drivers are files that tell AutoCAD how to relate to peripheral devices, such as plotters. Release 14 now has a feature called OLE/ADI printing, which lets you print or plot on a nonsystem Windows printer or plotter. However, this feature is *not* part of the typical installation of AutoCAD, and you may not have installed it. To install it, follow these steps:

1. Put the AutoCAD CD into your CD drive.

2. Start the setup program using the instructions in the CD-ROM case.

3. At the first screen, click Next.

4. At the next screen, click Add to add to your current installation.

5. At the next screen, check OLE/ADI Plot.

6. Continue to follow the onscreen instructions.

 Tip: *If you have Windows NT 3.51, you need Service Pack 2 or later to print or plot OLE objects using ADI drivers. You can download this free of charge from Microsoft's FTP site at ftp.microsoft.com.*

 Note: *OLE objects do not rotate when you set the plot rotation to anything other than 0 degrees. You may be able to rotate the plot using the plotter's landscape mode or other available plotter commands.*

! *Caution:* *The OLE/ADI feature creates a configuration for a system printer called Phantom AutoCAD OLE/ADI Printer. Do not change or delete these settings; you won't be able to plot OLE objects and AutoCAD may crash during plotting. Also, the OLE/ADI installation sometimes sets the Phantom driver as the default Windows system printer, in which case you may need to change the default printer by choosing Start | Settings | Control Panel | Printers. To make a printer the default printer, click it and choose File | Set as Default.*

Determining the Nature of the Object

ADI drivers do not print OLE objects that are raster images. A raster image is a bitmap graphic. The solution is to embed the object as a Metafile, a Windows vector file format. To embed an object as a Metafile, choose Edit | Paste Special (the PASTESPEC command) and choose Metafile from the list of file types. Click OK.

Note: *If necessary, delete the OLE object and reinsert it as a Metafile.*

Tip: *To find out what type of OLE object you have in a drawing, right-click the object to open the OLE Object menu. You can often use this menu to convert the image to another format. To do so, choose Convert Picture Object and choose the format in the Convert dialog box.*

You may have trouble plotting an OLE object that contains another OLE object. For example, if you paste an Excel spreadsheet into a Word document and then paste that document into AutoCAD, the ADI driver may not be able to plot the OLE object. Therefore, try to avoid these *nested* OLE objects. Also, when plotting, you may get better results using the Display option in the Plot Configuration dialog box instead of the Limits or Extents options.

Note: *OLE objects are not even displayed if they are contained in inserted blocks or drawings or are in externally referenced drawings, nor are they printed.*

4.   I created a new toolbar button and it looked fine, but now when I open AutoCAD the toolbar button just shows a little yellow smiley face. Why did this happen and where is the original button?

The button is somewhere on your hard drive (or network), but not in a location that AutoCAD can find. When you create a new toolbar button, AutoCAD saves it as a bitmap (.BMP) file. AutoCAD looks for this file in its *support file search path,* which by default is the \Support subfolder in the folder where you installed AutoCAD. If the location is not in AutoCAD's support file search path, the next time you open AutoCAD you will see a yellow smiley face like the one shown here, instead of your button.

Tip: You can designate any additional folder or folders to be in the support file search path. For more information, see the next box, "Adding a Folder to the Support File Search Path." It is very useful to put support files you have created in a separate folder and place that folder in AutoCAD's support file search path.

When you create your own button, you use the button editor, shown in Figure 1-3. Clicking Save As opens the Save As dialog box, which lets you save your button under any name in any location. Take care to place the new bitmap file in one of AutoCAD's support directories listed on the File tab of the Preferences dialog box or add the folder to the support file search path. You can easily lose your bitmap file if you use the Save As button to save a new button. Of course, if your button is missing, maybe you or someone else moved the bitmap file.

Another way to "lose" a bitmap file is to edit the Toolbars section of your menu file directly and specify a bitmap file for a toolbar button that is not in the support file search path. The solution is to find the correct bitmap file and move it to a

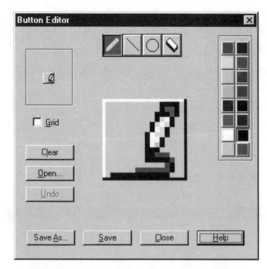

Figure 1-3 When you create a new button using the Button Editor, AutoCAD saves the image as a bitmap file

folder in the support file search path. Then close and reopen AutoCAD. Your toolbar will be back to normal.

 Tip: *An easy way to find bitmap files is to use Windows' Find feature. In Windows 95 and Windows NT 4.0, choose Start | Find. In the Named box, type ***.bmp** to find all the bitmap files on your system or in the location you specify in the dialog box.*

 Tip: *It's easy to look at bitmap files. You can view them with Microsoft Paint, which comes with Windows 95 and NT. Also, if you have Microsoft Word, choose Insert | Picture. When you find a bitmap file, click it. The bitmap appears in the preview box, making it easy to tell if that file is the one you want.*

5. When I open a drawing from the network, I get a message that says the file is 'read only.' How can I edit the file?

If another user has the drawing file open, you cannot edit the drawing. Therefore, AutoCAD opens the drawing in read-only

Adding a Folder to the Support File Search Path

To add a folder to AutoCAD's support file search path, choose Tools | Preferences and click the Files tab. Click the plus sign next to Support File Search Path to open up the list of current folders in the search path. Click Add. You can now either type a new folder (including its path) or click Browse to choose the folder from a dialog box.

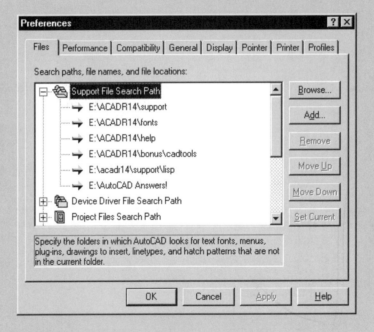

mode. This prevents one user from saving over another user's changes. You can wait until the other user closes the file, or you can choose File | Save As to make a local copy that you can edit. However, be aware that there are now two versions of the drawing on the network.

There are also other possible causes for this problem. See the last question in the "Incorporating External References

(Xrefs)" section in Chapter 5. User permission settings on a network might also limit file opening to read-only access. Check with your system administrator if you are not able to edit drawings in a specific folder.

On a stand-alone system, if you open a drawing in AutoCAD and then try to open the same drawing in a second instance of AutoCAD, you will get a message saying that the file is in use and asking if you want to open the drawing as read only.

Working with More Than One Release of AutoCAD

If you are working with more than one release of AutoCAD, you can get unexpected results when you try to open a drawing in a network environment.

- If the drawing is already open in Release 14 and you try to open it in Release 13, you get a message that AutoCAD cannot open the file.

- If the drawing is already open in Release 14 and you try to open it in Release 12, AutoCAD opens the drawing.

- If the drawing is already open in an earlier release of AutoCAD that has file locking on, you cannot open the drawing. However, if file locking is off, you can open and edit the drawing. Each user can overwrite the changes made by the other. For this reason, you should turn file locking on in the earlier releases.

 ### 6. How do I limit access to my drawings by other users?

AutoCAD does not provide a password security system. If you are using AutoCAD on a network, use the network operating system's password setup. If you are not on a network and wish to secure your drawings, use Windows NT, which provides more security features than Windows 95.

See the section "Using AutoCAD on the Internet" in Chapter 5 for a discussion of DWF files, which let you restrict access to drawings that you publish on a Web site.

 Note: *Release 14 no longer includes file locking to protect open drawings on a network. You must use the network operating system for this function.*

 ## 7. What's the best way to organize all the standard parts or symbols that I use?

You should create a parts or symbols library. There are two types of libraries that you can choose from and two methods of creating the parts or symbols. You design your library according to the method that best fits your needs.

Parts or symbols that are inserted into your drawing are called blocks. If you need to know how to create a block, see the box "Creating and Inserting Blocks" in Chapter 5.

The first type of library consists of a separate drawing file for each part or symbol. Generally, you place all these files in one folder and place the folder in AutoCAD's support file search path. Be sure to zoom into the part and make sure that a preview image will be created by setting the system variable RASTERPREVIEW to 1 before saving the file. You may want to plot each drawing, label it, and place the plots in a binder for easy reference. You can use AutoCAD's Batch Plot Utility for this purpose. To insert a part or symbol, follow these steps:

1. Choose Insert | Block to start the DDINSERT command.

2. Choose File from the Insert dialog box, shown in Figure 1-4.

3. From the Select Drawing File dialog box, choose the drawing file you want to insert and click Open. The preview on the right of the dialog box will help you to identify the symbol you want.

4. If you want to pick the insertion point for the block onscreen, leave Specify Parameters on Screen checked and click OK. In your drawing, specify the insertion point.

Figure 1-4 The Insert dialog box lets you insert both blocks and drawing files

5. On the command line, specify the scale and rotation angle for the block.

AutoCAD inserts the file as a block in your drawing.
    The second type of library puts all your parts or symbols in one drawing file. Again, you will probably want to place labels next to each part or symbol and print out the drawing for reference. The advantage to this type of system is that you have fewer files to keep track of, perhaps only one. To insert a part or symbol from this library file, follow these steps:

1. Choose Insert | Block.

2. Choose File from the Insert dialog box.

3. From the Select Drawing File dialog box, choose the drawing file you want to insert and click Open.

4. In the Insert dialog box, make sure that Specify Parameters on Screen is checked and choose OK.

5. At the "Insertion point:" prompt, press ESC.

AutoCAD has now inserted the block definitions into the drawing database without actually inserting the drawings. From now on, to insert any of your parts or symbols, choose Insert | Block and click Block in the Insert dialog box. All the

blocks are now listed and you can choose the one you want. You won't see a preview image of the blocks, however—just a list of the block names.

Tip: *Later on, you can eliminate the definitions of all the blocks you don't use with the PURGE command.*

Many block libraries store blocks at full size; this is probably the most common method. However, if you often scale and/or rotate your parts or symbols, you may want to use the *unit-block* method. Unit blocks are parts or symbols created at the size of one unit. You can then easily insert these unit-sized blocks at any scale or rotation. The unit-block method can be used with either type of library described above to store one block per file or many blocks per file.

8. I would like my laser printer to print out my drawing all in black rather than in shades of gray. How do I do this?

Choose Start | Settings | Printers and right-click your laser printer's icon in the Printers window. Click Properties. Different printers have different dialog boxes, but one common method is to click Graphics. Find the Dithering option and click None or turn it off. Click OK and close the Printers window.

If you still get poor results, here's another option:

1. Choose Tools | Preferences and click the Printer Tab.

2. Choose Default System Printer from the list of printers and click Modify.

3. In the Reconfigure a Printer dialog box, click Reconfigure.

4. In the AutoCAD System Printer Configuration dialog box, uncheck Allow Dithered Output and click OK.

5. AutoCAD opens the AutoCAD Text Window and asks you if you want to make any further changes. Press ENTER to accept the No default.

6. Click OK twice to return to your drawing.

9. What's the quickest way to bring an AutoCAD drawing into my word processor document?

You cannot use drag-and-drop to drag individual AutoCAD objects into another application. The copy and paste method works best: select and copy the objects to the clipboard in AutoCAD by choosing Copy to Clipboard on the Standard toolbar and paste them in your word processor. If you use Paste Special, you can import the AutoCAD drawing as an AutoCAD object, a picture (WMF format), or a bitmap.

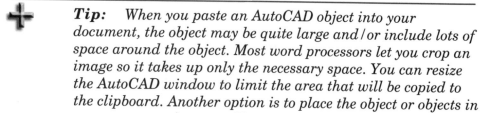

Tip: *When you paste an AutoCAD object into your document, the object may be quite large and / or include lots of space around the object. Most word processors let you crop an image so it takes up only the necessary space. You can resize the AutoCAD window to limit the area that will be copied to the clipboard. Another option is to place the object or objects in a paper space viewport. (For more information on paper space viewports, see Chapter 4.)*

If you choose Paste Link, changes in your drawing will be shown in your word processing document. Each time you open the document, your word processor will search for the AutoCAD drawing and reload it.

10. I found an AutoLISP routine on the Internet that I hope will solve all my problems. Now, how do I use it?

AutoCAD supports the programming language AutoLISP. AutoLISP programs can help you automate your work. For more information on AutoLISP, see Chapter 8.

Many AutoLISP routines that you download from the Internet come in a zipped file. If this is the case, you first need to use PKZIP, WinZIP, or another decompressing utility to unzip the file. You will often find instructions on how to use the file either at the top of the .LSP file itself or in a separate text file. Use a text editor such as WordPad to view the contents of the file. If this doesn't help, you may have to contact the developer who wrote it to ask some questions.

There are two basic ways to use an AutoLISP program.

Loading an AutoLISP File

If the routine is in its own file, copy this to a folder in AutoCAD's support file search path. You can load the routine in one of two ways:

● Load the file in a drawing by typing (**load** "*filename*") and pressing ENTER. Don't forget either the parentheses or the quotation marks. You don't need to specify the .LSP extension. AutoLISP responds by displaying the last command of the file on the command line. For example, if the file is REVLINE.LSP, you would type (**load "revline"**). If the file is not in AutoCAD's support file search path, you need to specify the path. Use forward slashes instead of backslashes to separate the parts of the path (for example, c:/mystuff/revline) because backslashes are reserved for special use in AutoLISP.

● Another way to load an AutoLISP file is to use the APPLOAD command. Choose Tools | Load Application. In the Load AutoLISP, ADS, and ARX Files dialog box (shown in Figure 1-5), you will see a list of previously loaded routines (if Save List is checked). If the routine you want to load is not on the list, click File to choose the routine from a dialog box. Find the file, select it, and click Open. Now select the routine from the Files to Load list and click Load.

You can now use the command that you want from the AutoLISP file. If the command you want was not the last command and so was not displayed, check the instructions or read through the AutoLISP code itself. Sometimes, brief instructions are displayed on the command line when you load the file. Press F2 to open the Text Window if they scrolled by too quickly.

Loading the Routine in ACAD.LSP

If you don't want to load the routine each time you start an AutoCAD session, or even a new drawing (if Reload AutoLISP between drawings is checked on the Compatibility tab of the Preferences dialog box), you can place the routine in ACAD.LSP. AutoCAD automatically loads ACAD.LSP

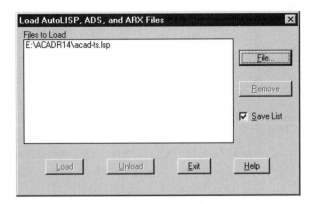

Figure 1-5   The Load AutoLISP, ADS, and ARX Files dialog box

whenever you open a new or existing drawing, so routines in this file are always ready for you to use.

 Tip: *Put routines that you use regularly in ACAD.LSP but keep others that you use occasionally in separate files to reduce the memory load.*

Follow these steps to place a routine in ACAD.LSP:

1. Open the file containing the routine.
2. Select the entire routine and copy it to the clipboard.
3. Open ACAD.LSP in Notepad from AutoCAD's \Support folder and press CTRL+V. If the file doesn't exist, open Notepad directly and paste the routine into a new file.
4. Save the file. If it is an unnamed file, save it as ACAD.LSP in AutoCAD's \support folder or another folder in AutoCAD's support file search path.

Chapter 8 covers AutoLISP files in greater detail.

Chapter 2

Getting Started with AutoCAD

Answer Topics!

Getting Started with AutoCAD @ a Glance

Installing AutoCAD is much easier in Release 14 than in earlier releases. Just put in the CD-ROM and choose one of the four types of installation: full, custom, typical, and compact. AutoCAD offers a wide array of bonus commands and utilities, which are installed only in a full or custom install. They add a number of customer-requested capabilities that you may find useful. Once the installation is done, you may still need to configure your plotter or digitizer before you can get down to work. Unfortunately, installing AutoCAD on a network is more involved and uses a different installation routine.

You can customize AutoCAD so that it opens in the folder you use most often. While you can't open Release 14 drawings in Release 13, you can save Release 14 drawings in Release 13 format.

You'll probably start out by using the online help a lot, whether you're a new user or just upgrading. Help has some new features that may seem strange, such as the inclusion of all its VBA (Visual Basic for Applications) terms. VBA is a programming language that Release 14 now supports. Help offers complete lists of commands and system variables and a fairly extensive list of How To's.

You can customize the toolbar placement and display any of the available toolbars to make your work easier. Right-click any toolbar to open the Toolbars dialog box. Check the toolbar you

want to display. You can display flyouts as toolbars if you want to see them permanently. As with any Windows program, you can drag toolbars anywhere on the screen and dock them at any of the four sides of the screen.

For Release 14, most configuration of AutoCAD is done in the Preferences dialog box, found under the Tools menu. Here you can set the location of supporting files, configure many settings that affect how AutoCAD functions, configure your pointing device and plotter, and create user profiles.

Release 14 offers several new features for the ever-present command line. Best of all is that you can now edit it, so you don't need to retype your entire entry when you make a mistake. You can also paste previous entries into the current command line. Pressing F2 opens the AutoCAD Text Window, which lets you see the command-line history for the entire drawing session.

As always, AutoCAD offers many options for viewing and specifying coordinates. To set the type of unit measurement, choose Tools | Units. Pressing F6 toggles between dynamic absolute, dynamic polar, and static absolute coordinate display on the status bar. Coordinates can be *absolute*—relative to 0,0 in the user coordinate system—or *relative*—relative to the last point you specified. You indicate relative points by placing the @ character before the coordinate. In 3-D drawings, you can also use cylindrical and spherical coordinates. The default way of measuring coordinates is based on the world coordinate system, where 0,0 starts at the lower-left corner of your screen and the X axis is horizontal and increases to the right, while the Y axis is vertical and increases upward. You can create your own user coordinate system (UCS) to meet your needs. UCSs are especially helpful for 3-D drawing.

INSTALLING AND UPGRADING AUTOCAD

 How much disk space do I need for AutoCAD Release 14?

AutoCAD offers four installation options. Choose the option that best meets your needs and available hard drive space.

Installation Type	Required Hard Drive Space
Typical	82MB
Full	112MB
Compact	46MB
Custom	Varies—up to 112MB

A typical installation installs the most commonly used tools. However, it doesn't install the bonus routines or the textures (used for rendering). A full installation installs everything. A compact installation would be ideal for a laptop or a situation where you have limited hard drive space. A custom installation lets you individually choose the items you want to install.

How do I decide which type of installation to do?

In order to decide which type of installation you should do, you really need to know which features are included in a typical installation. Table 2-1 lists the items available for installation and whether or not they are included in a typical installation.

From this chart, you can easily see if you need any of the items not automatically included in a typical installation. You may also find that you do not need some of those items, such as the samples and the learning tools. In either case, you should do a Custom installation. You can always go back later and add or delete items.

Use a compact installation if you are tight on hard drive space and a full installation if you have no hard drive constraints and think you'll use most of the features. If you're still not sure, do a Typical installation, which provides what Autodesk thinks most users need.

How do I set up a digitizer?

A *digitizer* is a flat, rectangular tablet that you use for both drawing and executing commands. It comes with a puck that you use instead of a mouse. Setting up a digitizer is a multistep process. For most work, you use a small area for

Option	Description	Included in Typical Installation
Program files	Executables, menus, toolbars, help files, templates, TrueType fonts, and additional support files. These constitute the basic AutoCAD program	Yes
Fonts	Non-TrueType fonts, for example, SIMPLEX.SHX	Yes
Samples	Includes sample drawings, ActiveX examples, database examples, and AutoLISP examples	Yes
Learning tools	AutoCAD tutorials	Yes
Bonus routines and applications	A set of additional commands and routines	No
Dictionaries	Spelling dictionaries	Yes
External database	Lets you access external databases using the AutoCAD SQL Environment	No
ADSRx	ADS is a programming language that lets you create your own applications that work with AutoCAD. It is being superseded by the ObjectARX programming language	No
Batch plotting	Batch Plotting Utility for doing mass plotting	Yes
Texture maps	Materials and textures used in photorealistic rendering; also landscape objects for rendering	No
Internet	Internet Utilities for creating drawings that you can display on the Web	No
OLE/ADI printing	Lets you plot OLE objects on a plotter or any nonsystem Windows printer	No

Table 2-1   AutoCAD Release 14 Installation Options

your drawing area and the rest for commands. When you want to *digitize* a drawing (translate a drawing from hard copy to electronic form), you may decide to recalibrate the digitizer so that the entire digitizing tablet is available for drawing.

AutoCAD provides a sample tablet drawing called TABLET14.DWG, which is found in the \Sample subfolder of your AutoCAD installation folder. This drawing, shown in Figure 2-1, is a good basis for creating your own customized tablet drawing.

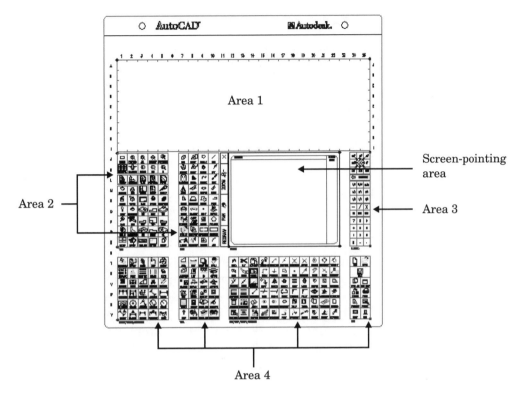

Figure 2-1 AutoCAD's default tablet drawing

Each of the small boxes represents a command. The top area is blank so that you can insert your own customized commands. AutoCAD's menu, which you can customize, includes a tablet section that corresponds to all the small boxes in this drawing. For more information on customizing AutoCAD's menu, see Chapter 7.

Configuring a Digitizer

To configure your digitizer for use as both a drawing tool and a menu, follow these steps:

1. AutoCAD comes with a plastic template for the default tablet menu, which you can place on your digitizer. It fits an 11×11-inch tablet. If you're not familiar with

how to customize AutoCAD's menus, start with the default tablet.

Tip: *If you want to customize the commands and placement—and most people do—open TABLET14.DWG, make the desired changes, save it under a new name, and print it. For a different size digitizer, you need to enlarge the drawing or completely redesign it to meet your needs. For example, if you have a larger digitizer, you might want to significantly increase the drawing area section. Print out the drawing and carefully tape the drawing to your digitizer. If the digitizer has a glass plate, place the drawing under the glass.*

2. To tell AutoCAD how to relate the template to its menu, choose Tools | Tablet | Configure. The tablet menu has four sections, corresponding to the four menu sections of the template. AutoCAD asks you for the number of tablet areas you want. Type **4** if you are using the default template. If you are customizing the tablet menu, you can use from 0 to 4 areas.

3. AutoCAD asks if you want to align the tablet menu areas. Type **y** and press ENTER.

4. Now AutoCAD prompts you to digitize (pick) the upper-left, lower-left, and lower-right corners of the first area of the tablet. These three corners are enough to specify an exact rectangle for each area. Use the digitizer's puck to pick each corner. The three points must create a 90-degree angle. If they don't, AutoCAD rejects the points and asks you to digitize them again.

Note: *The default template and drawing include filled circles (donuts) to indicate these points. The upper-left corner of area 2 is the same as the lower-left corner of area 1. Similarly, several other filled circles are used for two areas.*

5. AutoCAD asks you for the number of columns for the first area. The default template has 25 columns, so type **25** if you are working with that template.

6. AutoCAD asks you for the number of rows for the first area. The default has 9 rows.

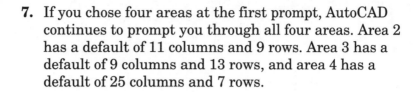

7. If you chose four areas at the first prompt, AutoCAD continues to prompt you through all four areas. Area 2 has a default of 11 columns and 9 rows. Area 3 has a default of 9 columns and 13 rows, and area 4 has a default of 25 columns and 7 rows.

Note: *Area 3 looks like it has only 3 columns, but it includes an empty column to the left, and each column is configured to be narrower than those of the other areas. For this reason, use the default of 9 columns if you are working with the default template and tablet menu.*

8. AutoCAD now asks if you want to respecify the screen-pointing area. Type **y** and press ENTER.

9. AutoCAD prompts you to pick the lower-left and upper-right corners of the screen-pointing area, that is, the drawing area.

10. The TABLET prompt now asks if you want to specify a floating screen-pointing area. You use this for digitizing paper drawings into AutoCAD. Type **y** and press ENTER.

11. AutoCAD asks if you want the floating screen-pointing area to be the same size as the fixed screen-pointing area. Type **y** for general use of the digitizer. You can press F12 to switch to the floating screen-pointing area. When you use the floating screen-pointing area, you can access menu commands from anywhere on the digitizing tablet so that you can both digitize and use commands.

12. The prompt asks if you want to specify a button to toggle the floating screen area. You can type **n** and press ENTER to use the F12 key, or type **y** to specify one of the buttons (but not the pick button) on your digitizing puck.

Note: *If you use both a mouse and a digitizer, select Tools | Preferences and choose the Pointer tab. In the "Accept input from" section, choose "Digitizer and mouse."*

If you use your digitizer to digitize paper drawings, you need to calibrate the digitizer as well. For more information, see the box, "Calibrating a Digitizer."

Calibrating a Digitizer

When you want to digitize a drawing, you usually need more space than the small drawing area you have specified for general use. In addition, you need to match the scale of the drawing to the size of the digitizer. Then, when you pick points on the drawing, they are turned into full-scale objects in your drawing.

To calibrate a digitizer, follow these steps:

1. Tape the paper drawing to your digitizer. If it doesn't fit, you will have to digitize the drawing in sections, being careful to match the section corners.

2. Decide on at least two points on the drawing whose coordinates you can calculate. If the drawing is dimensioned, you should be able to find two points on an object, set one point to 0,0 and calculate the other point based on the dimension. Otherwise, measure an object with a ruler, apply the scale factor, and calculate the appropriate coordinates. If the drawing has not been stretched or distorted in any way and is scaled accurately, two points are enough, although three points can provide greater accuracy. You can pick more points if you wish. If the x and y dimensions are distorted, you need at least 3 points. If you want to translate a perspective drawing (so that converging parallel lines are made truly parallel), you need at least four points. Again, you can pick more.

3. Choose Tools | Tablet | Calibrate to start the TABLET command with the Calibrate option.

4. AutoCAD asks you to digitize point #1. Pick the point carefully, placing the puck crosshairs directly over the point.

     Tip: *It helps to stand up and look directly down at the point.*

5. AutoCAD asks you for the coordinates of point #1. Type an x,y coordinate.

6. AutoCAD asks for the same information for point #2. Pick the point and type an x,y coordinate.

7. AutoCAD asks for the same information for point #3. You can press ENTER to end calibration or continue to specify points. Note that AutoCAD's calculations for four or more points can take awhile.

8. If you specified only two points, AutoCAD uses an orthogonal *transformation,* or means of translating the points into coordinates. If you specified three or more points, AutoCAD computes all three types of transformations and provides a table showing the results for each type of transformation. You can then choose the orthogonal transformation or one of two other transformations:

   ● Use Affine when horizontal dimensions are stretched relative to vertical dimensions. Lines that are supposed to be parallel should actually be parallel, that is, there should not be any perspective distortion.

   ● Use Projective when you want to correct parallel lines that appear to converge. The typical example is a set of railroad tracks that become closer and closer, giving the impression of distance.

9. AutoCAD uses the transformation you requested and ends the TABLET command.

10. At the command line, type **tablet** and press ENTER. Then type **on** and press ENTER. You can also usually press CTRL+T to toggle the tablet on and off. You can use the command line to issue commands or press F12 if you need to use a menu or toolbar. Press F12 again to return to picking points.

11. Start a drawing command as described in the previous step and pick points on your drawing to specify the object. Continue in this manner until the drawing is complete. Save the drawing.

12. Do any necessary cleanup, such as attaching lines that do not exactly meet, adding text and dimensions, and so on.

Caution: *The tablet calibration is not stored. When you close AutoCAD, the calibration is lost. If you need to leave your work, you may want to leave AutoCAD running.*

 ## I use Windows NT 3.51. Is this a problem?

No, AutoCAD Release 14 runs on Windows NT 3.51. To install, insert the CD-ROM, choose File | Run in Program Manager, and type *d*:**setup** where *d* is your CD-ROM drive. If you install the Internet Utilities (using a full or custom installation), you must also update your Windows NT by installing Service Pack 4 or 5, available from Microsoft (www.microsoft.com).

How do I install AutoCAD on a network?

Before installing AutoCAD on a network, you need to know the following:

- Where the file server and the workstations will be
- Where the main AutoCAD program files, such as ACAD.EXE, will be
- Which protocol you want to use for license management, TCP/IP or IPX
- The maximum number of people who will use AutoCAD at one time
- What the server and workstation operating systems will be

AutoCAD uses its Autodesk License Manager (AdLM) to monitor the number of concurrent AutoCAD users at any one time. AdLM won't allow more instances of AutoCAD to be opened than were purchased. The AdLM program should be installed on the server, not a workstation.

To start installing AutoCAD on a network, sit at the computer where you will load AdLM, and use the setup program in the \Netsetup folder on the CD. If the regular setup program starts automatically when you insert the AutoCAD R14 CD, exit it. You can start the network setup program by choosing Start | Run and typing *D*:**Netsetup\ SETUP.EXE** (where *D* is your CD-ROM drive) in the Open text box. You must have Administrator rights on your file server to run the network setup program. Choose Autodesk License Manager Installation Only, and select Install License

Manager Files and Tools. Choose the protocol you want to use.

The second phase is to run AdLM Admin, which generates a server code. You then need to contact Autodesk to get a network authorization code (call them at 800-551-1490). You should be able to provide Autodesk with the Host Name, Server Code, and your AutoCAD serial number(s). When you receive the authorization code, type it where indicated in the AdLM Admin dialog box. You can now close the dialog box.

Choose Start | Settings | Control Panel, and double-click the new AdLM icon. Choose Automatic Startup and click Launch, then OK. Close the Control Panel. AdLM does a self-diagnosis and starts itself.

The third phase is to install AutoCAD on the workstations. Go to a workstation, log in as an administrator, start the Network Setup program as you did earlier on the server. This time choose Network and AdLM installation. Follow the instructions to specify folders for Client Deployment (the setting up of AutoCAD on a workstation) and for Server File location. Choose the protocol you used on the server, and choose installation of AutoCAD R14 files. You can then start AutoCAD from that workstation by double-clicking the R14 icon. Repeat these steps for each workstation.

Note that there are two installation options. A Network Deployment runs AutoCAD from the file server. Network Deployments save workstation disk space and are easier for the network administration to update. A Client Deployment installs all the files necessary to run AutoCAD on the workstation. Client Deployments result in less network traffic and therefore faster performance.

How do I know if I want to install the bonus routines?

The bonus routines are actually user requests that didn't make it into the official program. Some of them are quite useful and one might be just what you've been missing. Here's a brief description of each and you can decide for yourself. Table 2-2 lists the bonus commands on the Bonus Standard toolbar.

Bonus Routine	Description
Extended Change Properties	Adds capabilities to the Change Properties command, using a dialog box interface that allows you to change the width and elevation of polylines and change the height and style of text objects.
Multiple Entity Stretch	Lets you use multiple crossing windows or crossing polygons to define a stretch of more than one object.
Move Copy Rotate	Moves, copies, rotates, and scales multiple objects using one base point.
Extended Trim	Trims objects to a cutting edge that can be a line, circle, arc, or polyline.
Extended Clip	Clips blocks, external references, or images to a cutting edge that can be a circle, arc, or polyline. Similar to the XCLIP or IMAGECLIP commands, but approximates a curved clipping edge by creating short line segments.
Multiple Pedit	Edits multiple polylines. Can convert multiple lines and arcs to polylines.
Copy Nested Entities	Copies objects that are nested in external references or blocks.
Trim to Block Entities	Lets you use a block or external reference as a cutting edge in a trim operation.
Extend to Block Entities	Lets you use a block or external reference as a boundary edge in an extend operation.
Wipeout	Lets you hide a portion of your drawing as defined by a polyline. Wipeout actually fills the polyline with a solid fill that matches the background color of your drawing.
Revision Cloud	Creates a *revision cloud*, a cloud shape indicating that a revision was made.
Quick Leader	Opens a four-tab dialog box (after you press ENTER at the "First Leader point or press ENTER to set Options:" prompt), enabling you to set leader options.
Pack 'n Go	Copies all dependent files for a drawing to the desired location so you can include them when you send someone a drawing.
List Xref/Block Entities	Displays the object type, name, layer, color, and linetype of nested blocks or external references.

Table 2-2   Bonus Commands on the Bonus Standard Toolbar

Table 2-3 lists the bonus commands on the Bonus Text Tools toolbar. All these commands assist you in creating and editing text.

Table 2-4 lists commands on the Bonus Layer Tools toolbar. All these commands help you manage layers.

Besides the three toolbars, there is a bonus menu. Most of these items duplicate those found on the toolbars, but

Bonus Routine	Description
Text Fit	Changes the width factor of text to fit it between two specified points.
Text Mask	Creates a wipeout (see the Wipeout bonus command in Table 2-2) behind text so that text that crosses objects is easier to read.
Change Multiple Text Items	Globally changes the properties (height, justification, location, rotation, style, text string, and width) of one or more text objects.
Explode Text	Changes text to lines and arcs. You can then give them thickness or elevation. Note: This command does not work well with all TrueType fonts.
Arc Aligned Text	Aligns text along an arc. It's also possible to select previously created arc-aligned text and edit it. A dialog box lets you choose from the many available options.
Find and Replace Text	Uses a dialog box to find and, if you wish, replace text created with TEXT or DTEXT. You can specify the search to be case sensitive and you can make global changes.
Explode Attribute to Text	Explodes block attributes to single-line text. (The EXPLODE command explodes attributes to their tag and you lose the attribute's value.) The text takes on the attribute definition's layer and style.
Global Attribute Edit	If you have one block with attributes inserted several times in a drawing, this command lets you globally change an attribute value for every instance of that block.

Table 2-3   Commands on the Bonus Text Tools Toolbar

Bonus Routine	Description
Layer Manager	Uses a dialog box to name and save *layer states,* which are configurations of the states (on/off, thawed/frozen, locked/unlocked, current) of your layers. You can then restore the configuration whenever you want. You can also save the layer state configuration to a file (*.LAY) and import it when you want, so that you can use the configuration in other drawings. Installing the bonus routines also installs eight sample LAY files in the \Bonus\Cadtools subfolder of your AutoCAD folder. These files are designed to meet AIA (American Institute of Architects) standards for architects.
Match Object's Layer	Changes the layer of selected objects to match a layer whose name you type or the layer of an object you select.
Change to Current Layer	Changes selected objects to the current layer.
Isolate Object's Layer	Turns off all layers except the layer of the object you select.
Freeze Object's Layer	Freezes the layer of the object you select. Does not work on the current layer.
Turn Object's Layer Off	Turns off the layer of the object you select. Three options let you determine how blocks, *xrefs* (external references), and objects nested in blocks and xrefs are handled.
Lock Object's Layer	Locks the layer of the object you select.
Unlock Object's Layer	Unlocks the layer of the object you select.

Table 2-4 Commands on the Bonus Layer Tools Toolbar

Table 2-5 lists those commands that are found only on the menu.

Finally, there are a few specialized commands that are available on the command line only. These are listed in Table 2-6.

Actually, there are more items; AutoCAD also adds a few drivers, utilities, the SHP files for the SHX font files, some SHP and SHX Asian fonts, and additional sample drawings. All in all, the bonus item adds many useful functions to AutoCAD.

 Note: *To install the bonus routines, you must also install Batch Plotting, because they share certain files.*

Bonus Routine	Description
Turn All Layers On	Turns all layers on.
Thaw All Layers	Thaws all frozen layers.
Extended Explode (XPLODE)	Not a new command for Release 14, XPLODE lets you control the resulting color, linetype, and layer for the new objects. You can explode objects individually or globally.
Attach Leader to Annotation	Attaches an existing leader line to existing multiline text, a tolerance, or a block.
Detach Leaders from Annotation	Detaches an attached leader line from multiline text, a tolerance, or a block.
Global Attach Leader to Annotation	Attaches multiple leaders to the most likely annotation object.
Get Selection Set	Creates a selection set with the specified layer and/or type of object.
Pline Converter	Permanently converts polylines to Release 14 lightweight polylines.
Command Alias Editor	Provides a dialog box to edit command aliases that are stored in the ACAD.PGP file.
System Variable Editor	Provides a dialog box to change system variable values. You can also save the settings to an SVF file and later use it as a script file to restore all the saved system variable values.
Xdata Attachment	Attaches extended data to objects. (Extended data is data attached to an object in addition to the object's properties already contained in the drawing database. You can then retrieve this data and manipulate it. Extended data is usually created using ARX or AutoLISP.)
List Entity Xdata	Lists extended data of objects.
Dimstyle Export	Saves dimension styles to a file.
Dimstyle Import	Imports saved dimension styles.
Pop-Up Menu	Lets you use one of the drop-down menus as a cursor menu for easy access.

Table 2-5   Bonus Commands on the Bonus Menu

If you uninstall the bonus item and then reinstall it, the bonus menu and toolbars do not automatically load. Type **bonusmenu** at the command prompt to load the menu and toolbars.

Bonus Routine	Description
ASCPOINT	Creates line segments, a polyline, a 3-D polyline, multiple copies of a selection set of objects, or points based on coordinates from a text file.
BLK_LST.LSP	This AutoLISP routine contains four commands that list blocks and attributes.
BLOCKQ	Lists objects contained in a block.
COUNT	Creates a table listing the number of insertions of each block you select. (You can select the entire drawing to get a drawing-wide listing.)
CROSSREF	Lists blocks that contain the specified layer, linetype, style, dimstyle, mlinestyle, or block.
DBTRANS	An aid for translating text from Release 11 or earlier drawings.
DOSLIB	A library of DOS functions you can use in AutoLISP.
JULIAN	Routines to convert to and from Julian dates.
PQCHECK	An AutoLISP parenthesis and quotation mark checker.
SSX	Creates a selection set of objects matching a selected object. You can use the filter options to adjust the properties matched.

Table 2-6 Command-Line-Only Bonus Commands

What are the main new features of Release 14?

Many of the new features of Release 14 are designed to help you work more quickly and efficiently, but there are a number of added functionalities as well. Here is a summary of the major new features of Release 14:

● AutoCAD has been enhanced to reduce the time it takes to open, save, and display files.

● The graphics system requires less memory. Also, there are two new objects, the lightweight polyline and the new hatch object, which are stored more efficiently in the database. However, they function the same way as before.

● Displaying paper space doesn't require a regeneration. You can now zoom and pan in paper space just as you do in model space. Paper space is covered in Chapter 4.

● Object snaps are now displayed using AutoSnap, which provides a geometric marker, a Snap Tip (like a ToolTip), and a magnetic pull of the cursor toward the object snap. The OSNAP button on the status bar turns on and off running object snaps. See Chapter 3 for more on object snaps.

- Tracking lets you locate a new point based on the coordinates of existing points. Tracking is explained in detail in Chapter 3.

- Release 14 offers complete support for raster (bitmap) images, including scanned graphics and photographs. There is a new Image dialog box that lets you manage images in one location.

- Layer and linetype management has been simplified and enhanced on the Object Properties toolbar. Chapter 3 includes more on working with layers and linetypes.

- There is a new button on the Object Properties toolbar, Make Object's Layer Current, that lets you set the current layer to the layer of a selected object.

- There is a new button on the Standard toolbar, Match Properties, that copies properties such as color and linetype from one object to another.

- There is a new Toolbars dialog box that lets you display and customize toolbars from one location. See Chapter 7 for more on customizing toolbars.

- There are a number of shortcut menus that appear when you click the right mouse button. These appear when you right-click selected objects with grips, any toolbar, the command line, embedded objects, and certain dialog boxes.

- You can finally edit the command line. Details are provided later in this chapter.

- You can pan and zoom in real-time, just by moving the cursor. Chapter 3 offers some tips for zooming and panning.

- The Multiline Text Editor has new features, such as Character, Properties, and Find/Replace tabs, and a drop-down box to insert symbols. In addition, there is support for True Type font styles such as bold and italic. Chapter 4 has more information about creating text.

- There are new wizards to help you set up your drawing. Chapter 3 explains how to set up a drawing.

- Release 14 uses templates instead of prototype drawings for saving settings and standardized objects and text. The template is a different file type than a drawing, with an extension of .DWT. Chapter 3 includes more information on templates.

- You can finally use the hatching feature to create solid fills.

- All the features of AutoVision, previously a separately sold application, are now part of the rendering module. Specifically, you can now create shadows, transparent materials, and realistic reflections. There is also a sun locator so that you can place a light where the sun would be at a specific geographic location, date, and time. Chapter 6 details some of these new features.

- There is a new External Reference dialog box that lets you manage external references (xrefs) in one location and see their relationships to each other and your drawing. There are also enhancements to the display of large xrefs. See Chapter 5 for more information on xrefs.

- There is a whole new set of commands to let you create DWF (Drawing Web File) files. You can attach links, as well as insert and open drawings. There is a new button on the Standard toolbar that launches your Web browser. See the section "Using AutoCAD on the Internet" in Chapter 5 for several questions and answers on the DWF file format.

- The new Preferences dialog box lets you configure AutoCAD in one location. This multitabbed dialog box significantly improves the management of your AutoCAD system. You can save named sets of preferences, called *profiles*, so that different users can quickly change to their preferred settings. Setting Preferences is covered later in this chapter.

- The Batch Plot Utility lets you plot any number of drawings at one time. One suggested use is to create a set of draft plots overnight.

- Release 14 supports ActiveX automation, a means of customizing and integrating applications. You can

therefore create programs that integrate AutoCAD with other applications that support ActiveX. Release 14 includes VBA (Visual Basic for Applications), a programming language that you can use with ActiveX. See Chapter 8 for more details.

As you can see, Release 14 has many new features for you to explore. You will find this release both quicker and easier to use. Most of these new features are well covered in this book.

OPENING AUTOCAD

When I open AutoCAD and start the OPEN command, the dialog box always defaults to displaying my AutoCAD R14 folder. How can I get AutoCAD to default to a folder of my choice?

Right-click the shortcut that you use to start AutoCAD. From the menu, choose Properties to open the Properties dialog box. Click the Shortcut tab, shown in Figure 2-2. In the Start in text box, type the path of the folder you want to start in.

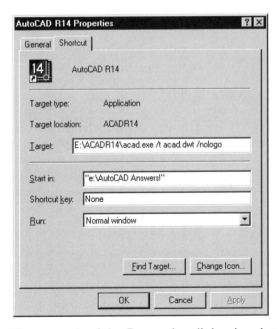

Figure 2-2   The Shortcut tab of the Properties dialog box lets you change where AutoCAD starts when you open a drawing

From now on, when you start AutoCAD and open a drawing, the Open dialog box will start with the folder you specified.

  Note: *If you open a drawing from a different folder, then for subsequent OPEN commands in the same drawing session, AutoCAD uses that different folder as the default.*

 ### Some of our clients still have AutoCAD Release 13. Can they use my Release 14 drawings?

They can't open Release 14 drawings in Release 13, but you can save your drawings in Release 13 format. Features that are unique to Release 14 (such as solid fill hatches) will not be displayed. To save a Release 14 drawing in Release 13 format, follow these steps:

1. Choose File | Save As.
2. In the Save Drawing As dialog box, click the Save as type drop-down arrow and choose AutoCAD R13/LT95 Drawing (*.DWG).

 ***Note:***   *You can also save a drawing in R12 / LT2 format.*

3. Type a name for the drawing in the File name text box or accept the default.
4. Click Save.

  Caution: *If you save your drawing again, on closing AutoCAD or opening another drawing, AutoCAD automatically saves the drawing in Release 14 format. To keep the Release 13 drawing as a separate drawing, give it a different name from the Release 14 drawing.*

GETTING HELP

 ### I see AIG, AUG, and ACG after topics in Help. What do these mean?

AIG is the AutoCAD Installation Guide, AUG is the AutoCAD User's Guide, and ACG is the AutoCAD

Customization Guide. These were once three separate books and have maintained their identities in the online help.

I see some pretty weird stuff listed in the Help index, like ActiveDimStyle property and LoadShapeFile method. What are these?

Release 14 has a new programming language that it supports—VBA (Visual Basic for Applications). These are keywords that you would use in VBA code. See Chapter 8 for more information on using VBA.

Where can I find a list of system variables?

Choose Help | AutoCAD Help Topics | Contents and double-click Command Reference. Double-click System Variables to get a complete listing. To see all the system variables as they are currently set in your drawing, use the System Variable Editor bonus tool.

Where can I find easy instructions for completing basic tasks?

The How To section of Help is very useful if you want to know how to complete a basic task. Choose the Contents tab and double-click How To. Scroll down the list and choose the item that best fits what you want to do. Double-click the item's book icon and a further list opens up. The list doesn't include basic drawing tasks but covers nearly everything else.

USING TOOLBARS

What's the easiest way to open and close a toolbar?

Right-click any toolbar to open the Toolbars dialog box. Scroll down to find the toolbar you want and click its check box. Click Close to close the Toolbar dialog box.

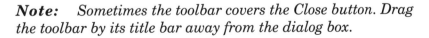

Note: *Sometimes the toolbar covers the Close button. Drag the toolbar by its title bar away from the dialog box.*

The easiest way to close a toolbar is to click its Close button at its top-right corner. If the toolbar is docked, it

doesn't have a Close button. In that case, drag the toolbar from its border onto the drawing area to undock it, and then click the Close button.

 What do I do if I want a flyout, such as the Zoom flyout, to remain visible all the time?

In Release 14, all the flyouts are also toolbars. Just right-click any toolbar and choose the flyout from the Toolbar list and it appears! You can dock it at any side of the screen for permanent use.

✳ ***Note:*** *For more information on customizing toolbars, see Chapter 7.*

SETTING PREFERENCES

 Are there any items in Preferences that should not be left at the default setting?

Yes, you should change the automatic save time from 120 minutes (every two hours!) to every 15 or 20 minutes. Choose Tools | Preferences and the General tab. Make sure Automatic save is checked and change the Minutes between saves text box to 15 or 20.

 My coworker and I use AutoCAD on the same computer. One of us wants a black screen, the other wants a white screen, and we have several other varying preferences. How can we set up AutoCAD so we don't have to change all the settings each time we sit down to work?

This is one of the top ten frequently asked questions. See question #2 in Chapter 1 for the answer.

 How do I change the screen color from black to white?

In Release 14, all configuration changes are made from the Preferences dialog box. To change the screen color, follow these steps:

1. Choose Tools | Preferences.

2. Click the Display tab.

3. In the AutoCAD window format section, click Colors to open the AutoCAD Window Colors dialog box, shown in Figure 2-3.

4. At the top right of the dialog box, choose Graphics window background from the Windows Element drop-down box. (To change other elements, choose one of the other options.)

5. For any basic color, such as white, click the colored square you want. You will see the result in the Graphics Window preview at the left. If you want an exotic color, use the RGB controls to change the color.

6. Click OK twice to return to your drawing.

Note that you cannot change the background color of the preview in the Open dialog box or the Print Preview window.

How do I get the full-screen crosshairs back?

You're not alone in wanting the crosshairs the way they used to be. Choose Tools | Preferences and click the Pointer tab. In the Cursor size section change the Percentage of screen size text box to 100. Click OK.

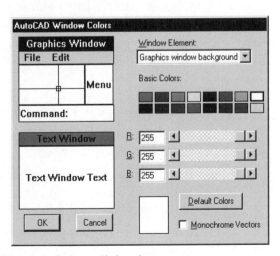

Figure 2-3 The Window Colors dialog box

 I changed the color of my screen and now I can't see the crosshairs. Where did they go?

You probably changed the color of the screen to that of the crosshairs. You can either change the color of the screen to be different from the crosshairs or change the color of the crosshairs. See "How do I change the screen color from black to white?," two questions back, for instructions on changing the screen color.

To change the color of the crosshairs, choose Tools | Preferences | Display and click Color. In the Window Element drop-down list, choose Crosshair color. Click the color swatch for the color you want. Click OK twice to return to your drawing.

 What is the support file search path and why is it useful?

The support file search path is the folder where AutoCAD searches for support files such as AutoLISP files, fonts, hatch patterns, linetypes, and so on. By default, this is the \Support subfolder in your AutoCAD folder. However, you can add a folder to this path if you want to place files that you've created or obtained in a separate folder. That way AutoCAD will be able to find your files. Follow these steps:

1. Choose Tools | Preferences and click the Files tab.
2. Click the plus sign to the left of Support Files Search Path. All the current folders in the search path are displayed.
3. Click Add.
4. A new row opens so you can type the new path.
5. Since it's easier to locate the folder in a dialog box than to type it, click Browse.
6. In the Browse for Folder dialog box, locate and select the folder you want to add to the search path. Click OK. Your folder appears on the list of folders in the search path.
7. Click OK to return to your drawing.

❓ Is there any way to continue to use CTRL+C to cancel a command as I did in DOS Release 12?

Autodesk hasn't forgotten you old-timers. Choose Tools | Preferences and click the Compatibility tab. In the Priority for accelerator keys section, click AutoCAD classic. (No, it's not a kind of cola.) Click OK.

❓ The Windows taskbar is taking up precious room on my screen. Can I get rid of it?

You can't actually get rid of it but you can hide it. There are two ways to do this. To set the properties of the taskbar, right-click on any unused area of the taskbar and choose Properties. This opens the Taskbar Properties dialog box, shown in Figure 2-4.

The most common setting is to check both Always on top and Auto hide. The result is that the taskbar is hidden when the mouse cursor is not over it, but when you move the mouse

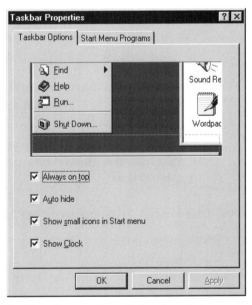

Figure 2-4   The Taskbar Properties dialog box lets you customize how the taskbar functions

cursor to the bottom of the screen, it appears. This setting
lets you have the taskbar always available when you need it,
without it taking up space when you don't need it.

The only problem with this setting is that you may find
that when you want to use AutoCAD's status bar buttons,
such as SNAP or OSNAP, you inadvertently display the
taskbar, which then hides the status bar. This can be very
frustrating if you're not careful where you place the cursor.

The other setting that hides the taskbar is checking only
Auto hide. This hides the taskbar, but you don't have access
to it as long as AutoCAD, or any other application, is
maximized—that is, takes up the entire screen. To access the
taskbar, you have to click the Maximize button as it appears
in a maximized application. This reduces the size of the
application and frees up space for the taskbar, which appears
when you move the cursor to the bottom of the screen.

WORKING WITH COMMANDS

 ### How can I reuse an earlier command-line entry so I don't have to retype it?

Release 14 offers new options to make command-line entry
easier. Here are the two basic techniques:

- To reuse the last line you entered, press the UP ARROW,
  and then press ENTER to execute the command.

- To reuse earlier lines, press F2 to open the AutoCAD Text
  Window. Scroll to the entry you want and highlight it.
  Right-click and choose Paste To CmdLine from the menu
  that pops up.

How can I edit the command line?

Editing the command line is a new feature for Release 14.
You can edit the command line using standard Windows
editing keys. The following table shows how these keys work:

Key	Action
LEFT ARROW	Moves cursor to the left
RIGHT ARROW	Moves cursor to the right
BACKSPACE	Erases character to the left of the cursor
DELETE	Erases character to the right of the cursor
HOME	Moves cursor to the far left
END	Moves cursor to the far right
INSERT	Toggles between insert and overwrite modes

My plotting dialog box has disappeared! I now have to use the command line. Where did the dialog box go?

Somehow, the CMDDIA system variable was set to 0. This usually is done by an AutoLISP routine. The AutoLISP routine should set CMDDIA back to 1, but if you canceled operation in the middle, it could remain at 0, and the Print/Plot Configuration dialog box will not appear. To get it back, type **cmddia** and press ENTER. At the prompt, type **1** and press ENTER.

My Save Drawing As and Open dialog boxes have disappeared? What happened?

The FILEDIA system variable was set to 0. This is usually done by an AutoLISP routine. To get back the dialog boxes that ask for files, type **filedia** and press ENTER. At the prompt, type **1** and press ENTER.

One of my custom toolbars at the right of my screen disappeared. Where did it go and how can I get it back?

If the reason it disappeared is that it is just not being displayed, right-click any toolbar to open the Toolbars dialog box. Find your missing toolbar in the list and check its box. Click Close to close the dialog box.

If the toolbar is not listed, it may be in a different menu group. Click the Menu Group drop-down box and choose the toolbar's menu group. This should display the toolbar in the Toolbars list.

If the missing toolbar's box in the list is checked and the toolbar still doesn't display, it could be that someone changed the resolution of the screen, perhaps from 1,024×768 to 800×600, and there is no longer room for the toolbar on the screen. Uncheck the toolbar in the list in the Toolbars dialog box and try the following:

1. With the Toolbars dialog box open, choose the toolbar's name in the list and click Properties. The Toolbar Properties dialog box opens, as shown here:

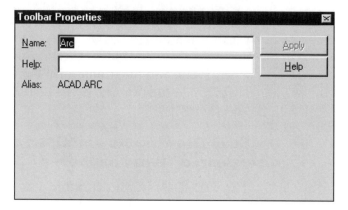

2. Find the toolbar's alias. In the illustration above, it is ACAD.ARC.

3. Click the Close button to close the Toolbar Properties dialog box and close the Toolbars dialog box.

4. On the command line, type **-toolbar**. This executes the TOOLBAR command on the command line. (Note that without the hyphen, a dialog box will open instead.)

5. At the first prompt, type the alias of the toolbar.

6. At the next prompt, type **f** (for Float) and press ENTER.

7. At the next prompt, press ENTER to accept the default position. This will display the toolbar at the top left of the screen.

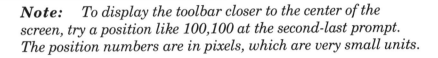

8. At the final prompt, press ENTER to display the toolbar in one row.

9. You should now see the toolbar at the top left of your screen, and you can drag it to any location.

Note: *To display the toolbar closer to the center of the screen, try a position like 100,100 at the second-last prompt. The position numbers are in pixels, which are very small units.*

How can I find out the name of a command?

If you know the menu or toolbar location of a command that you want to use, choose the menu item or toolbar button. The command name appears on the command line. You can then press ESC to exit the command if you wish.

Tip: *If a command starts with DD, it opens a dialog box. However, many commands that don't start with DD also open dialog boxes.*

USING COORDINATES AND COORDINATE SYSTEMS

Is there any way to use Direct Distance Entry at unusual angles? It seems to be useful only for right (orthogonal) angles.

Direct Distance Entry is a great way to specify distances, such as the length of a line or the distance to move an object. Just point the cursor in the direction you want and type the distance instead of the usual x,y format. Generally, it works best with ORTHO on, so you can control the direction of the cursor. But what if you want to move the cursor at a 10-degree angle? For just one distance, it's probably easiest to use polar coordinates (for example, @3.5<10). However, if you have several distances at the same angle (or at angles that are 90 degrees from each other such as 10, 100, 190, and 280 degrees), the easiest method is to change the snap angle. To do so, choose Tools | Drawing Aids to open the Drawing Aids

dialog box. Figure 2-5 shows the Snap Angle set to 10 degrees. Click OK to return to your drawing. You will see that the crosshairs are at an angle. Notice, however, that the user coordinate system (UCS) icon remains unchanged.

Tip: *When working with rotated snap angles, it's often helpful to use full-screen crosshairs. Choose Tools | Preferences and click the Pointer tab. In the Cursor size section, set the Percentage of screen size to 100.*

If you turn on ORTHO, you can now easily create lines at a 10-degree angle and at its 90-degree increments, as shown here:

Of course, Direct Distance Entry can also be used for moving, copying, or any editing commands where you need to specify a distance.

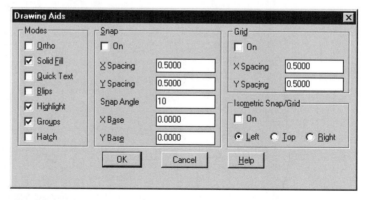

Figure 2-5 The Drawing Aids dialog box

Another possibility is to create a user coordinate system (UCS). By changing the UCS you change the entire coordinate system. If you need to do quite a bit of work at a different angle, a UCS, while more difficult to understand, can be easier to work with. For example, if you tilt the X and Y axes 10 degrees, you can think in terms of the more familiar 0-, 90-, 180-, and 270-degree angles but get the same results as if you had changed the snap angle.

To create a user coordinate system, use the UCS command by choosing Tools | UCS and selecting one of the submenu options. If you're working in 2-D and want to rotate the X and Y axes 10 degrees as in the previous example, the Z Axis Rotate option is easiest. The origin remains the same and AutoCAD displays the "Rotation angle about Z axis <0>:" prompt. Just type **10** and press ENTER. Notice that the UCS icon is now rotated along with the crosshairs. Turn on ORTHO and you can use Direct Distance Entry at the angles of the axes.

How are architectural units typed? I'm confused about where to put hyphens and spaces, especially for fractional inches.

The reason you are confused is that the way you type architectural units is different from the way they appear on the status bar. Architectural notation uses fractions for parts of inches. You must separate the fraction from the whole inches with a hyphen. You cannot use any spaces because AutoCAD interprets a space as equivalent to pressing ENTER and ends your input. However, the status bar places a hyphen between the feet and the inches and a space between whole and fractional inches. This use of a hyphen gets particularly complex when you are typing in negative numbers that also use a hyphen to indicate the negative value. Here you see some architectural notation as you need to type it in, and as shown on the status bar:

Typed Format	Status Bar Format
13'3-1/2"	13'-3 1/2"
-1'2-3/8"	-1'-2 3/8"

 Is there a way to use CAL (AutoCAD's calculator) to evaluate a mathematical expression inside a relative coordinate?

Yes. To create a coordinate using CAL, place it in square brackets as in the following example:

1. Start the LINE command.
2. At the first prompt, pick any From point.
3. At the next prompt, type **'cal** and press ENTER. AutoCAD starts the calculator.
4. At the final prompt, type your calculation, for example **[@(3.25+1.61)<30]**, and press ENTER.

In this case, AutoCAD draws a line that is 4.86 units long at an angle of 30 degrees from the start point. You can include any valid CAL expression to represent a distance in a coordinate.

 I want to draw a line in 3-D, but I don't know the length of the line. If the line I want to draw is like the hypotenuse of a right triangle, I know only two sides of the triangle. Is there a way to do this?

AutoCAD has a method of specifying coordinates just for this situation, called cylindrical coordinates. See Chapter 6 for a detailed explanation of both cylindrical and spherical coordinates.

I want to use the last point I specified at the prompt, let's say for the center of a circle. Can I do this if I'm not sure where the last point is?

Just type @ at the prompt, which means *last point*. If you are drawing a line, you can also press ENTER at the prompt to start the line from the last point.

Chapter 3

Starting to Draw

Answer Topics!

Starting to Draw @ a Glance

When you are ready to start drawing in AutoCAD, you need to set up your drawing to suit your needs. Release 14 offers a new feature—drawing templates. These are similar to the templates used in many other Windows programs, allowing you to save unit and angle types, layers, text styles, dimension styles, blocks, and other system variables. Also, because you draw at full size in AutoCAD but often plot at a different scale, you need to understand how to calculate the scale factor and apply it to text, dimensions, and noncontinuous linetypes so that they appear in an appropriate size when you plot your drawing.

AutoCAD offers numerous drawing aids to speed up your drawing. The most commonly used tool is object snaps. You can snap to endpoints, midpoints, intersections, centers, and many other geometric points. You can set running object snaps to make it even easier to find the points you need. Tracking is a new feature that lets you quickly locate a new point based on existing points. It can be faster than using point filters, but there is a trick to getting the right point each time. Point filters are still necessary for 3-D work, however.

Layers are the mechanism you use to manage object properties—specifically, color and linetype. The Object Properties toolbar, which lets you control layers, colors, and linetypes, has been updated in Release 14 to work more like other Windows programs. The Layer & Linetype Properties dialog box is also new, providing a one-stop layer management feature. A helpful feature when you have dozens of layers is the ability to filter the list of layers to suit your needs. You can also give a layer a noncontinuous linetype.

AutoCAD keeps track of the properties of every object in your drawing. You can use the LIST or DDMODIFY command to get information about an object.

 AutoCAD offers many ways to display your drawing. New for Release 14 are real-time zoom and pan, a definite time saver. Also, most of the familiar ZOOM options are still available in Release 14. Aerial View is a quick way of panning and zooming in one operation and is especially useful for very large drawings. Tiled viewports are also useful for viewing large drawings; they divide up the screen into two or more windows, and you can set the view in each one. Floating viewports are used to lay out your drawing for printing or plotting. You can save configurations of tiled and floating viewports for future use.

SETTING UP A DRAWING

 ### How do I transfer all my Release 13 prototype drawings to Release 14 templates?

Release 14 adds a new file format, .DWT, for template files. It works like your word processor's template. To use your Release 13 prototype drawings as templates, follow these steps:

1. Open each prototype drawing in Release 14.

2. Choose File | Save As.

3. In the Save as type drop-down box at the bottom of the dialog box, choose Drawing Template File (*.DWT).

4. In the File name text box, type a name. Leave out the filename extension. AutoCAD will automatically give the file a .DWT extension.

5. If you want your templates to appear in the Start Up dialog box so you can easily choose them, double-click to open the \Templates subfolder in your AutoCAD folder. You will see all the default templates.

6. Click Save.

7. In the Template Description dialog box, type a description of the template and click OK. AutoCAD saves the template.

Follow this procedure for all your prototype drawings.

 Tip: *To create a new template from scratch, apply all the drawing settings you need in a new Release 14 drawing; then follow the same procedure.*

To use a template from within AutoCAD, follow these steps:

ew on the Standard toolbar.

reate New Drawing dialog box, choose Use late.

the template you want from the Select a te list. For each template, you will see the tion you created at the bottom of the dialog box. D also shows you a preview of each template hlight.

K. AutoCAD opens a new drawing, initially DRAWING.DWG, based on the template.

ur templates when launching AutoCAD, start d in the Start Up dialog box choose Use a hoose the template you want and click OK.

include in a template drawing?

hould include some or all of the following:

Purpose	How to Set
Sets the unit and angle types.	Use one of the Setup Wizards or choose Format I Units.
Sets the height and width of a drawing.	Use one of the Setup Wizards or choose Format I Drawing Limits.
Layers	Organizes your drawing by color and linetype.	Choose Layers from the Object Properties toolbar.
Text styles	Defines font, font style, height, and other text properties.	Choose Format I Text Style.

Item	Purpose	How to Set
Blocks, including a title block	Loads the blocks you will need. You can include the title block.	Choose Make Block from the Draw toolbar, or choose Insert Block from the Draw toolbar if the block already exists.
Multiline styles	Loads multiline styles.	Choose Format I Multiline Style.
Dimension styles	Includes dimension styles in your drawing.	Choose Dimension I Style.
Drawing aid settings	Presets drawing aids (snap, grid, ortho, osnap, and so on).	Choose Tools I Drawing Aids.
Profiles	Stores all the settings from the Preferences dialog box.	Choose Tools I Preferences and click the Profiles tab.

How do I calculate a scale factor so I can create text and dimensions of the proper size?

Scale factors are used for regular text, dimensions (including the text, arrows, etc.), and noncontinuous linetypes. In a drawing that will be greatly scaled down at plot time, you need to know the scale factor or these objects will be too tiny to see! This is especially true of architectural and civil engineering drawings that are plotted to scales like 1:48, 1:96, or even higher.

Remember that you draw full size in AutoCAD. But objects like text, dimensions, and noncontinuous linetypes are not real objects. You use them to make the drawing clearer but they have no true size by themselves. Your only concern is that these elements are clearly visible when they are plotted to a scale. Assuming you are scaling down at plot time, you need to make these items bigger by the same factor you use at plot time so that the end result is that they are the proper size on the sheet of paper.

Calculating the Scale Factor

To get the right results, you need to calculate the scale factor. But first, you need to figure out what scale you are going to use when you plot your drawing. A scale is generally written

in the syntax *plotted size:actual size*. The actual size is the same as the drawing size, since you draw full scale.

Here's an example: Let's say you're drawing the layout of a house that's 40 feet by 30 feet. You want to plot it on size B paper which is 11×17 inches. For the standard sheet sizes, see the table below. A typical architectural scale is ¼"=1'. This means that 40 feet would plot out at 10 inches, and 30 feet would plot out at 7¼ inches. This would give you plenty of room for the house, dimensions, any necessary annotation, and a title block.

To calculate the scale factor, transform the scale into the format 1:*f* where *f* is the scale factor and both sides of the scale are in the same units. Therefore, ¼"=1' is the same as 1:48 because one foot is 48 times the length of ¼ inch.

To calculate the scale, you need to know both the size of the drawing (including allowances for a title block, dimensions, annotation, various views, etc.) and the size of the paper (with an allowance for margins) that you will plot on. Here are the standard sheet sizes:

Standard English Sheet Sizes (in inches)			Standard Metric Sheet Sizes (in mm)		
Size	Width	Height	Size	Width	Height
A	11	8½	A4	297	210
B	17	11	A3	420	297
C	22	17	A2	594	420
D	34	22	A1	841	594
E	44	34	A0	1,189	841

Using the Scale Factor

To use the scale factor in text, set the text height to the scale factor and multiply by the desired height. If you want the text to be the default of .2 inches on the paper, and you have a scale factor of 48, set the height to 9.6. You can set the text height when you create a text style. (If you set the text height of the style to 0, AutoCAD prompts you for a height when you use the style.)

To use the scale factor in dimensions, the easiest way is to create a dimension style. Choose Dimension Style from the

Dimension toolbar. In the Dimension Styles dialog box, click Geometry. The Geometry dialog box opens as shown in Figure 3-1.

In the Scale section, you simply type the scale factor. AutoCAD then automatically multiplies the scale factor by all appropriate settings, such as text height and arrowhead sizes.

 Note: *Use the Scale to Paper Space check box when you are creating floating viewports that have different zoom scales. AutoCAD automatically assigns a scale factor based on the difference in the zoom scale between the paper space viewport and the current model space viewport (which is your entire model space drawing if your drawing is not divided up into tiled viewports).*

To use the scale factor for noncontinuous linetypes you can change the global linetype scale. Choose Linetype from the Object Properties toolbar. AutoCAD opens the Linetype

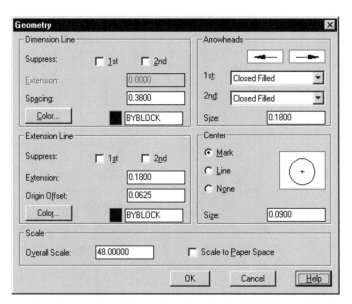

Figure 3-1 The Geometry dialog box lets you quickly assign the scale factor to all appropriate dimension measurements

tab of the Layer & Linetype Properties dialog box, shown in Figure 3-2.

Type the scale factor in the Global scale factor text box. When you change the scale factor, AutoCAD regenerates the drawing and changes all noncontinuous linetypes.

Also in this dialog box, you can change the current object scale for new objects. AutoCAD multiplies the current object scale by the global object scale. The result is that individual objects' scales can differ from the global scale factor. Use this for problematic situations where the global scale doesn't provide the results you need. For example, a line might not be long enough to display the dots and/or dashes of a noncontinuous linetype. When you have finished setting the current object scale for an object or objects, change the setting back to 1.

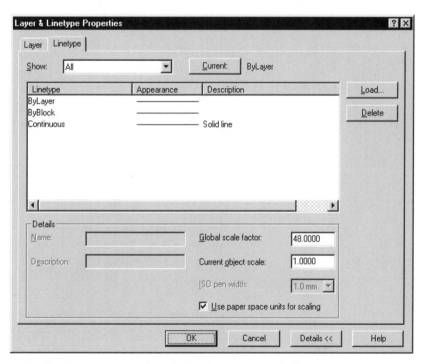

Figure 3-2 You can set the global linetype scale factor on the Linetype tab of the Layer & Linetype Properties dialog box

You can change an existing object's linetype scale by selecting the object and choosing Properties from the Object Properties toolbar. Type the new linetype scale for the object in the Linetype Scale text box.

 ## What are the different units you can use in a drawing?

When you set up a drawing, one of the first steps is to choose the type of unit format you want to use. Choose Format | Units to open the Units Control dialog box, shown in Figure 3-3.

You can set both the unit and angle types in this dialog box.

Tip: *You can also format unit and angle type by choosing Use a Wizard from the Start Up dialog box when you start AutoCAD. Then choose Advanced Setup. The choices are the same as in the Units Control dialog box, although they are presented slightly differently.*

Unit Type

The following table shows the unit types and their formats. Note that the display of partial units also depends on the

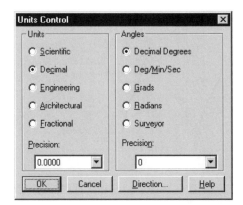

Figure 3-3 The Units Control dialog box lets you set the format of the units you want to use in your drawing

precision that you have specified in the Units Control dialog box.

Unit Type	Format	Example
Scientific	Base number plus exponent	5.6750E+01
Decimal	In any units; partial units are in decimals. This is the default unit type.	56.75
Engineering	In feet and inches; partial inches are in decimals	4'-8.75
Architectural	In feet and inches; partial inches in fractions	4'-8 3/4"
Fractional	In any units; partial units in fractions	56 3/4

Angle Type

The following table shows the available angle types and their formats. The display of partial angles also depends on the precision that you have specified.

Angle Type	Format	Example
Decimal Degrees	Degrees (partial degrees are in decimals)	20.50
Deg/Min/Sec	Degrees (partial degrees are in minutes; partial minutes are in seconds)	20d30'
Grads	Grads, which equal 1/100 of a right angle	22.78g
Radians	Radians, which equal 57.32 degrees	0.36r
Surveyor	Surveyor units, which measure angles in degrees, minutes, and seconds from North or South in either the East or West direction	N 69d30' E

USING DRAWING AIDS

 When I use Tracking to locate a point, sometimes I get the wrong point. What am I doing wrong?

Release 14's new Tracking feature is a great time saver, but it can be tricky to use properly. However, once you get the technique down, you can locate the point you want every time.

Tracking locates a point determined by the x and y coordinates of two existing points. A common problem arises, because for any two existing points, tracking can locate two possible other points. Figure 3-4 shows how this works.

Suppose you want to draw the two dashed lines in Figure 3-4. You want to start drawing a line from the filled donut at the bottom left of Figure 3-4, labeled "First existing point used for tracking." You want to use tracking to find the endpoint of the line, which should be at the point object marked "First possible new point." You want to use the donut on the right, labeled "Second existing point used for tracking," as your second tracking point. But tracking can find either of the two points that share x and y coordinates with your two tracking points. One is the point you want and the other is marked "Second possible new point" in Figure 3-4. It also shares x and y coordinates with your two tracking points. To get the point you want in Figure 3-4, you should follow these steps:

1. Start the LINE command.

2. At the "From point:" prompt, use the Endpoint object snap to start the line at the donut marked "First existing point used for tracking."

3. At the "To point:" prompt, choose tracking from the Object Snap flyout of the Standard toolbar. (You can also find tracking on the cursor menu—press SHIFT and right-click.)

4. At the "First tracking point:" prompt, again use the Endpoint object snap to pick the donut marked "First existing point used for tracking."

5. Move the cursor up in the direction of the point you want to locate. This is the crucial instruction that locates the point you want.

6. At the "Next point:" prompt, and only after you have moved the cursor toward the desired point, use the Endpoint object snap to pick the donut marked "Second existing point used for tracking."

7. Press ENTER to end tracking. AutoCAD finds your point.

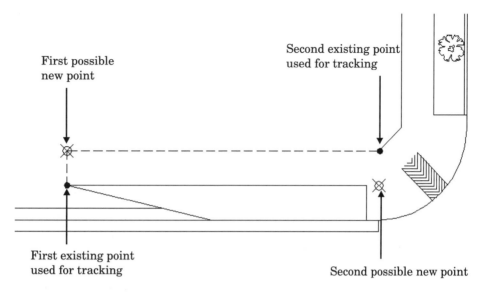

First possible new point

Second existing point used for tracking

First existing point used for tracking

Second possible new point

Figure 3-4 Tracking using two existing points (indicated by the filled donuts) can locate one of two possible new points, indicated by the x-in-a-circle point objects

If you move the cursor to the right in step 5, tracking locates the other point, marked "Second possible new point" in Figure 3-4.

When you start tracking, AutoCAD constrains the cursor so that you can move it only at right angles (orthogonally) from the first tracking point. The direction you move the cursor at this time determines which of the two points tracking locates.

 ## When can you use Tracking and when do you need to use point filters?

You need to use point filters if your tracking points are not all in the plane of the current user coordinate system. Tracking is meant for 2-D use only. Because tracking using two points can locate two new points, sometimes it may be clearer to use point filters where you specify which coordinate (x or y) you want to use from your existing points.

 How do I locate the center of an arc?

You locate the center of an arc or of a circle in the same way, using the Center object snap (also called the Center osnap). When you need to specify the center of the arc or circle, hold down SHIFT and right-click anywhere in the drawing area to get the cursor menu. Choose Center. At the "_cen of" prompt pick any point on the circumference of the arc or circle. Notice the symbol—called a *marker*—that indicates the Center osnap. A SnapTip also appears with the word "Center."

There are three other ways to specify the Center osnap (or any other osnap for that matter). You can choose any osnap from the Object Snap flyout on the Standard toolbar, shown here, which by default displays the Tracking button. You can also type the object snap on the command line. You can generally enter the abbreviation of an object snap by typing its first three letters. For example, you can type **cen** for the Center object snap. Finally, you can set a running object snap. For more information, see the box, "Working with Running Object Snaps."

Working with Running Object Snaps

Release 14 introduced a new way to work with object snaps, called AutoSnap, which makes it much easier than previously to find the object snap you want. Another new feature for Release 14, the OSNAP button on the status bar, makes it much more practical to use *running object snaps*. Running object snaps stay on until you turn them off, unlike regular object snaps, which are active only during the current prompt on the command line. By setting one or more running object snaps, you can speed up the process of locating object snaps as you draw. There are two ways to set running object snaps:

- If no running object snaps are set, double-click the osnap button on the status bar. AutoCAD opens the Osnap Settings dialog box with the Running Osnap tab on top, as shown in the following illustration. Choose the running object snaps that you want and click OK.

Osnap Settings ? X

Running Osnap | AutoSnap(TM)

Select settings

- Endpoint
- Midpoint
- Center
- Node
- Quadrant
- Intersection
- Insertion
- Perpendicular
- Tangent
- Nearest
- Apparent Int
- Quick

Clear all

Aperture size

OK   Cancel   Help

● If running object snaps *are* set, and you wish to add or clear one or more of them, choose Tools | Object Snap Settings to open the Osnap Settings dialog box. Add or clear any of the object snaps and click OK.

Once you have running object snaps, you can toggle them off and on at any time by double-clicking the OSNAP button on the status bar. Regardless of the running osnaps you have set, you can always specify an object snap for any particular prompt. You can also type coordinates on the command line, which by default take precedence over object snaps in Release 14.

Is there a quick way to find the point where two other lines would meet if extended?

Yes, use the Apparent Intersection object snap. You can find it on the cursor menu and the Object Snap flyout. Its command line abbreviation is app. When you use this object snap, AutoCAD prompts you to identify the two objects for which you want to find the apparent intersection.

How can I snap to a point object?

The Node object snap finds point objects.

I have blocks whose insertion point is not on one of the block objects. Sometimes I need to check if the block was inserted at the right coordinate. How can I do this?

There are two ways to check the insertion point of a block. Select the block and choose Properties on the Object Properties toolbar, or use the LIST command on the block. If you want to draw an object from the insertion point, use the Insert object snap. These same methods also apply to the insertion point of text.

USING LAYERS, COLORS, AND LINETYPES

 The Layer Control drop-down box sometimes shows the current layer, and sometimes it shows another layer. In Release 13, it only showed the current layer. Sometimes the box is blank, showing no layer at all. What's going on?

This change in Release 14 can be confusing at first. However, it can also be useful and it brings AutoCAD in line with other Windows applications. You may have noticed that while you are typing in a word-processing program, the Formatting toolbar shows the current style, font, and font size. However, when you select text that is different from the current formatting, the Formatting toolbar shows the features of the selected text. AutoCAD Release 14 now works the same way. If no object is selected, the Object Properties toolbar shows you the current layer, linetype, and color. However, when an object is selected, this toolbar indicates the layer, linetype, and color of the selected object. Furthermore, if you have selected several objects with different layers, colors, and/or linetypes, one or more of the boxes on the Object Properties toolbar is blank. For more information on organizing objects and their properties, see the box, "Using Layers to Manage Object Properties."

Using Layers to Manage Object Properties

Layers are the primary means of managing the properties of objects—colors and linetypes. Every object must be on a layer and every layer must have a name, a color, and a linetype. Layer names can be up to 31 characters and cannot contain spaces.

To create a new layer, choose Layers from the Object Properties toolbar and click New. AutoCAD adds a new layer to the layer listing with the default color of black/white and the default linetype of continuous. The layer's default name (Layer1, Layer2, etc.) is highlighted so you can immediately type a new name. Click the color

swatch to choose a new color, and click the linetype to load and choose a new linetype. Click OK to return to your drawing.

To use the layer, click the Layer Control drop-down box and choose the layer. The layer you choose becomes the current layer and is used for all objects you subsequently draw, until you change the current layer again.

To change an object's layer, select the object and click the Layer Control drop-down box. Choose the layer you want.

Layers also have states:

- **On/Off**   When you turn a layer off, it is hidden, but the layer is regenerated when the drawing is regenerated.

- **Thawed/Frozen**   When you freeze a layer, it is hidden and the layer is not regenerated with the drawing. The purpose of this state is to save regeneration time in large drawings.

- **Unlocked/Locked**   When you lock a layer, it is visible but cannot be edited.

You can change a layer's state by clicking the Layer Control drop-down box and clicking the appropriate icon next to the desired layer. For more information on the columns in the Layer Control drop-down box, see the question, "There are several columns in the Layer & Linetype Properties dialog box. What are they for and how do you use them?," later in this chapter.

It is standard practice to assign color and linetype by controlling the layer, not by directly assigning a color and linetype to an object. This ensures that all objects on the Centerline layer have the same color, for example, making it easier to understand the drawing.

 I want all objects to take on the color of their layer, but I have old drawings that have many objects whose color was set using the COLOR command. Is there any quick way to make this change?

The best way to organize a drawing is to set the color of each object to *ByLayer*, which means that the object takes on the color of the layer. The quickest way to do this is to follow these steps:

1. If there are any frozen layers, thaw them.
2. Do a ZOOM Extents.
3. Select all the objects in your drawing, using a large crossing window.
4. From the Object Properties toolbar, click the Color Control drop-down box.
5. Choose ByLayer.

I sometimes have dozens of layers in my drawings, especially if I've attached an xref. How can I easily find the layers I need in the Layer & Linetype Properties dialog box?

You can filter the layer list in any way you please. From the Layer & Linetype Properties dialog box, click Show to see the drop down list shown here. If one of the AutoCAD-provided filters suit your needs, choose it.

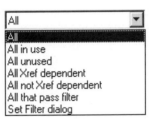

If you need a customized filter list, choose Set Filter Dialog to open the Set Layer Filters dialog box, shown in Figure 3-5.

You can use this dialog box to set complex filters by name, status, color, and linetype. For name filtering options, see the box, "Filtering Layer Names, Colors, and Linetypes." To filter by status, use the drop-down lists. For example, you can choose to list only layers that are set on or layers that are

Figure 3-5 The Set Layer Filters dialog box

locked. Once you create a filter and click OK, AutoCAD automatically uses the filter on the layer list.

There are several columns in the Layer & Linetype Properties dialog box. What are they for and how do you use them?

The Layer & Linetype Properties dialog box, shown in Figure 3-6, has a column for each possible property of a layer, but the columns are so narrow that you can't read their titles. To help you out, when you place the cursor over one of the icons in a column, a ToolTip for that column appears.

However, you can also widen the columns to see the column headings. Place the cursor over any vertical line

Filtering Layer Names, Colors, and Linetypes

AutoCAD offers some very advanced capabilities for filtering layer names, colors, and linetypes. You are probably familiar with using a question mark (?) to match any single character and an asterisk (*) to match any number of characters. There are several other filtering characters you can use, as shown in the following table. The examples assume you are using the filtering characters in the Layer Names text box, but you can use them in the Colors and Linetypes boxes as well. If you don't want to use these characters, you can just type a specific name, color, or linetype in the appropriate text box.

Character	Function
#	Matches any numeral
@	Matches any alphabetical character
*	Matches any number of characters
?	Matches any single character
~ (Tilde)	Matches anything but the pattern; for example, ~no* matches all layers that don't start with *no*
[ ]	Matches any one of the characters within the square brackets; for example, [no]t matches *nt* and *ot*
[~]	Matches any character not enclosed in the brackets; for example, [~no]t matches *pt* but not *nt* or *ot*
[-]	Specifies a range for a single character; for example [n-s]* matches layers that start with *n, o, p, q, r,* and *s*
` (Reverse quote)	Reads next character(s) literally; for example, `$no matches *$no* Note: The reverse quote is different from an apostrophe. It may be located under the tilde (~) on your keyboard.

between two column headings. Press and drag to the right to widen the column to the left.

Table 3-1 explains the meaning of all the columns.

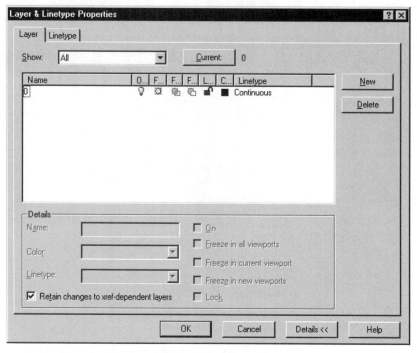

Figure 3-6   The Layer tab of the Layer & Linetype Properties dialog box

Column Name	Description
On/Off	By default, layers are on, which means they are visible. When you turn a layer off, it becomes invisible but is regenerated when the drawing is regenerated. Turn a layer off when you don't want to see or plot objects on that layer. Because turning a layer back on doesn't cause a regeneration, you may want to use the on/off states when you need to change objects from visible to invisible often.
Freeze/Thaw in all viewports	By default, layers are thawed, which means they are visible. Frozen layers are invisible but are not regenerated when the drawing is regenerated. Freeze a layer when you don't want to see or plot objects on that layer. Keep in mind, though, that when you thaw a layer, the drawing regenerates.
Freeze/Thaw in current viewport	This state is used for floating viewports. Freeze a layer in the current viewport when you have some object that you want to appear only in that viewport. A common use is for annotation or dimensions that you want to appear only in one viewport.

Table 3-1   Layer Status Columns in the Layer & Linetype Properties Dialog Box

Column Name	Description
Freeze/Thaw in new viewports	This state sets the freeze/thaw status of a layer for floating viewports that you have not yet created. It leaves the freeze/thaw status of layers in existing viewports unchanged. You should freeze a layer in new viewports when you are about to create a new floating viewport in which you don't want the layer to appear.
Lock/Unlock	By default, layers are unlocked. Locked layers are visible but not editable. Lock layers when you want to refer to them while making sure that they can't be modified.
Color	By default, new layers are black. Click the color swatch to choose a new color.
Linetype	By default, new layers are continuous. Click the Linetype to load and choose a new linetype.

Table 3-1   Layer Status Columns in the Layer & Linetype Properties Dialog Box (*continued*)

 ## Can I print out a list of my layers?

Yes, there are several ways of creating a list of layers. One simple way is to follow these steps:

1. Type **-layer** and press ENTER. Don't forget this hyphen before the command name. It executes the LAYER command on the command line, without the dialog box.

2. At the prompt, type **?** and press ENTER.

3. At the "Layer name(s) to list <*>:" prompt, press ENTER to request a list of all the layers. AutoCAD opens the AutoCAD Text Window and lists all the layers and their properties, as shown in Figure 3-7.

4. Select the text in the Text Window and right-click to open the shortcut menu.

5. Choose Copy to copy the text to the Windows clipboard.

6. Open any word processor, or Notepad, and press CTRL+V to paste the text into a new document.

7. Print the document.

Another way is to enable the log file, which keeps a record of all the text in the text window. To enable the log file,

```
Command: -layer
?/Make/Set/New/ON/OFF/Color/Ltype/Freeze/Thaw/LOck/Unlock: ?

Layer name(s) to list <*>:

    Layer name        State        Color        Linetype
--------------------  ---------    -----------  ------------
0                     On           7 (white)    CONTINUOUS
CENTERLINE            On           3 (green)    CENTER
HIDDEN                On           4 (cyan)     HIDDEN
PARTS                 On           7 (white)    CONTINUOUS
TEXT                  On           1 (red)      CONTINUOUS

TITLEBLOCK            Frozen       5 (blue)     CONTINUOUS

Current layer: PARTS
```

Figure 3-7   You can use the -LAYER command to get a listing of all the
layers in a drawing

choose Tools | Preferences and click the General tab. Check
Maintain a log file. Click OK.

 Note: *To set the name and location of the log file, click the*
Files tab and click the plus sign next to Menu, Help, Log, and
Miscellaneous File Names. Then click the plus next to Log file.
By default, this file is named ACAD.LOG and is located in
your AutoCAD Release 14 folder. Type a new path and
filename and click OK.

Now follow steps 1 through 3 previously listed. The layer
listing will go into the log file, which you can open and print.

Often, the reason you need a layer listing is to give it to a
colleague who will be working on the drawing. The bonus
commands include a Layer Manager that saves *layer states*.
(See Chapter 2 for more information about the bonus
commands.) A layer state includes the properties and state of
each layer in a drawing. You can then restore the saved layer
states when needed. You can even export a layer state listing
to a .LAY file and send it along with the drawing to your
colleague who can import the .LAY file and restore the layer
states. Figure 3-8 shows a sample .LAY file.

As you can see, the listing uses codes and is not as clear
as the listing using the -LAYER command. However, if the
reason you want the listing is to restore layers and their
states, the Layer Manager can be very useful.

```
(1000 . "{LAYER_STATE1")
(1070 . 0)
(1070 . 7)
(1000 . "CONTINUOUS")
(1000 . "LAYER_STATE1}")
(1000 . "{BEARINGS")
(1070 . 0)
(1070 . 7)
(1000 . "CONTINUOUS")
(1000 . "BEARINGS}")
"PARTS"
(1000 . "{LAYER_STATE1")
(1070 . 0)
(1070 . 1)
(1000 . "CONTINUOUS")
(1070 . 1)
(1000 . "LAYER_STATE1}")
(1000 . "{BEARINGS")
(1070 . 0)
(1070 . 7)
(1000 . "CONTINUOUS")
(1070 . 1)
(1000 . "BEARINGS}")
"HIDDEN"
(1000 . "{BEARINGS")
(1070 . 0)
(1070 . 4)
(1000 . "CONTINUOUS")
(1000 . "BEARINGS}")
"CENTERLINE"
(1000 . "{BEARINGS")
(1070 . 0)
```

Figure 3-8 A .LAY file lists layers, their properties, and their states. The file can be imported into a drawing and the layer states can be restored

My dashed linetypes sometimes look continuous. How can I fix this problem?

This is a common problem and there are three ways to fix it. The problem may occur because the line is too short to adequately display the dashes and/or dots, or because of an incorrect linetype scale, or because of an inappropriate linetype.

Use a Different Linetype

Some of AutoCAD's most commonly used linetypes come in three variations: short, medium, and long. These linetypes are listed here:

Border, Border2, Borderx2
Center, Center2, Centerx2

> Dashdot, Dashdot2, Dashdotx2
> Dashed, Dashed2, Dashedx2
> Divide, Divide2, Dividex2
> Dot, Dot2, Dotx2
> Hidden, Hidden2, Hiddenx2
> Phantom, Phantom2, Phantomx2

Often you can simply choose another variation of the same linetype to get the results you want.

Some companies use ISO linetypes to meet the specifications of the International Standards Organization. However, these linetypes are much longer than AutoCAD's other, comparable definitions. You may need to make adjustments to the linetype scale when using an ISO linetype.

Change the Global Scale

If all the noncontinuous linetypes look continuous, change the global linetype scale. For more information on scale factors, see the section, "Setting Up a Drawing," earlier in this chapter.

To change the global linetype scale, click Linetype on the Object Properties toolbar to open the Linetype tab of the Layer & Linetype Properties dialog box. In the Details section, change the value in the Global scale factor text box. Choose a smaller scale to create more repetitions of the pattern per unit and a large scale to create fewer repetitions of the pattern per unit, as shown in Figure 3-9.

Sometimes the problem is localized to a specific object. The linetype scale might be fine for most objects, but one object is too small to display the linetype pattern. In this case, you can change the linetype scale of an individual object. Choose Properties from the Object Properties toolbar, and type a new linetype scale in the Linetype Scale text box. Other objects remain unchanged.

 Note: *For the object whose linetype scale you changed, AutoCAD multiplies the object's linetype scale times the global linetype scale.*

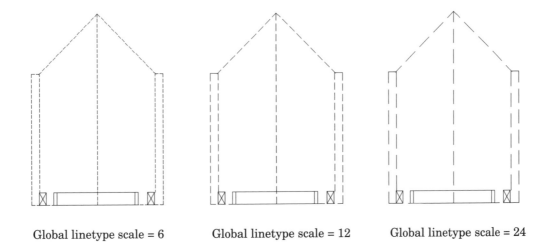

Global linetype scale = 6   Global linetype scale = 12   Global linetype scale = 24

Figure 3-9   The number of repetitions of a noncontinuous linetype
pattern per unit varies with the global scale factor

 **Is there a quick way to create a custom linetype
without opening up a text file and learning all about
customization?**

Yes, but if you make a mistake, you still have to open the
linetype file with a text editor and edit the linetype. Here's
the code:

Dash	A positive number. The number is the length of the dash in units.
Dot	Zero
Space	A negative number. The number is the length of the space in units.

To create a custom linetype "on the fly," follow these steps:

1. Type **-linetype** and press ENTER. The hyphen forces
    AutoCAD to use the command-line version of the
    command.

2. At the "?/Create/Load/Set:" prompt, type **c** and
    press ENTER.

3. At the "Name of linetype to create:" prompt, type the name of your linetype. The name cannot have any spaces in it. AutoCAD asks you to wait while it checks to see if the linetype is already defined.

4. AutoCAD opens the Create or Append Linetype File dialog box. For easy access, accept the default of ACAD.LIN, which is the file that contains all the linetypes that AutoCAD provides. Click Save.

Note: *You can create a new linetype file at this point. Its filename extension must be .LIN. To load the linetype, choose Linetype from the Object Properties toolbar. Click Load and locate and choose your linetype file from the Load or Reload Linetypes dialog box.*

5. At the "Descriptive text:" prompt, type a description of up to 47 characters. The description can have spaces.

6. At the "Enter pattern (on next line):" prompt, AutoCAD places "A," on the next line. All linetype definitions start with an A and a comma. Type your definition after the comma and press ENTER. AutoCAD tells you that the new definition was written to the file. For example, the code you see here:

   ```
   A,.5,-.25,.5,-.25,0,-.25
   ```

   creates a linetype with two dashes and a dot, as shown here:

   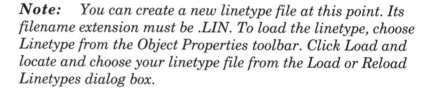

7. AutoCAD repeats the "?/Create/Load/Set:" prompt. To use your linetype, you need to load it. Type **l** and press ENTER.

8. At the "Linetype(s) to load:" prompt, type the name of your linetype. AutoCAD opens the Select Linetype File dialog box. Accept the default of ACAD.LIN or locate and choose the linetype file where you saved your linetype. Click Open. AutoCAD loads the linetype.

9. Press ENTER to end the LINETYPE command.

10. To draw with your new linetype, create a new layer. You can now choose the linetype for the layer.

GETTING INFORMATION ABOUT A DRAWING

 What's the best way to get information about an object?

There are two methods. If all you want is information, use the LIST command. You can select as many objects as you want.

 If you might want to change one of the properties of the object, select the object and click Properties on the Object Properties toolbar. This executes the DDMODIFY command. The Modify dialog box that appears will be specific to the object you chose, such as Modify Circle. You can then change any of the modifiable properties of the object.

 How can I get the length of an arc?

The easiest way is to choose Properties on the Object Properties dialog box and choose one arc only. The Modify Arc dialog box lists the arc's length. You can also start the LENGTHEN command and choose the arc. The arc's length will be displayed on the command line.

If the arc is a polyline, you can use the AREA command to get the arc's length (as well as its area, calculated as if a line were drawn from the arc's start point to its endpoint). The LIST command will also give the length of an arc that is a polyline.

DISPLAYING YOUR DRAWING

 My circles look like stop signs, but they plot fine. How do I get them to look smooth?

Use the REGEN command. You can also check the view resolution. Type **viewres** at the command line and press ENTER. At the "Do you want fast zooms? <Y>" prompt, press ENTER. At the "Enter circle zoom percent (1-20000) <100>:" prompt, type a number between 1 and 20,000. The default is

100. If someone has changed the circle zoom percent to a low number, however, your circles will look like stop signs. AutoCAD automatically regenerates the drawing after you change this setting.

Is there a way to return to the zoom I had two zooms ago?

Yes, you can use Zoom Previous twice to return to your second-last display. The Zoom Previous button is on the Standard toolbar. You can go back up to ten times.

I do a lot of zooming and panning. Is there any way to save zooming and panning time?

There are several techniques that can save zooming and panning time. Release 14's new Real-time zoom and pan are faster than the previous ZOOM and PAN commands. A very useful technique is to save views. You may want to save several standard views of a large drawing, for example, immediately after you create the title block. These views will help you navigate your drawing throughout the drawing process. To save a view, follow these steps:

1. Display the desired view.
2. Choose Named Views from the View flyout of the Standard toolbar (or choose View | Named Views) to call up the DDVIEW command.
3. In the View Control dialog box, shown in Figure 3-10, click New.
4. In the Define New View dialog box, type a name of up to 31 characters with no spaces.
5. Click Save View.
6. Click OK.

To restore a view, open the View Control dialog box, choose the view you want from the list, click Restore, then click OK.

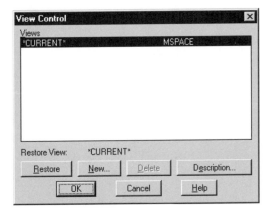

Figure 3-10   The View Control dialog box

Can I change my drawing area to white and my white objects to black?

Yes. You can change the color of any aspect of the screen, including the command-line text, the drawing area, the screen menu (if you display it), and the text window. White objects on a black background automatically become black objects when you choose a white drawing area. For example, choose Layers from the Object Properties dialog box and open the Details section by clicking Details. Choose any layer with a white (or black) color. The Color drop-down box lists the layer's color as white but shows a box that is half white and half black, as shown in Figure 3-11, to indicate that the layer can be displayed either as black or as white, depending on the color of the drawing area.

To change your drawing area to white, follow these steps:

1. Choose Tools | Preferences and click the Display tab.

2. In the AutoCAD window format section, click Colors to open the AutoCAD Window Colors dialog box, shown in Figure 3-12.

3. In the Window Element drop-down box, choose "Graphics window background."

86

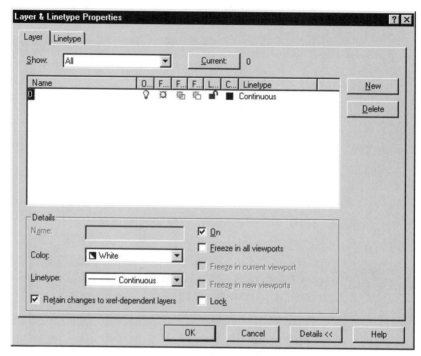

Figure 3-11   The Layer tab of the Layer & Linetype Properties dialog box lists the color of a layer as white, but the square shows it as both black and white

4. From the Basic Colors color swatches, click the white color swatch. The large color swatch at the bottom of the dialog box also changes to white.

5. Click OK twice to return to your drawing. AutoCAD changes the color of the screen and all white objects become black.

My layers are set for different colors, but all my objects are monochrome. Why can't I get the proper colors?

Assuming all your other Windows programs are displaying proper colors, follow these steps:

1. Choose Tools | Preferences and click the Display tab.

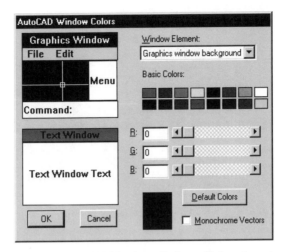

Figure 3-12   Use the AutoCAD Window Colors dialog box to change the colors on your screen

2. Click Colors from the AutoCAD window format section of the dialog box.

3. In the AutoCAD Window Colors dialog box, shown in Figure 3-12, uncheck Monochrome Vectors.

4. Click OK twice.

My grid and crosshairs are rotated 45 degrees. How do I get them back to normal?

Choose Tools | Drawing Aids to open the Drawing Aids dialog box, shown in Figure 3-13. In the Snap section, change the Snap Angle to 0, then click OK. This probably happened because you ran an AutoLISP program that changed the snap angle. For some reason the program was interrupted and didn't reset the snap angle back to normal.

I can't pick a window to zoom in using Aerial View. What am I doing wrong?

Aerial View is great for heavy-duty panning and zooming but it works a little differently than the ZOOM command.

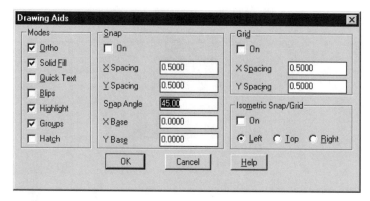

Figure 3-13 The Drawing Aids dialog box

First, you need to make sure the Aerial View window is active. When you open Aerial View, the window is not active, so click anywhere in the window to activate it. You can tell it's active because the title bar is blue (by default) instead of gray.

To quickly zoom in, click the Zoom button. To pick your zoom window, you need to press and drag. That means, click a point at one corner of the desired window, keep the pick button down, and drag to the opposite corner. When the thick box includes the portion of the drawing that you want to see, release the pick button. This action is different from using ZOOM with the Window option, for which you pick one point and then pick the opposite point of the window.

You can set AutoCAD to use press and drag whenever you specify a window (using either a window or a crossing selection) to select objects. Choose Tools | Selection to open the Object Selection Settings dialog box shown in Figure 3-14. Check the Press and Drag option and click OK. This option is not on by default, but AutoCAD offers Press and Drag because it matches the selection method used by most other Windows programs.

Figure 3-14 The Object Selection Settings dialog box lets you select objects using the Press and Drag method of specifying a window

What's the difference between tiled viewports and floating viewports?

While there are a number of differences between tiled and floating viewports, the most important one is their purpose. Tiled viewports are an aid to viewing your drawing while you draw and edit. Floating viewports help you lay out your drawing for printing or plotting. If you are in the drawing/editing process and need an easier way to view different parts of your drawing or to see close-in detail without losing your view of the entire drawing, use tiled viewports. If you are ready to lay out your drawing for plotting, use floating viewports. Table 3-2 explains the major differences between the two types of viewports.

Once you have created a floating viewport in paper space, you can return to model space and continue to draw and edit. When you are in model space, floating and tiled viewports are

Tiled Viewports	Floating Viewports
Created in model space	Created in paper space
Always take up the entire screen	Can take up only a portion of the screen
The crosshairs only appears in the active viewport	The crosshairs can appear anywhere on your screen
The user coordinate system (UCS) icon, if on, appears in each viewport	The UCS icon appears only once on your screen
Tiled viewports are not objects and cannot be edited as objects	Floating viewports are objects and can be moved, copied, given a layer, resized, etc. Their layer can be frozen or turned off
Cannot have individual settings for layer visibility in each port	Can set layer visibility for each viewport individually
AutoCAD only plots the active viewport	AutoCAD plots all viewports
Cannot show some viewports with hidden lines and others without	Can show and plot some viewports with hidden lines and others without

Table 3-2 Tiled and Floating Viewport Characteristics

more similar. For example, only one viewport can be active at a time, and whatever changes you make in one viewport immediately show up in other viewports, provided those viewports show that portion of your drawing.

Chapter 4 covers paper space, floating viewports, and plotting in more detail.

 I created a configuration of tiled viewports that I like, but it's not one of AutoCAD's standard setups. How can I save it so I don't have to create it over and over?

It's easy to save a configuration of tiled viewports. Choose View | Tiled Viewports | Save, type a name for the configuration, and press ENTER. To use your saved configuration, choose View | Tiled Viewports | Restore and type the name of your configuration. If you've forgotten the name, type **?** and press ENTER twice. AutoCAD lists all the saved viewport configurations.

For more information on creating your own tiled viewport configurations, see the box, "Creating Tiled Viewport Configurations."

Creating Tiled Viewport Configurations

The easiest way to create tiled viewports is to choose View | Tiled Viewports | Layout. This opens the Tiled Viewport Layout dialog box, shown in the following illustration. Here you can pick the best configuration by clicking one of the image tiles.

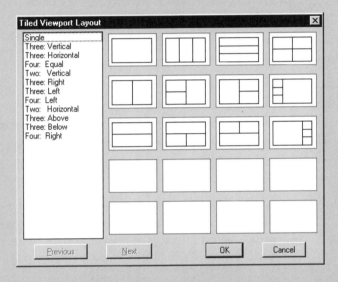

To create your own configuration, start with this dialog box and choose the configuration that most closely matches what you want. Then use the tiled viewport options to make the adjustments you need. These options are all available from the View | Tiled Viewports submenu.

- To divide an existing viewport into smaller viewports, click the viewport to make it current. Then choose View | Tiled Viewports. From the submenu, choose the number of viewports you want to create. You can divide a viewport into two through four smaller ones. If you choose two or three viewports, AutoCAD further prompts you to specify how you want those viewports to be laid out.

- To join two viewports together, choose View | Tiled Viewports | Join. AutoCAD asks for the dominant viewport. Pick the viewport you want to keep or press ENTER to use the current viewport. Then pick the viewport you want to join with the first viewport. AutoCAD joins the two viewports, keeping the view of the dominant viewport.

 Tip: *You can save a viewport configuration that you like in your template.*

 I created a configuration of tiled viewports that I want to use for floating viewports in paper space. Is there an easy way to do that?

Yes! A nice feature is that when you are in paper space, you can restore viewport configurations that you created in model space using tiled viewports. Once you have saved the tiled viewport configuration you like, follow these steps:

1. Double-click TILE on the status bar to enter paper space.

2. Choose View | Floating Viewports | Restore.

3. At the "?/Name of window configuration to insert <*ACTIVE>:" prompt, type the name of your tiled viewport configuration and press ENTER.

4. At the "Fit/<First Point>:" prompt, type **f** and press ENTER to cover the entire screen with the viewports, or pick two diagonally opposite points to define a rectangle that will contain the viewport configuration.

AutoCAD restores your configuration in paper space.

 I'm working in 3-D and have a viewpoint that I like. But the annotation isn't readable from that viewpoint. How can I place some text so it's readable?

There are two ways to handle this problem. If you simply want to save a view and have readable text, create a new UCS (user coordinate system) using the View option of the UCS command. (Choose Tools | UCS | View.) The View option places the UCS parallel to your current view. You can then write text that looks flat. Figure 3-15 shows text drawn in the old UCS and new text drawn in a new UCS using the

View option. Note that the model appears after using the HIDE command.

Note: *The HIDE command hides lines that would be hidden if you were looking at a real object. It helps you see what's in back and what's in front. For example, in Figure 3-15, you can see that the back of the bracket is obscured by the front, as it would be in real life. Before you use the HIDE command, you see the back lines too.*

Another way to deal with this issue is to go into paper space. Follow these steps:

1. Double-click TILE on the status bar to go into paper space.

2. Choose View | Floating Viewports | 1Viewport to create a floating viewport.

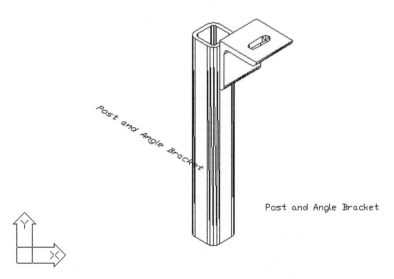

Figure 3-15 You can draw text parallel to the current view using the View option of the UCS command

3. Double-click PAPER on the status bar to return to model space but still view your floating viewport.

4. Choose View | Named Views and restore the view you created in model space.

5. Place any previously existing text on its own layer and freeze that layer.

6. Double-click MODEL on the status bar to return to paper space.

7. Use MTEXT or DTEXT to create text on a separate, visible layer.

Figure 3-16 shows the results of placing the text in paper space. The viewport's layer has been frozen and the model is shown after using the HIDE command.

Post and Angle Bracket

Figure 3-16 You can also use paper space to place readable text next to 3-D models viewed at an angle

Chapter 4

Drawing and Editing in 2-D

Answer Topics!

Drawing and Editing in 2-D @ a Glance

AutoCAD offers two kinds of construction lines: xlines and rays. Another object used in constructing a drawing is the point, which can be set to one of 20 styles. AutoCAD offers quick shortcut commands for creating both rectangles and polygons.

AutoCAD offers an array of selection options that make it easy to select whichever objects you need. You can also customize how AutoCAD handles object selection. Some of the more common editing commands let you move, copy, scale, rotate, and mirror objects. You can also create chamfered corners and extend lines to others they don't actually meet.

When you pick an object before starting an editing command, it appears with grips—small boxes that can be used to edit the object. Click one of the grips to make it *hot* and use that grip as the base point for moving, scaling, rotating, stretching, or mirroring the object.

AutoCAD lets you create single-line and multiline text with many formatting options. Release 14 offers more complete support for TrueType fonts than before, including bold and italic versions of most fonts. You can import text from a word processing document so you don't have to retype it, and use your word processor's dictionary for spell checks in AutoCAD. You can also align text along an arc, and create stacked fractions.

Most drawings contain dimensions and AutoCAD lets you format dimensions to meet the needs of all disciplines. You save the formatting in a dimension style. You can dimension lines, arcs, circles (radii and diameters), and angles. You can also rotate dimensions, create custom arrows, specify exceptions to the dimensioning styles, and copy dimension styles from other drawings.

AutoCAD lets you create several types of complex objects. For example, you can create areas called *hatches,* filling them in with a solid color or a pattern of parallel lines. *Polylines* are collections of line segments and arcs that are treated as one object. *Splines* are curves defined by a series of points that you specify. *Multilines* are sets of parallel lines that you can draw at one time. To create a multiline, you first define a multiline style.

When you are ready to print or plot your drawing, you should first lay out your drawing so that models are presented in an easy-to-understand manner. Paper space lets you create viewports that display different views of your model. This chapter tells you how to create the effect of nonrectangular viewports and how to hide lines of 3-D models in some viewports but not in others. When you are ready to plot, you can change the line thickness used to print or plot the objects in the drawing. AutoCAD lets you save your print/plot settings in a configuration file so you don't have to create the settings each time.

DRAWING BASIC OBJECTS

 What are xlines and rays and how are they used?

Xlines and rays are both used as *construction lines*. Construction lines indicate geometric features of objects but don't actually exist in the real objects you are portraying. They are almost universal in mechanical drawings. Examples are center lines, which show the center of an object, and hidden lines, which indicate a line that would otherwise be hidden from the viewpoint used in the drawing. Construction lines can also be used to indicate relationships, for example, to point out equivalent parts of an object that appear twice in a drawing in different views, or to show how different objects line up.

How do you choose which type of construction line to use? Here is a brief summary of the features of each type of construction line:

- *Xlines are infinite lines.* They have no endpoint. No matter how far you zoom out, the xline extends to the edges of your screen. AutoCAD also calls xlines construction lines.

- *Rays have one endpoint but the other end is infinite.* Use a ray when you want your construction line to start at a specific point.

Figure 4-1 shows a simple drawing containing both an xline and a ray.

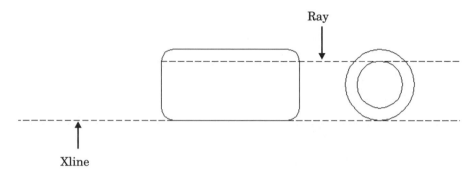

Figure 4-1 You can use xlines and rays to clarify relationships between views of objects or to indicate hidden features

To create an xline, choose Draw | Construction Line.
At the "Hor/Ver/Ang/Bisect/Offset/<From point>:" prompt, pick the first point through which you want the xline to pass, or choose one of the options. If you pick a point, AutoCAD prompts you for a through point. Pick this second point and AutoCAD creates the xline. The XLINE command continues to prompt you for through points so you can create additional xlines if you wish. Press ENTER to end the command.
Here are the other options:

● If you choose the Hor option, AutoCAD confines the xline to being horizontal and prompts you for a through point to draw the xline. The XLINE command continues to prompt you for through points so you can create additional xlines if you wish. Press ENTER to end the command.

● Choose the Ver option to confine the xline to being vertical. At the "Through point:" prompt, enter one point to create the xline. Continue to specify through points if you wish, and press ENTER to end the command.

● Choose the Ang option to specify the angle of the xline. For example, type **45** to get only 45 degree xlines. At the "Through point:" prompt, enter one point to create the xline. Continue to specify through points if you wish, and press ENTER to end the command. You can use the Reference suboption to specify the angle from an object. For example, if you select a 45-degree line and specify a 45-degree angle, your xline will be at a 90-degree angle.

- Use the Bisect option to create an xline that bisects an angle. You first specify the angle's vertex, then the start and end points of the angle. XLINE continues to prompt you for angle endpoints. Press ENTER to end the command.

- The Offset option creates an xline at a specified offset from a line, xline, ray, or polyline. To use the Through option, type **t**, specify the line object you want to offset, and then specify the point through which the xline should go. Alternatively, type an offset distance. Then select an object and pick which side of the object you want the xline to be drawn on. Press ENTER to end the command.

Note: *Xlines and rays are not considered when you do a ZOOM All or ZOOM Extents — it would be hard to zoom out to infinity!*

If you trim an xline at either end, it turns into a ray. If you trim a ray at its infinite end, it turns into a line.

When I change the point style, my existing points remain as they were before. How do I change them to the new point style?

Just do a regen (choose View | Regen). All your points will change to the new point style. For details on creating point styles, see the box, "Creating Point Styles."

Can I use more than one point style in my drawing?

No. AutoCAD only stores one point style at a time. You can display more than one type of point style by using one point style, changing the point style, and then using the new point style. However, as soon as you do a regen or plot, all the points will change to the new point style.

Here are a couple of workarounds:

- You could use an external reference (xref) to attach a drawing using another point style.

- You could create block symbols for each point style you want to use and use them instead of, or in addition to, points.

For more information on xrefs and blocks, see Chapter 5.

Creating Point Styles

Points are objects used for reference. You can snap to them using the Node object snap. Both the DIVIDE and MEASURE commands can use points to divide up an object. AutoCAD offers 20 point styles. To select a point style choose Format | Point Style to open the Point Style dialog box, shown in the following illustration. Then choose the point style you want. The default style is a simple dot, but it is not easily visible. The second style is no point. If you use points for reference while drawing, you can change the style to no point, do a regen, and then plot without having to erase all your points. (You could also put them on a different layer and freeze or turn off that layer.)

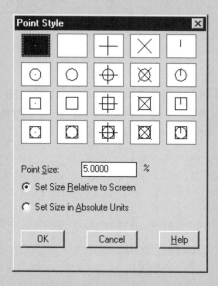

You can also set the point size. By default, a point is set to 5 percent of the screen. That means that no matter how far in or out you zoom, the apparent size of the point is constant. This provides an easily identifiable size for all your drawing situations and is appropriate when you are using the points for reference only.

However, if the points indicate real objects, you can set the size in absolute units. Then, if you zoom in, the points appear larger and vice versa.

When you are done setting the point style, click OK to return to your drawing.

 How can I create a polygon whose bottom edge is not horizontal?

When you create a polygon with the POLYGON command, you first specify the center and whether the polygon should be inscribed in a circle or about a circle. AutoCAD then prompts you for a radius. If you type the radius, the bottom edge is always horizontal. However, if you pick a point to indicate the radius, you can rotate the polygon at any angle. Just move the cursor around and click when you get the results you like.

The problem with this method is that you can't specify an exact radius. Direct Distance Entry doesn't work—if you place the cursor at an angle and type a radius, the bottom edge is still horizontal.

The secret is to change the snap angle. If you want the bottom edge at a 36-degree angle, choose Tools | Drawing Aids, type **36** in the Snap Angle text box, and click OK. Now create the polygon and type the radius. The bottom edge will be at a 36-degree angle, as shown here:

 The RECTANG command has lots of new options in Release 14. What do they mean?

You can now create a lot of variations on the rectangle theme in one fell swoop. In order to understand all the options, it helps to understand that a rectangle consists of segments of a single polyline rather than four separate lines. The command displays the "Chamfer/Elevation/Fillet/Thickness/Width/ <First corner>:" prompt. Here's how to use the options:

● The default options are to specify the two corners of the rectangle. Note that for the second corner you can use relative coordinates to specify the width and height of the rectangle. For example, if you specify @5,3 for the

second corner, the rectangle will be five units wide and 3 units high.

● Use the chamfer option to chamfer all four corners of the rectangle by specifying first and second distances. If you specify two different distances, AutoCAD cuts the corners as if you had picked the two lines (as you have to do if you use the CHAMFER command) going counterclockwise. There is no angle method available. The rectangle shown here has a first chamfer distance of .5 and a second chamfer distance of 1.

● The Elevation option is used for 3-D drawings and gives the entire rectangle a Z coordinate equal to the elevation you specify. The option doesn't change the current elevation of the drawing but *does* affect subsequent rectangles, which are all drawn at the same elevation.

● The Fillet option fillets the entire rectangle using an arc with the radius you specify. A *fillet* is a rounded corner. This radius affects subsequent rectangles that you draw.

● The Thickness option is also used for 3-D drawings. It gives a thickness to the entire rectangle, turning it into a 3-D surface object, as shown here after using the HIDE command. The thickness setting affects subsequent rectangles.

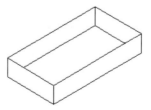

● Use the Width option to create a wide polyline object, as shown here:

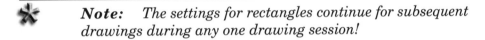

You can combine options, for example to create a wide, filleted rectangle.

✳ ***Note:*** *The settings for rectangles continue for subsequent drawings during any one drawing session!*

SELECTING AND EDITING OBJECTS

Is there a quick way to deselect an object that I've selected in error?

Yes, press SHIFT and pick the object. This method is much quicker than using the Remove option when you are selecting objects. You can use the SHIFT key method either after you have started a command at the "Select objects:" prompt, or before choosing a command.

Whenever I click the screen by accident, AutoCAD expects me to create a window, and I have to click another point or ESC to continue working. Is there any way to stop this feature?

Yes. Choose Tools | Selection to open the Object Selection Settings dialog box. Click Implied Windowing to uncheck the box and click OK. Now try clicking an empty space on your screen. AutoCAD doesn't ask you for the other corner.

The downside to this choice is that to create a selection window, regular or crossing, at the "Select objects:" prompt after you have started a command, you need to type **w** or **c**. However, implied windowing is always on before a command—

even if you have turned it off—so that you can use grips. For more information, see the next box, "Customizing Object Selection."

 In my other Windows programs, I'm used to pressing SHIFT to select additional objects. Can I set AutoCAD that way?

You certainly can. Choose Tools | Selection to open the Object Selection Settings dialog box. Click Use Shift to Add and click OK. For more information, see the following box, "Customizing Object Selection."

Customizing Object Selection

There are a number of ways you can customize how AutoCAD selects objects. Choose Tools | Selection to open the Object Selection Settings dialog box, shown here:

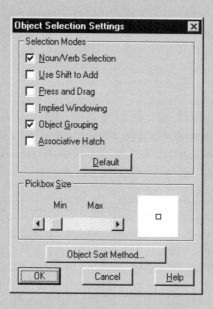

These options are explained here:

Option	Description
Noun/Verb Selection	Turning on this option lets you choose objects (nouns) before starting a command. You still have the option of starting the command first. Note that, regardless of how this option is set, not every command lets you choose objects first. Noun/Verb Selection is on by default.
Use Shift to Add	This option allows you to press SHIFT and click to select more than one object. This type of selection is typical of other Windows programs but is off by default in AutoCAD.
Press and Drag	Press and Drag determines how you create a selection window. With this option on, you pick the first corner of the window, hold down the mouse (or puck) button, move the cursor to the opposite corner, and release the button. This type of selection is typical of other Windows programs but is off by default in AutoCAD.
Implied Windowing	Implied windowing means that when you pick a point on your screen that is not on an object, AutoCAD starts a selection window—a regular window that selects objects completely within the window if you pick from left to right, and a crossing window that selects objects all or partially within the window if you pick from right to left. If you turn implied windowing off and pick a point not on an object, AutoCAD simply notes, 0 found. Implied windowing is always on before choosing a command, so turning it off only affects object selection after you choose a command.
Object Grouping	Object Grouping lets you select named sets of objects that have already been defined as a Group. Turn object grouping off if you want to select objects within a group individually.
Associative Hatch	When this option is on, if you select an associative hatch pattern, AutoCAD automatically selects its boundary as well.

You can click the Default button in the Object Selection Settings dialog box to quickly return all the settings to their default values.

The lower part of the dialog box lets you customize the size of the pickbox that appears when you select objects. Use the slider bar to adjust the size.

Choose Object Sort Method to tell AutoCAD to sort objects in the order in which they were created for certain operations, such as object selection, object snaps, redraws, regenerations, plotting, and PostScript output. By default, object sorting is on only for plotting and PostScript output.

 ### How can I scale an object when I only know the final size I want, not the amount I want to scale it?

The Reference option of the SCALE command was made for this purpose. Follow these steps:

1. Start the SCALE command.

2. Select the object you want to scale.

3. Pick the *base point,* the point from which AutoCAD scales the object. All other points on the object change when scaled, but the base point is fixed.

4. At the "<Scale factor>/Reference:" prompt, type **r** to use the Reference option. AutoCAD prompts you for the reference length.

5. Pick the start point on the object (such as the endpoint of a line or one quadrant of a circle), usually by using object snaps.

6. At the "Second point:" prompt, pick the opposite end of the object (such as the other endpoint of a line or the opposite quadrant of a circle). Together these two points indicate the current length of the object.

7. At the "New length:" prompt, type in the length you want. AutoCAD scales the object to be the length you specified.

In Figure 4-2a, the rectangle has been scaled so that the bottom edge is 2.25 units. Figure 4-2b shows the two endpoints of the bottom edge of the rectangle that were used to specify the reference length.

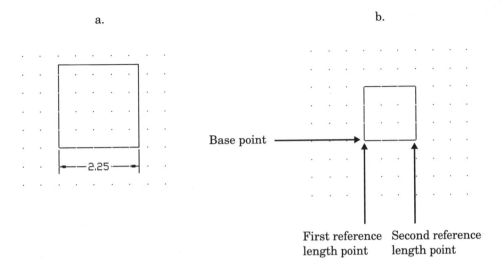

a.

b.

Base point ⟶

First reference   Second reference
length point   length point

Figure 4-2   Scaling an object with the Reference option lets you specify
the desired size instead of the change in size

How do I rotate an object when I only know the final angle I want, not how much I want to rotate it?

By default, AutoCAD asks you how much you want to rotate the object. However, by using the Reference option, you can specify the final angle you want. Follow these steps:

1. Start the ROTATE command.
2. Select the object you want to rotate.
3. Pick the base point.
4. At the "<Rotation angle>/Reference:" prompt, type **r** to use the Reference option. AutoCAD prompts you for the reference angle.
5. Pick two points, usually on the object, that specify the current angle of the object in the current UCS (user coordinate system). The simplest example is the two endpoints of a line. Note that you need to pick the two points in the proper order—AutoCAD measures the second point counterclockwise from the first point.
6. At the "New angle:" prompt, type in the angle you want for the object.

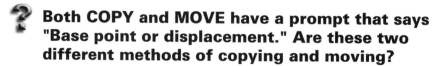

Both COPY and MOVE have a prompt that says "Base point or displacement." Are these two different methods of copying and moving?

Yes, they are. Most people don't realize that you can specify the distance and angle for a move or copy in two ways, as listed here:

- **Base point method** This method requires you to specify a base point and then a second point. AutoCAD moves or copies the object(s) the distance and angle indicated by the difference between the two points. Use this method when you want to point to coordinates, for example with object snaps.

- **Displacement method** Use the displacement method when you know the difference between the two points in terms of the change in x and y coordinates. For example, a displacement of 3,4 moves the object(s) 3 units to the right and 4 units up. Type the displacement *without* using the @ symbol, press ENTER, and then press ENTER again at the "Second point of displacement:" prompt.

When I mirror text along with other objects, it comes out backward! How can I mirror the text but leave it reading from left to right?

The MIRRTEXT system variable determines whether text is mirrored. By default, MIRRTEXT is set to 1 (on), which means text is mirrored. Set it to 0 (off) if you don't want to mirror text. To change the mirror setting, type **MIRRTEXT** at the command line, press ENTER, type in the new value, and press ENTER. Figure 4-3 shows the result of mirroring text with MIRRTEXT both on and off.

How do I chamfer two lines when I only know how much I want to cut off each line, but not the angle of the chamfer?

You need to use the Distance method of chamfering. The CHAMFER command has two methods of specifying the chamfer: distance and angle. Here's how they work:

● **Angle** You specify the distance for the first line, and then the angle between the first line and the desired chamfer line.

● **Distance** You specify the length that you want cut off of the first line, then the length that you want cut off of the second line, with both lengths being measured from the corner to be chamfered.

When you start the CHAMFER command, AutoCAD either displays two distances or a length and an angle. If you see two distances, then the distance method is current. If you see a length and an angle, the angle method is current. Use the Method option to change the method. You can then use the Distance or Angle options to set the desired parameters.

To specify the two distances, use the Distance option by typing **d** at the "Polyline/Distance/Angle/Trim/Method/<Select first line>:" prompt. Then, at the "Enter first chamfer distance <0'-0 1/4">:" prompt, type the distance by which you want to shorten the first line. At the "Enter second chamfer distance <0'-0 1/2">:" prompt, type the distance by which you want to shorten the second line.

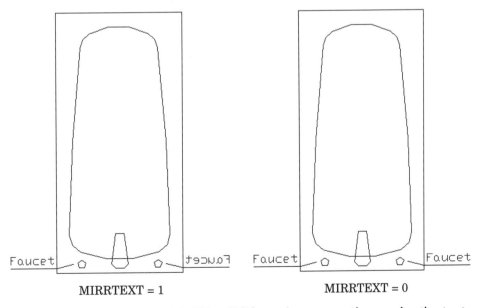

MIRRTEXT = 1   MIRRTEXT = 0

Figure 4-3 When MIRRTEXT is off (0), a mirror operation copies the text but leaves it reading from left to right

 Tip: *If you set the two chamfer distances to 0, you can use CHAMFER to trim or extend two lines so they meet perfectly.*

Remember that when you set the parameters, AutoCAD ends the command. Start the command again to actually chamfer and select the two lines you want to chamfer. If you specified two different distances, first select the line to be shortened by the first distance, and then select the line to be shortened by the second distance.

Can I extend a line to another line that won't actually meet the first line?

Yes, using the Extend Edge mode of the EXTEND command. When you start EXTEND, you will see the "Select boundary edges:" prompt. You will also see a message that looks something like this: (Projmode = UCS, Edgemode = Extend). This tells you that EXTEND is set to recognize boundary edges that would meet your object if the boundary edge were extended. To change the Edge mode, follow these steps:

1. Start the EXTEND command.

2. At the first prompt, choose the boundary edge that you want to extend to. It's okay if even when you extend your object, it won't actually meet the boundary edge. Press ENTER to end object selection of boundary edges.

3. At the "<Select object to extend>/Project/Edge/Undo:" prompt, type **e** for the Edge option.

4. AutoCAD displays the "Extend/No extend <Extend>:" prompt. (The default inside the angled brackets is the current setting.) Type **e** or **n** to choose either the Extend or the No extend option. In this case, type **e** to choose the Extend option, allowing you to extend an object—Object 1—to an object—Object 2—that Object 1 would meet only if Object 2 were extended.

5. AutoCAD repeats the previous prompt. Now you can select the object to extend.

 Note: *Remember to pick the object you want to extend on the side you want extended.*

When I try to select an object for an editing command, the crosshairs disappear and I can't select the object. Even when I'm not in a command, the crosshairs don't have the customary pickbox. What's wrong?

This can happen when the pickbox size gets set to a very large number. The pickbox is there but it's so big that you can't see it. To get it back, type **pickbox** and press ENTER. The current size is shown in the angle brackets. If it's large, type a smaller number such as **3**, the default, and press ENTER. This should bring back your crosshairs and pickbox.

Another possible cause is that grips might be disabled. Choose Tools | Grips and make sure that Enable Grips is checked in the Grips dialog box.

EDITING WITH GRIPS

Can I copy an object by using grips?

Yes, but copying using grips is a little confusing. The grip options are Stretch, Move, Rotate, Scale, and Mirror. However, each of those choices has a Copy suboption. The easiest way to copy by using grips is to use the Move option with the Copy suboption. Follow these steps:

1. Select an object or objects.
2. With the left (pick) button, click the grip that you want to use as the base point for the copy operation. It turns red (by default, but you can customize the color). This is called a *hot grip*.
3. Right-click anywhere to open the cursor menu.
4. With the left button, choose Move.
5. Right-click again and choose Copy with the left button. (You are choosing the Copy suboption of Move.)
6. At the "<Move to point>/Base point/Copy/Undo/eXit:" prompt, pick a point. This point is equivalent to the second point of displacement in a regular move operation. AutoCAD moves the object(s).

Although grips are supposed to make certain editing operations easy and intuitive, copying by using grips is not necessarily easier than using the COPY command—but if you like grips, you can copy objects with them.

When I mirror using the MIRROR command, the default is to keep the original object. But when I mirror using grips, the original disappears. How can I keep the original object?

You need to use the Copy suboption. Once you have chosen the Mirror option (either on the command line or using the cursor menu), choose the Copy suboption. Now, when AutoCAD mirrors, you will get a copy and the original object will remain.

I'd like to be able to access the grips of objects inside blocks. Is that possible?

Yes. To access grips within objects, choose Tools | Grips to open the Grips dialog box, shown in Figure 4-4.

In the top section of the dialog box, choose Enable Grips Within Blocks, and click OK. This setting is off by default because some blocks have so many objects that the grips become overwhelming. You can turn this setting on and off as you need it. For more information on customizing grips, see the box, "Customizing Grips."

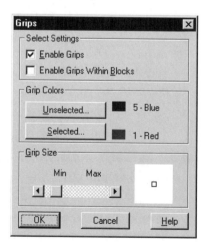

Figure 4-4   The Grips dialog box

Customizing Grips

You can use the Grips dialog box, shown in Figure 4-4, to customize how grips work. At the top of the dialog box, you can turn grips off completely by unchecking the Enable Grips check box. As mentioned in the previous question, you can also turn on grips for objects within blocks.

In the middle of the dialog box, you can customize grip colors. Choose Unselected to open the Select Color dialog box. Use this dialog box to change the color of unselected grips. To change the color of selected (hot) grips, click Selected. Again, you use the Select Color dialog box to choose a color of your choice.

At the bottom of the dialog box, use the slider bar to change the size of your grips. When you are done customizing grips, click OK to return to your drawing.

CREATING TEXT

 How do I control the way my text looks?

Text is controlled using text styles. To create a text style, follow these steps:

1. Choose Format | Text Style to start the STYLE command and open the Text Style dialog box, shown in Figure 4-5.

2. Click New and type a name for the text style. The name can have a maximum of 31 characters and may not include spaces. Click OK.

3. Click the Font Name drop-down list to choose a font.

4. Some fonts support font styles. If the Font Style drop-down list is active, you can choose a font style, such as bold or italic.

5. In the Height text box, type the desired height in units. If you want to be able to quickly vary the text's height while keeping the other properties of the text style

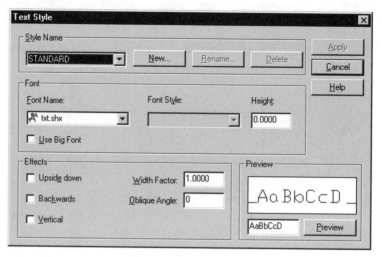

Figure 4-5 The Text Style dialog box

constant, leave the height at zero. Then, when you use the DTEXT or TEXT commands, AutoCAD will prompt you for a height.

6. In the Effects section of the dialog box, check if you want the text to be upside down, backward, or vertical. Only a few fonts support vertical text.

7. Type a width factor. A value of 1, the default, is standard text. A value less than one creates narrower characters, and a value of more than one creates fatter characters.

8. If you want to angle the characters, as in italic text, change the oblique angle. A positive angle creates italic characters, and a negative angle creates backward slanting characters.

9. Click Apply to make the text style current if you wish.

10. Click Close to close the dialog box.

 Is there a way to change the properties of all my text at once?

There are two ways to globally change text. The first is to change the text style. When you change a text style, AutoCAD regenerates the drawing and changes all the existing text that was using that text style. This method is nevertheless not very complete, because, while AutoCAD processes changes to the font, font style, and orientation, it ignores changes to the height, width, and oblique angle. When you change a text style, all new text you add will conform completely to the new definition, however.

To change a text style, choose Format | Text Style and choose the style you want to change from the Style Name drop-down list. Make your changes as you would when creating a text style, click Apply, then Close.

The other way to globally change text is to use the bonus command, CHT. Choose Bonus | Text | Change Text. Select the text objects you want to change. At the "Height/Justification/Location/Rotation/Style/Text/Undo/Width:" prompt, you can choose to change any of the listed options. The next prompt lets you change the property you chose either globally (for all selected text objects) or individually. You can continue to change other properties if you wish.

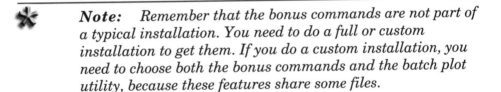

Note: *Remember that the bonus commands are not part of a typical installation. You need to do a full or custom installation to get them. If you do a custom installation, you need to choose both the bonus commands and the batch plot utility, because these features share some files.*

Sometimes I get a drawing from a colleague that contains fonts I don't have, and AutoCAD always reports that it is substituting another font. How can I control which fonts are used in place of the fonts I don't have?

There are two mechanisms that AutoCAD uses to handle text in fonts that it can't find—the font mapping table and the FONTALT system variable.

The Font Mapping Table

The font mapping table is a text file that lists substitution fonts. Font substitutions are made whether or not the original font being replaced is available. The default file, set in the Preferences dialog box, is ACAD.FMP. Each line of the

file contains a font filename, a semicolon, and the name of a font file to substitute. For example, if you want to substitute SIMPLEX.SHX for TIMES.TTF (a TrueType font), put the following line in ACAD.FMP or your own .FMP file:

```
times.ttf;simplex_.shx
```

Notice the underscore character in the simplex file. In order to create a substitution font, you need to use the actual filename. These filenames are generally found in the \Fonts subfolder of your Win95 folder, *not* in any AutoCAD R14 folder. Use Windows Explorer to locate the \Fonts subfolder and find the font you want to use. The second column lists the actual font filename.

If you want to use your own font mapping file, follow these steps:

1. Choose Tools | Preferences and click the Files tab.
2. Click the plus sign next to Text Editor, Dictionary, and Font File Names.
3. Click the plus sign next to Font Mapping File.
4. Click the current file and click Browse.
5. In the Select a File dialog box, locate your .FMP file and click Open.
6. Click OK to return to your drawing.
7. Type **regen** and press ENTER to convert existing text to the substitution font.

Tip: *You can use this method to alternate two .FMP files to change complex fonts to simpler ones while you are drawing and back to nicer ones just before plotting.*

Using the FONTALT System Variable

If your drawing includes a font that you don't have, AutoCAD looks for the value of the FONTALT system variable, which is SIMPLEX.SHX by default. You can change FONTALT to any font you wish by typing **fontalt** and entering a font.

How do I import text from a word processor document?

There are several ways to do this. The first method is to import unformatted text (files with the extension .TXT) or rich text format files (files with the extension .RTF) in the Multiline Text Editor. Follow these steps:

1. Start the MTEXT command.

2. At the prompts, specify two corners to place the text. AutoCAD opens the Multiline Text Editor.

3. Click Import Text.

4. In the Open dialog box, locate and click the file you want. Remember, it must have an extension of .TXT or .RTF. Click Open. AutoCAD places the text in the Multiline Text Editor.

5. Format the text as you wish, and click OK.

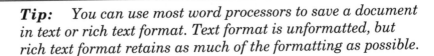

Tip: *You can use most word processors to save a document in text or rich text format. Text format is unformatted, but rich text format retains as much of the formatting as possible.*

To avoid having to save a word processing document in text or rich text format, you can skip the Import Text button and do the following:

1. Start the MTEXT command.

2. At the prompts, specify two corners to place the text. AutoCAD opens the Multiline Text Editor.

3. Go to your word processor document. If it's already open, use the Windows taskbar. Otherwise, open your word processor and the document.

4. Select the text you want and press CTRL+C to copy it to the clipboard.

5. Use the taskbar to return to your drawing. With the cursor in the Multiline Text Editor, press CTRL+V. AutoCAD pastes the text.

6. You can change the formatting of the text by using the Multiline Text Editor's tools if you wish. When you are done, click OK to place the text in your drawing.

Another method is to cut (or copy) and paste directly into the drawing. Open the file containing the text and select the desired text. Press CTRL+C to copy the text to the clipboard. If AutoCAD is not open, start it. Otherwise, click the AutoCAD button on the taskbar. What you do next, and the results you get, depend on the text and the format you want for the text in AutoCAD. Table 4-1 explains your options.

 I used Paste Special to paste formatted text into AutoCAD as AutoCAD entities, but it appeared in Greek letters! How do I get my text back in English?

Sometimes AutoCAD gets confused. This generally happens when there is a symbol in the text. (Notice in the following example, there is an arrow symbol used in the text.) You might get something like what is shown here:

1. Εξπλοδε τηε τεξτ. Ωηεν ψου παστε ιτ ιντο ΑυτοΧΑΔ ιτ ισ ιμπορτεδ ασ α βλοχκ.
2. Σελεχτ αλλ τηε τεξτ υσινγ α ωινδοω.
3. Χηοοσε Φορματ → Τεξτ Στψλεσ το οπεν τηε Τεξτ Στψλε διαλογ βοξ.

Action	Type of Text	Results
Click Paste on the Standard toolbar	Formatted	The text is pasted as an OLE frame, which can only be moved and resized (using the handles). However, you can double-click it to edit it in the original word processor.
Click Paste on the Standard toolbar	Unformatted	The text is pasted as multiline text. You can edit the text as you would any text you created using MTEXT.
Choose Edit | Paste Special	Formatted	You can choose the format AutoCAD uses to paste the object. If you choose AutoCAD Entities, you can explode it into AutoCAD text and maintain the formatting. If you choose Text, you can explode it into AutoCAD text, but you lose the formatting.

Table 4-1 Options for Pasting Text into AutoCAD

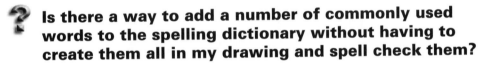

Here's how to get back your English text:

1. Explode the text. When you paste it into AutoCAD, it is imported as a block.

2. Select all the text using a window.

3. Choose Format | Text Styles to open the Text Style dialog box.

4. Click the Style Name drop-down list. Notice that AutoCAD has created one or more new styles that start with WMF. AutoCAD created as many styles as it calculated were necessary to retain the original formatting. If you see a style called WMF-SYMBOL0, that's the cause of your problem. AutoCAD changed your letters to symbols!

5. Choose another style, such as WMF-0, to maintain the text's original formatting as closely as possible. You can also choose a style that you have created.

6. Click Close to return to your drawing and see your text in English.

Is there a way to add a number of commonly used words to the spelling dictionary without having to create them all in my drawing and spell check them?

Yes, but in order to do so, you need to open the Check Spelling dialog box. However, the only way to open the Check Spelling dialog box is to have a misspelled word. The trick is to create a misspelled word! Then follow these steps:

1. Choose Tools | Spelling and select the misspelled word. AutoCAD opens the Check Spelling dialog box.

2. Choose Change Dictionaries (even though you don't want to change dictionaries) to open the Change Dictionaries dialog box, shown in Figure 4-6.

3. In the Custom dictionary words text box, type a word to add to the custom dictionary. Click Add. The word disappears from the text box but is added to the dictionary.

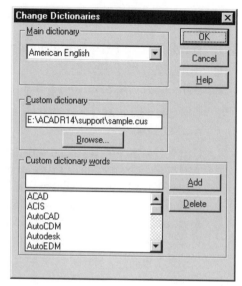

Figure 4-6   The Change Dictionaries dialog box lets you add a number of words at one time to the custom dictionary

4. Continue to type words in the text box and click Add until you have finished.

5. Click OK to return to the Check Spelling dialog box. If you wish to correct the word you intentionally misspelled, do so now. Close the Check Spelling dialog box to return to your drawing.

Can I use my word processor's custom dictionary for spell checking?

Yes, you can. Your word processor's custom dictionary may already have most of the special words you use in your drawings. Here's how to use it for your AutoCAD spell checking:

1. Locate the custom dictionary for your word processor. Microsoft Word's dictionary is called CUSTOM.DIC but yours might be different. If you know the name or extension, you can use Windows' Find feature (Choose Start | Find).

2. Use Explorer to copy the file to the AutoCAD \Support folder.

Tip: *Press CTRL as you drag it from its current folder to AutoCAD's \Support folder.*

1. Click the AutoCAD \Support folder in the left Explorer pane to list all the files in the right pane.

2. Choose your word processor's custom dictionary file to highlight it.

3. Click the file once more so you get a border around the name. You can now change the name.

4. Change the file's extension (the part after the period) to .CUS and press ENTER. Windows then asks if you are sure you want to do this. Click Yes.

5. Create a misspelled word and choose Tools | Spelling.

6. In the Check Spelling dialog box, choose Change Dictionaries to open the Change Dictionaries dialog box.

7. In the Custom dictionary text box, type the name of the dictionary file or choose Browse to locate it.

8. Click OK to return to the Check Spelling dialog box.

9. Click Cancel to return to your drawing.

From now on, AutoCAD will use your word processor's custom dictionary for checking spelling.

Once you have changed the filename extension of the dictionary you want to use, you can also tell AutoCAD to use that dictionary by choosing Tools | Preferences and clicking the Files tab. Click the plus sign next to Text Editor, Dictionary, and Font File Names. Now click the plus sign next to Custom Dictionary File. You can now type the path and name of the new dictionary, or click Browse to choose it from a dialog box.

I'd like to create some fancy text effects. Is there any way to do that in AutoCAD?

The only real text effect available is creating text along an arc, by using one of the bonus commands. Remember that the

bonus commands are not part of a typical installation. For more information on installing the bonus commands, see Chapter 2. Figure 4-7 shows an example of arc-aligned text.

Don't forget that you can import raster images of anything you want. For example, you can create fancy text or a logo in any program, save it as a bitmap file, and import it into AutoCAD. However, you can't edit the raster image in AutoCAD.

With Release 14's better support for TrueType fonts, you can get some nice effects with fonts alone. Look in the \Sample subfolder of your AutoCAD folder for TRUETYPE.DWG and open it or print it out. It contains samples of AutoCAD's TrueType fonts. In addition, AutoCAD can use any of your existing TrueType fonts. You probably have quite a few if you have a word processor on your system, so try them out!

In addition, you can use the MTEXT command to create varying colors, sizes, and fonts within a paragraph or even within a word. Highlight the text you want to change and choose the effect for that text.

How can I create stacked fractions and control their sizes?

To create stacked fractions, start the MTEXT command and specify the two corners of the text area to open the Multiline Text Editor. Type the fraction using a forward slash (/). Now, select the fraction and click the Stack/Unstack button. This button is grayed out (unavailable) until you select a fraction.

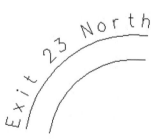

Figure 4-7   Arc-aligned text, created using the ARCTEXT bonus command

The Stack/Unstack button is a toggle, which means that it stacks unstacked fractions and unstacks stacked fractions.

When you stack a fraction, the numbers above and below the fraction line retain their original size. This generally makes the fraction, as a whole, too big for the rest of the text. To change the height of the fraction, select it and use the font height box to change the height. Try cutting the height in half so that the fraction matches the rest of the text. Click OK to close the Multiline Text Editor.

DIMENSIONING A DRAWING

 How do I control the size of stacked fractions in dimensions?

Setting the height of stacked fractions in dimensions is different from setting the height of regular text. You need to use the Annotation dialog box to control how fractions appear in dimensions. Follow these steps to create stacked fractions and control their height:

1. Start the DDIM command by choosing Dimension | Style.

2. Click Annotation in the Dimension Styles dialog box.

3. In the Annotation dialog box, choose Units from the Primary Units section.

4. In the Primary Units dialog box, click the Units drop-down list and choose Architectural (Stacked) or Fractional (Stacked). Architectural (Stacked) displays measurements in feet and inches. Fractional *inches* are stacked. The Fractional (Stacked) choice displays measurements in units. Fractional *units* are shown as stacked fractions instead of as decimals.

5. Click OK once to return to the Annotation dialog box.

6. In the Height text box of the Tolerance section, change the height. The default is 1. Use .5 if you want the total fraction to equal your other text. (The height value specifies the proportion of fractional text to regular text and is not in absolute units.)

7. Click OK.

8. If you want to save these settings as a new style, type the new style name in the Name text box and click Save. Then click OK to return to your drawing. Or click Save to save the current style with the new settings, then click OK.

Your dimensions will now show stacked fractions whose text is the proportion you specified, as shown here:

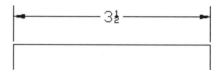

What's the best way to fit a dimension into a small space?

That depends on your situation and on the standards in your field of work. AutoCAD offers a number of ways to fit dimensions into small spaces. To find these settings, start the DDIM command (Dimension | Style), and click Format to open the Format dialog box, shown in Figure 4-8.

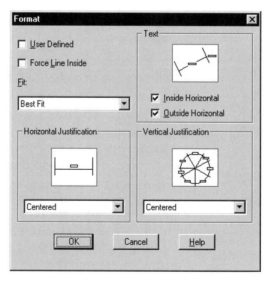

Figure 4-8   The Format dialog box offers options for fitting dimensions into small spaces

The top-left section of this dialog box is where you specify how you want AutoCAD to fit dimensions when there is not enough room for all the dimension elements. To review, here are the elements that must normally fit within the dimension:

- Dimension line
- Text
- Arrows

Table 4-2 shows how the settings in this section affect a dimension that cannot entirely fit within the length you are dimensioning.

Setting	Result
User Defined	Check this box to manually control the placement of dimension text that would otherwise be controlled by the horizontal justification setting. When User Defined is on, AutoCAD places the text where you specify for the dimension line location.
Force Line Inside	Places a dimension line between the extension lines even if there isn't room for arrows or text.
Text and Arrows	This option from the Fit drop-down list always places text and arrows together. Therefore, if there is not enough room for either text or arrows, both go outside the extension lines.
Text Only	The Text Only option from the Fit drop-down list places text inside if there is room, leaving the arrows outside the extension lines.
Arrows Only	The Arrows Only option from the Fit drop-down list places the arrows inside if there is room, leaving the text outside the extension lines.
Best Fit	This option from the Fit drop-down list fits either the text or the arrows inside if either one fits. If neither one fits, they both go outside.
Leader	The Leader option from the Fit drop-down list draws a leader if there isn't enough room for text. Text can be moved separately from the dimension line, unlike the previous options, giving you maximum flexibility for text placement.
No Leader	The No Leader option from the Fit drop-down list places the text above the dimension line with no leader if it can't fit within the extension lines. As with the Leader option, you can move the text anywhere.

Table 4-2   Fit Options for Dimensions

One of these options should provide you with the results you need. If you need to create different settings for different types of dimensions, see the box, "Creating Dimension Families."

Creating Dimension Families

Dimension styles help you control dimensions. Dimension families let you control dimension styles when you need different settings for different types of dimensions, such as linear, angular, diameter, radial, ordinate, and leader dimensions. A *child dimension style* is a group of settings that applies only to one dimension type. For example, you may want dimension text to be above the dimension line (as in architectural dimensions), but you may want leader text to be centered next to the line. By using families, you can have one vertical setting for linear dimensions and another for leaders. Here's how to create a family:

1. Start the DDIM command to open the Dimension Styles dialog box.
2. Click the type of child category you want, such as Linear, Angular, and so on.
3. Use the Geometry, Format, and Annotation buttons to make any desired changes in the dimension style setting.
4. In the Dimension Styles dialog box, click Save.

If you want to edit the child dimension style, be sure to click the child type in the Dimension Styles dialog box before making changes.

 What's the quickest way to move dimension text slightly if it's crossing another object?

Grips are the best way to move dimension text. Remember that some settings in the Fit drop-down list of the Format dialog box keep the text and dimension line together, so while you can move the text along the dimension line, you can't move it perpendicular to the dimension line. If you want to be sure you won't move the dimension line, turn on ORTHO as you move the text (double-click the ORTHO button on the status bar).

How do I move leader text to a better location?

One way is to explode the leader. The text is then a separate object that you can move. Or, you may be able to adjust the text's justification to your liking:

1. Select the leader and choose Properties from the Object Properties toolbar.
2. Click the Justify drop-down box in the dialog box and choose another justification.
3. Click OK.

I'm always exploding my dimensions. Is there any way to create dimensions that aren't blocks?

Yes, turn off the DIMASO system variable, which controls whether dimensions are associative or not. Associative dimensions are not only blocks, but they adjust automatically if you change the size of the object or objects you are dimensioning. To turn off the DIMASO system variable, type **dimaso**, press ENTER, type **off**, and press ENTER again. If you want DIMASO off permanently, you can save this value in your templates.

My arrowheads are not filled in. What is the problem?

Fill may be turned off. Type **fill**, press ENTER, type **on**, and press ENTER. Also, arrows do not show as filled after you use HIDE. Regen to return to a nonhidden view of the drawing.

 My radius and diameter dimensions aren't showing the radius or diameter symbol before the text. What's wrong?

The usual cause is that a prefix was set for the dimension style. To remove the prefix, follow these steps:

1. Choose Dimension | Style.

2. Click Annotation.

3. In the Prefix text box of the Primary Units section of the dialog box, select and delete any text, as shown in Figure 4-9.

4. Click OK.

5. In the Dimension Styles dialog box, click Save to save this change to the dimension style.

6. Click OK.

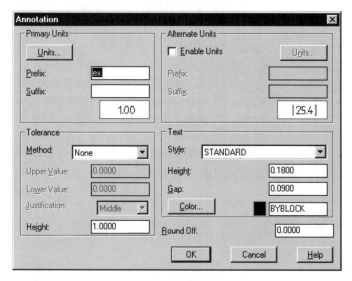

Figure 4-9   If your radius and diameter dimensions do not display the radius and diameter symbols, remove the prefix from the dimension style

 When I create my first dimension, AutoCAD creates a new layer, defpoints. What's this for?

The defpoints layer holds the definition points that AutoCAD uses to define the endpoints of the object you are dimensioning. AutoCAD uses these points to keep track of the measurements of the object so that if you stretch the object, AutoCAD can stretch the dimension and its measurement as well. When you pick a dimension, you will see a grip at each of the definition points. The defpoints layer is not plotted and cannot be deleted.

 How do I start setting up my drawing for dimensions?

There are several steps you should take before you start to dimension:

1. Create a dimension layer. Choose a color that contrasts with your objects.

2. Create a text style for your dimension text. Set the height to zero. You will specify the height when you create the dimension style. See the question "How do I control the way my text looks?," earlier in this chapter, for more details.

3. Set the running object snaps you will need, depending on the types of objects you need to dimension. See Chapter 3 for more information.

4. Create a dimension style.

5. Display the dimension toolbar.

6. If you use these settings a lot, save them in a template.

Now you're ready to dimension.

 I'm dimensioning a line at an angle. What's the difference between rotated and aligned dimensions, and which should I use?

A rotated dimension creates a linear dimension whose dimension line is not parallel to the line you are

dimensioning. As a result, the distance measured is not the same as the length of the line. Figure 4-10 shows a rotated dimension. The door, which is 3' long, is at a 45-degree angle, but the dimension has been rotated to 60 degrees and shows $2'-10^{3}/_{4}"$.

An aligned dimension's dimension line is parallel to the line you are dimensioning and always measures the line's actual length. Figure 4-11 shows the same door dimensioned with an aligned dimension.

Deciding which to use is not difficult. If you want to measure the actual length of a line at an angle, use an aligned dimension. Use a rotated dimension only if you want to measure a length at an angle that is different from the angle of the line.

To create a rotated dimension, use the DIMLINEAR command (Dimension | Linear). After specifying the extension line origins or selecting the object, type **r** and press ENTER at the "Dimension line location (Mtext/Text/Angle/Horizontal/Vertical/Rotated):" prompt. At the "Dimension line angle <0>:" prompt, type the angle you want for the dimension line angle (or specify two points that indicate the angle). You can then specify the location of the dimension line.

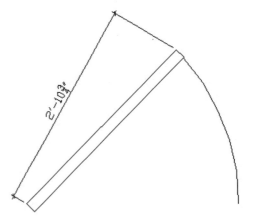

Figure 4-10 A rotated dimension

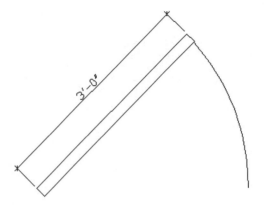

Figure 4-11   An aligned dimension

To create an aligned dimension, use the DIMALIGNED command. Specify the extension line origins or select the object. Then specify the location of the dimension line as you would for any linear dimension.

 When I dimension angles, I sometimes need to dimension the major (outside) angle, not the minor (inside angle). How do I do this?

To dimension the major angle created by two lines, follow these steps:

1. Start the DIMANGULAR command (Dimension | Angular).

2. At the "Select arc, circle, line, or RETURN:" prompt, press ENTER.

3. At the "Angle vertex:" prompt, pick the vertex of the angle.

4. At the "First angle endpoint:" prompt, press the first endpoint of the angle.

5. At the "Second angle endpoint:" prompt, press the second endpoint of the angle.

6. At the "Dimension arc line location (Mtext/Text/Angle):" prompt, move the cursor to the major angle side (outside the minor angle area) and pick a point.

AutoCAD dimensions the major angle, as shown here:

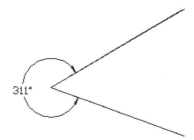

Can I tell AutoCAD to put mm after each dimension measurement?

Sure. Here are the steps to put any suffix after your dimension measurements:

1. Start the DDIM command (Dimension | Style).

2. Choose Annotation.

3. In the Suffix text box of the Primary Units section of the dialog box, type the suffix you want to add.

 Note: *You can also add a prefix in the Prefix text box.*

4. Click OK.

5. In the Dimension Styles dialog box, click Save if you want to save this change to your current dimension style.

6. Click OK to return to your drawing.

How do I create my own arrow for dimension lines?

You can create your own arrows for dimension lines if you like to be creative. Here's how:

1. In any drawing, create the arrowhead you want. The arrow should point to the right.

2. Scale the arrow so that its length is one unit.

3. Use the BMAKE command to turn the arrow into a block. Put the insertion point at the arrow's tip. Give it any name you want.

4. Use the WBLOCK command to save the block to a separate drawing file. Be sure to save the block to a folder in AutoCAD's support file search path.

5. Start the DDIM command (Dimension | Style), and click Geometry to open the Geometry dialog box, shown in Figure 4-12.

6. In the Arrowheads section, click the 1st drop-down list and scroll until you can choose User Arrow. The 2nd drop-down list automatically sets itself for a User Arrow, as well. The User Arrow dialog box opens.

7. In the dialog box, type the name of the block file you created in step 4, and click OK.

8. Type the desired size in the Size text box, and click OK to return to the Dimension Styles dialog box.

9. Click Save if you want to save the changed settings to the current dimension style.

10. Click OK to return to your drawing.

You can now dimension with your custom arrow. AutoCAD automatically reverses the block for the left end of

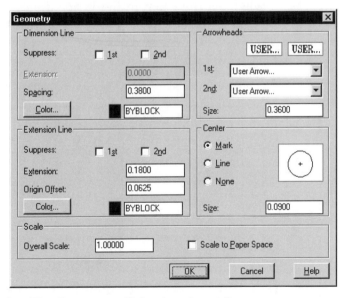

Figure 4-12 The Geometry dialog box is set for a user arrow

the dimension line and rotates the block appropriately for dimension lines at varying angles, as shown in Figure 4-13.

 ## Sometimes I need to make an exception for one setting of a dimension's style. How do I accomplish this?

It is common to need to adjust a dimension style for an unusual situation, such as a tight space or a location where one of the extension lines would interfere with another object in your drawing. This is called *overriding* a dimension style. Follow these steps:

1. Start the DDIM command.

2. Use the Geometry, Format, or Annotation dialog box to make the change (or changes) you want. Click OK.

3. In the Dimension Styles dialog box, do *not* click Save. Click OK to return to your drawing.

Your existing dimensions will now reflect the changes you made.

To continue to create new dimensions with your regular dimension style, start DDIM again and choose the current style from the Current list in the dialog box. When AutoCAD asks if you want to save the changes to the style, choose No.

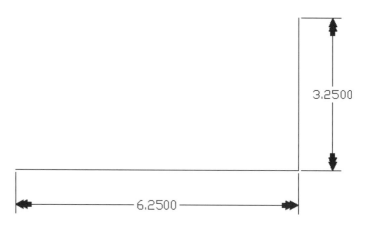

Figure 4-13 A large, fancy user arrow in two dimensions. The original block was created with a polyline of varying widths

Click OK to return to your drawing. Your new dimensions will be in the regular dimension style.

Can I copy dimension styles from other drawings?

Yes, you can. This is very useful, because dimension styles can be complex and hard to recreate. You may receive a drawing from a client and need to duplicate the dimension style. The easiest way to copy dimension styles is to use the bonus commands DIMEX, which exports dimension styles, and DIMIM, which imports dimension styles. Once the dimension style is exported as a file, your client can send it to you along with the drawing. You can then import the file into your drawing.

Note: *The bonus commands are not part of a typical installation. You need to do a full installation or a custom installation and choose both the bonus and batch plotting options.*

To export a dimension style, choose Bonus | Tools | Dimstyle Export, which opens the Dimension Style Export dialog box, shown in Figure 4-14.

Specify the filename, choose the dimension style, and pick one of the two text style options. Then click OK.

To import the file, copy it to a folder in the AutoCAD support file search path. Choose Bonus | Tools | Dimstyle

Figure 4-14 You can use the bonus command, DIMEX, to export a dimension style to a file

Import, select the desired .DIM file, and click OK. If there is an existing dimension file of the same name, you can choose to keep or overwrite the existing dimension style.

If you don't have the bonus commands installed and don't want to take the time to install them, you do have another option. Use the INSERT command and choose the drawing file containing the dimension style you want. In the Insert dialog box, Specify Parameters on Screen should be checked. Click OK. Press ESC to cancel the command. AutoCAD inserts all the styles from the other drawing but does not insert the drawing itself. You get not only the dimension styles, but also all the layers, text styles, blocks, and so on.

 Tip: *Now use PURGE to delete any unwanted styles and blocks.*

CREATING COMPLEX OBJECTS— HATCHES, POLYLINES, SPLINES, AND MULTILINES

 ### How do I control what areas are hatched when there are several overlapping objects?

If you want to hatch the entire portion of all of the objects, choose Select Objects from the Boundary section of the Boundary Hatch dialog box, shown in Figure 4-15. Then select each of the objects you want to be hatched.

If you want to hatch only certain portions of the objects, but each area you want to hatch is bounded by an object or a portion of an object, choose Pick Points from the Boundary section of the Boundary Hatch dialog box. At the "Select internal point:" prompt, pick any point inside the area you want to hatch. AutoCAD tries to find a *boundary*—an area bounded by objects or portions of objects. You can pick as many internal points as you want. Press ENTER when you're done to return to the Boundary Hatch dialog box.

If the area you want to hatch is not enclosed, you may have to enclose it by creating objects that join existing objects or by editing the objects so they meet.

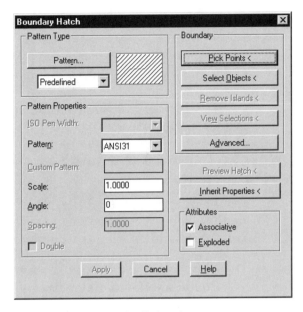

Figure 4-15 The Boundary Hatch dialog box

Can I create my own hatch pattern on the fly?

Not in the same way you can create linetypes on the fly. But you can create user-defined hatch patterns. These are hatches of parallel lines, and you can control their angle and spacing. To create a user-defined hatch pattern, follow these steps:

1. From the Draw toolbar, click Hatch. AutoCAD opens the Boundary Hatch dialog box.

2. Choose User-defined from the Pattern Type section of the dialog box.

3. Type an angle in the Angle text box.

4. Type the spacing between the lines in the Spacing text box. The number you type is the number of units between the lines.

5. Choose Double to cross-hatch, creating the hatch pattern you specified plus the same number of lines crossing at a 90-degree angle.

Apply your user-defined hatch as you would any other hatch.

 Note: *This hatch is not saved with your drawing.*

See Chapter 7 for information on creating your own custom-made hatches.

? How do I control the hatching of objects within other objects?

For the purposes of hatching, objects that are wholly inside another object are called *islands*. You can control how AutoCAD handles islands when hatching. Follow these steps:

1. Choose Hatch from the Draw toolbar to open the Boundary Hatch dialog box.

2. Choose Advanced to open the Advanced Options dialog box, shown in Figure 4-16.

3. In the Boundary Style section, click the Style drop-down list and choose the type of hatching style you want. The styles are described in Table 4-3.

4. If you want AutoCAD to recognize islands, make sure that Island Detection is checked in the Define Boundary Set section of the dialog box. By default, island detection is on.

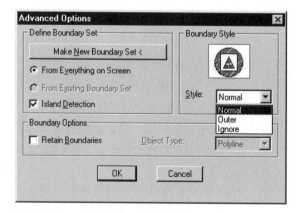

Figure 4-16 The Advanced Options dialog box, showing the hatching style drop-down list

Boundary Style	Result
Normal	AutoCAD alternates the hatching of islands within each other. The outside object is hatched, an island inside the outer object is not hatched, an island within the first island is hatched, and so on.
Outer	AutoCAD hatches just the outer object and does not hatch any inner islands.
Ignore	AutoCAD ignores islands and hatches all the area within the outer object.

Table 4-3   Hatching Boundary Styles

5. Click OK to return to the Boundary Hatch dialog box. Here you can continue to specify the hatch.

The Normal boundary style is shown here:

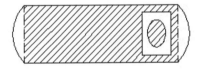

The Outer style is shown here:

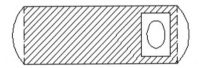

The Ignore style is shown here:

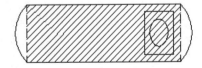

 When I select a hatch, I'd like the border to be selected as well. Can I set up AutoCAD to do this?

The PICKSTYLE system variable determines whether or not AutoCAD automatically selects the boundaries of hatches when you select the hatch itself. By default, PICKSTYLE is

set to 1, which means that when you select a hatch, the boundary is not automatically selected. Set PICKSTYLE to 3 if you want AutoCAD to automatically select the boundary when you select its hatch.

Sometimes I have trouble selecting a solid fill hatch. What's the problem?

Solid fill hatches are new for Release 14 and they take some getting used to. In order to select a solid fill, you need to use a crossing window (from right to left) or pick its edge. If you happen to pick its grip exactly, you can pick it with one click. Otherwise, a single pick will not select the solid fill.

I have some noncontinuous linetypes that I use on polylines, but they don't always appear properly. Sometimes they seem continuous or awkwardly displayed. Can I fix this?

Try changing the PLINEGEN system variable. By default PLINEGEN is off, which means that AutoCAD restarts the noncontinuous linetype's definition at each vertex of the polyline. If your polyline segments are short, the linetype may look continuous. When you turn PLINEGEN on by setting it to 1, AutoCAD generates the linetype continuously throughout the polyline.

How do I turn a series of line segments into a polyline?

Easy. Start the PEDIT command. At the "Select polyline:" prompt, choose a line. AutoCAD tells you that the line is not a polyline and asks if you want to turn it into one. Press ENTER to accept the Y default.

AutoCAD then continues with the regular PEDIT prompt. You can type **x** to exit. It is common to use the Join option to join other contiguous lines to the new polyline you just created.

 Splines seem to have control points, fit points, and fit data. I'm confused. What's the difference between these?

When you create a spline, you pick points to define the spline. These are fit points. Unless you set the fit tolerance to a number other than the default of zero, the spline passes through these fit points, as shown in Figure 4-17. When you select a spline, you see grips on the fit points. You can tell because they are usually on the spline (unless you set a tolerance).

AutoCAD calculates other points, called control points, to display the spline. These points are not on the spline, but are necessary to display the spline. In fact, once AutoCAD has created the control points, it doesn't need the fit points any more.

Finally, the fit data includes the fit points, the tolerance, and the tangents you specified when you created the spline.

When you start the SPLINEDIT command and select the spline, the grips displayed are on the control points, and some will seem to be very far from the spline itself. You can use the Fit data option to edit the fit points and see the grips back on the fit points again. If you purge the fit data or make other changes that require AutoCAD to discard the fit data, the Fit data option will not appear when you use SPLINEDIT on that spline. AutoCAD can also discard the fit data if you use the Refine option, or change the tolerance and move its control points.

Figure 4-17   When you draw a spline and then select it, you can see the grips on the fit points

 ## How do I go about creating multilines?

There are several steps to creating multilines:

1. Choose Format | Multiline Style to open the Multiline Styles dialog box. Type a new name for the style in the Name text box and click Add. Use the Element Properties and Multiline Properties buttons to specify the style, and then click OK. For further details, see the box, "Creating a Multiline Style."

2. Click Save to save the changes to the new style.

3. In the Save Multiline Style dialog box, choose a file. You can either save the style in the default file, ACAD.MLN, or create a separate multiline style file for your custom multilines. Click Save.

4. From the Multiline Style dialog box, click Load. In the resulting dialog box, choose your multiline style. Click OK to load the style.

5. Click OK again to return to your drawing.

6. To draw with the multiline, choose Multiline from the Draw toolbar to start the MLINE command. You can change the justification, scale, and style at the prompt.

7. Pick points to create the multiline. When you are finished, press ENTER to end the command.

 ## How do you edit multilines?

A multiline is all one object. The following editing commands do not work with multilines:

- BREAK
- CHAMFER
- EXTEND
- FILLET
- LENGTHEN

Creating a Multiline Style

Before you can use a multiline, you need to create a style. AutoCAD only comes with one standard multiline style—two black lines one unit apart. Multiline styles have two components: element properties, which determine the lines that make up the multiline; and multiline properties, which affect the multiline as a whole. Here's how you create your own multiline style.

1. Choose Format | Multiline Style.

2. Type a name in the Name text box and click Add.

3. Click Element Properties to open the Element Properties dialog box, shown here:

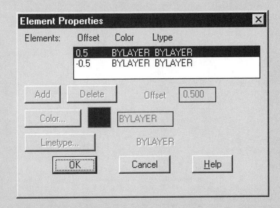

4. If the existing two lines of the Standard style don't suit your needs, select each one and click Delete. You can also select them and change their properties if that is easier for you.

5. To create a new line, choose Add.

6. Type the offset value in the Offset text box (for an existing element or a new one). The offset defines the distance in units that the line should be from the points you pick when you draw the line. An offset of 0 places the line on the pick point. A positive offset places the line above the pick point when the line is

horizontal and you are drawing from left to right. A negative offset places the line below the pick point. The offset maintains the same relationship to the pick point when you draw a multiline in other directions.

7. Click Color and choose a color for the line.

8. Click Linetype and choose a linetype.

9. Continue to add new line elements until you are done.

10. Click OK to return to the Multiline Styles dialog box.

11. Click Multiline Properties to open the Multiline Properties dialog box, shown here:

12. Click Display joints if you want AutoCAD to place a line across each vertex.

13. To place a closing line at the start and/or end of the multiline, check one or both of the Line check boxes. In the Angle text box, type an angle for the line.

14. To place an outer arc at the start and/or end of the multiline, check one or both of the Outer arc check boxes. An outer arc connects the outermost elements with an arc.

15. To place an inner arc at the start and/or end of the multiline, check one or both of the Inner arcs check boxes. An inner arc connects the matching inner elements with an arc, as shown here:

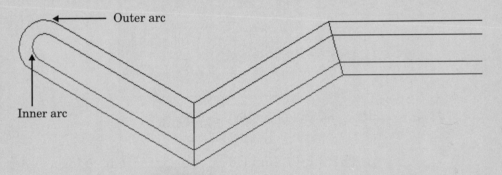

Outer arc

Inner arc

16. If you want the inside of the multiline filled, check On in the Fill section and choose a color.

17. Click OK.

18. In the Multiline Styles dialog box, click Save.

19. Click Load. Choose the new multiline style and click OK.

20. Click OK again to return to your drawing.

That is a lot of steps! Don't forget to load your multiline style or else you won't be able to use it!

AutoCAD offers a special command just for editing multilines: MLEDIT. Choose Modify | Object | Multiline, and AutoCAD opens the Multiline Edit Tools dialog box, shown in Figure 4-18.

 Tip: *Click any of the images to see its name at the bottom of the dialog box.*

- The first column creates three types of crossing intersections: the closed cross, the open cross, and the merged cross.
- The second column creates three types of T-shaped intersections: the closed tee, the open tee, and the merged tee.

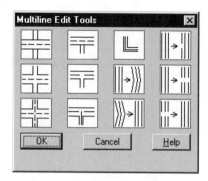

Figure 4-18 The Multiline Edit Tools dialog box

 The third column creates a corner joint, adds a vertex, or deletes a vertex.

 The last column cuts through one or all of the multiline elements, or removes cuts (called welding).

To edit the multiline, choose the type of editing operation you want and click OK. AutoCAD closes the dialog box and prompts you to pick the appropriate multiline. Once you do so, AutoCAD edits the multiline.

When you create intersections, AutoCAD asks you to select the first and second multilines. These can be two segments of one multiline. For intersections that involve editing one of the multiline segments, AutoCAD edits the first one you pick.

Tip: *If you want to move a vertex, the easiest way is to stretch it using grips.*

LAYING OUT AND PLOTTING A DRAWING

Why doesn't the Plot dialog box appear when I use the PLOT command?

If the Plot dialog box doesn't appear, then the CMDDIA system variable is turned off. Type **cmddia**, press ENTER, type **1**, and press ENTER again. Your dialog box should now appear. This can happen when an AutoLISP routine turns CMDDIA off and gets interrupted before turning it on again.

 I'm still confused about paper space. Are there any shortcuts to help me use it?

The MVSETUP command can help you set up a drawing in paper space. It's a bit obscure, but it can help you with the basics. Since MVSETUP is an old command, you provide your settings on the command line. The following steps don't explain each option in detail, but include the basics:

1. Type **mvsetup** on the command line.

2. At the "Enable paper space? (No/<Yes>):" prompt, type **y** and press ENTER. AutoCAD puts you into paper space and displays the main MVSETUP prompt, "Align/Create/ Scale viewports/Options/Title block/Undo:".

3. If you want to insert a title block in paper space, start by choosing Options, which affects how AutoCAD inserts the title block.

4. At the "Choose option to set — Layer/LImits/Units/Xref:" prompt, type **l** to specify the layer for the title block. You can name an existing or a new layer.

5. AutoCAD repeats the previous prompt. Type **li** and then type **y** or **n** to specify if you want AutoCAD to set the limits to the extents of the title block.

6. Type **u** to set the paper space units to feet, inches, meters, or millimeters.

7. Type **x** to specify if you want the title block to be an external reference or to be inserted as a block.

8. When you are done setting the options, press ENTER to return to the original MVSETUP prompt. Type **t** and press ENTER twice to insert (or xref) a title block. AutoCAD lists a full range of title block sizes in millimeters and inches.

9. At the "Add/Delete/Redisplay/<Number of entry to load>:" prompt, type the number of the title block you want, and press ENTER or choose one of the options. You can also add and delete title blocks. Once you have placed the title block, AutoCAD repeats the original prompt.

 Tip: *To add your own title block, create it and save it in a folder in AutoCAD's support file search path, such as the \Support folder. It must be saved as a drawing, not a template. Choose the Add option in MVSETUP, write a description (which will appear in the list of title blocks), and type the name of the drawing. You can also specify the default usable area for the title block. AutoCAD then relists the title blocks, including the one you added. You can then choose it from the list.*

10. You are now ready to create floating viewports. Type **c** and press ENTER twice. AutoCAD lists four choices: none; single; Std. Engineering, which creates four viewports with four differing viewpoints; and Array of Viewports, which lets you specify how many viewports you want along the X and Y axes.

11. Choose the option you want, and follow the prompts for the bounding area of the viewports and other options, depending on your choice. AutoCAD creates the viewports, and you can now see your drawing in them.

12. You can now type **s** to use the Scale viewports option and set the scale within each viewport. AutoCAD asks you to select the viewports you want to scale. Be sure to pick on the viewport's border to pick the viewport itself. Press ENTER to end selection.

13. AutoCAD asks you to specify the ratio of paper space units to model space units. This is very much like setting any plotting ratio because the view you see in paper space is equivalent to one sheet of paper. At the "Number of paper space units. <1.0>:" prompt, type the scale factor. For example, 48 and 96 are typical architectural scale factors.

14. At the "Number of model space units. <1.0>:" prompt, type a number. If you typed the scale factor in the previous prompt, you can usually press ENTER to keep the default of 1.

15. You can continue to use the Scale viewports option for all the viewports.

16. The final option, Align, lets you align objects in different viewports. Most alignments are horizontal or vertical. The viewport that you want to align should be current. Type **a** to start the option, and then choose either the Horizontal or Vertical alignment.

17. At the "Basepoint:" prompt, pick a point in the viewport you want to align to.

18. Click the viewport you want to align (change). At the "Other point:" prompt, pick a point that will then be aligned either horizontally or vertically with the base point.

19. Press ENTER to end the command.

✱ ***Note:*** *You will probably still have to go into each viewport and pan the view until it shows what you want. You may also want to resize or move the viewports themselves.*

Figure 4-19 shows a paper space layout created with MVSETUP. For more information about paper space, see the box, "Working in Paper Space."

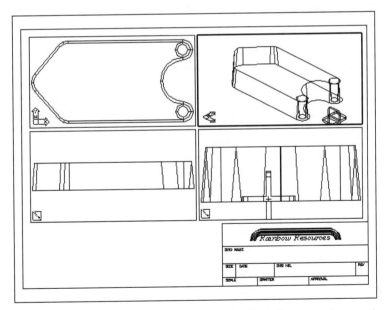

Figure 4-19 A paper space layout using the Std. Engineering option, created with the MVSETUP command

See the question "Is there an easy way to set up different views of a 3-D drawing in paper space?" in Chapter 6 for another way to set up a 3-D drawing in paper space—by using the SOLVIEW command.

Working in Paper Space

Working in paper space seems complex at first, but with a little practice you will feel quite comfortable. First, review the answer to the question "What's the difference between tiled viewports and floating viewports?" in Chapter 3 in the "Displaying Your Drawing" section.

The key to understanding paper space is to realize that there are actually three, not two, working modes. These are outlined here:

Mode	Description	How to Get There
Model space with no paper space layout	The default working space. You create your drawing here at full size without any thought of the final layout on a sheet of paper. The MODEL button shows on the status bar, and the TILE button is on.	All new drawings automatically open in model space. To get to model space from either of the other two modes, double-click TILE on the status bar.
Model space with paper space layout	After creating your paper space layout, you work in this mode to zoom and pan to get the right views. You can also freeze layers in individual floating viewports. This mode is similar to working with tiled viewports—to work in a viewport, click it to make it active. The MODEL button shows on the status bar, and the TILE button is off.	From paper space, double-click PAPER on the status bar.

Mode	Description	How to Get There
Paper space	Use paper space to create your floating viewports and/or insert a title block. You cannot work on your drawing, but you can add elements to the title block and annotation that reside in paper space. You can move and resize any viewport (which are all actual objects) by clicking on it, clicking a grip to make it hot, and specifying a new location for the hot grip. PAPER shows on the status bar, and the TILE button is off.	From model space with no paper space layout, double-click TILE on the status bar. From model space with paper space layout, double-click MODEL on the status bar.

Here is the usual procedure for creating a layout in paper space:

1. Create your drawing in model space with no layout.

2. Create layers for paper space. You usually use a separate layer for the floating viewports, so you can freeze them if you don't want to see the borders. If you will insert a title block in paper space, create a layer for that, too. You can also place text and dimensions in paper space if you wish.

3. Enter paper space (double-click TILE on the status bar).

4. Insert the title block if you want one.

5. Create the floating viewports (choose View | Floating Viewports). Resize or move them as needed.

6. Change to model space with paper space layout by double-clicking PAPER on the status bar.

7. For each viewport, click inside the border to make it active and set the scale. You can use Realtime zoom or use ZOOM with the Scale option to create an exact scale. For example, to create a 1:48 scale, type **1/48xp** at the "Enter scale factor:" prompt.

8. Pan to get the view that you need of your drawing.

9. You may also want to freeze layers in certain viewports. For example, you may want dimensions to show only once. Click the viewport, click the Layer Control drop-down list on the Object Properties toolbar, and click the Freeze/Thaw in current viewport for the layer you want to freeze.

> *Tip:* *The column headings are too narrow to read. Hold the cursor over each column and the heading pops up as a ToolTip.*

You can go back and forth among the three modes as necessary until you are satisfied with the results.

 Can I save the scale of a paper space viewport so that if I zoom in on it I can get back my original scale again?

Yes, you can use the DDVIEW command to save a view in paper space, including the zoom value.

 First, with your paper space viewports visible, go into model space by double-clicking the PAPER button on the status bar. Click the viewport you want to work in and set the zoom. For example, if you want to set a 1:2 zoom, start the ZOOM command and type **.5xp**.

Choose Named Views on the Standard toolbar to open the View Control dialog box, shown in Figure 4-20.

Click New to open the Define New View dialog box:

Define New View	☒
New Name:	
⦿ Current Display	
○ Define Window	
Window <	

First Corner	Other Corner
X: -7.3364	X: 19.3249
Y: -10.9972	Y: 10.3808

Save View	Cancel

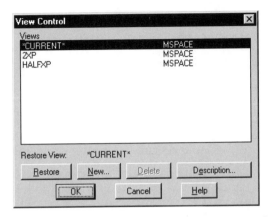

Figure 4-20   The View Control dialog box lets you save views in paper space viewports so you can restore them easily

Type a view name with no spaces in the New Name text box, and click Save View. Your view now appears on the list of views in the View Control dialog box.

 Note: *Although your view is in a paper space floating viewport, because you were in model space (with TILEMODE off) when you saved the view, the View Control dialog box correctly lists your view as being in model space. You can also save views in paper space, when the PAPER button on the status bar is displayed.*

To restore your view, open the View Control dialog box again (using the DDVIEW command), choose the desired view, click Restore, and click OK.

 I want to create an unusual-shaped floating viewport, because otherwise unwanted portions of the drawing show in that viewport. Can I do this?

No and yes. AutoCAD can only create rectangular viewports. However, there is a way to create the same effect, using the XCLIP command. The XCLIP command can create polygon-shaped boundaries that clip external references, or xrefs. For more information on xrefs, see Chapter 5. Here's

how to create the effect of an unusual-shaped floating viewport:

1. Start a new drawing.

2. In paper space, create the floating viewports you want on their own layer. Insert a title block if you want.

3. Double-click PAPER on the status bar to enter model space with the paper space layout.

4. Choose Insert | External Reference and click Attach.

5. Choose the file you want to plot and click Open. Click OK again to return to your drawing. AutoCAD displays the xref in all the floating viewports.

6. Click in the viewport with which you want to clip the xref. A top view is probably the easiest to work with.

7. Choose Modify | Object | Clip. At the "Select objects:" prompt, pick anywhere on the xref and press ENTER to end object selection.

8. At the "ON/OFF/Clipdepth/Delete/generate Polyline/<New boundary>:" prompt, press ENTER.

9. At the "Select polyline/Polygonal/<Rectangular>:" prompt, type **p** and press ENTER to specify a polygonal clipping boundary. The polygonal boundary gives you the flexibility to create an irregular border.

10. Start picking points around the part of the xref you want to keep. AutoCAD shows the entire boundary as you pick points. Press ENTER when you are done, and AutoCAD clips the xref. Anything outside the boundary is not shown. At the top of Figure 4-21 you can see a drawing with a small part that you may not want to plot. At the bottom you see the clipping boundary that has clipped off that small part.

11. Choose Modify | External Reference | Frame. The Frame menu item has a check next to it if your frame was visible, as in Figure 4-21. Choose Frame to turn off the frame.

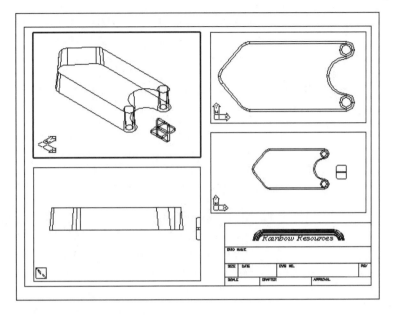

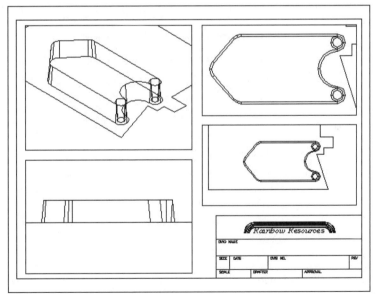

Figure 4-21 On the top you see the original drawing. The viewports display has been created by inserting an external reference. On the bottom you see the result of clipping the xref. The small part is no longer visible

12. Double-click the MODEL button to return to paper space and freeze the viewport layer. The result is shown in Figure 4-22.

Can I use varying line thicknesses when printing a drawing?

Line weights (thicknesses) are assigned to colors in your drawing. For most printers, you can assign different weights for any of the colors available in AutoCAD. To do this, follow these steps:

1. Make sure that your drawing is organized so that each color contains only objects that are to receive a particular line weight. Set the colors by defining layers. Any one color can only receive one line weight.

2. Start the PLOT command. In the Print/Plot Configuration dialog box, click Pen Assignments to open the Pen Assignments dialog box, shown in Figure 4-23.

3. Choose the color whose line weight you want to set.

4. In the Width text box at the right of the dialog box, type the new line weight.

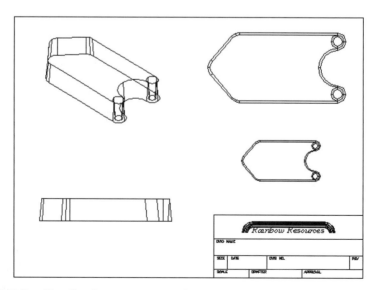

Figure 4-22 The final paper space views

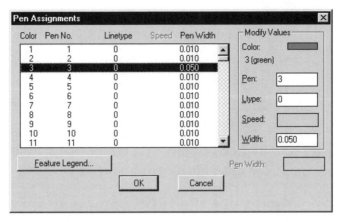

Figure 4-23 The Pen Assignments dialog box

5. Click OK.

6. Print or plot as usual.

 Note: *The new line weight may not show up in a plot preview.*

The table shown here lists the most commonly used colors and their numbers:

Color Number	Color Name
1	Red
2	Yellow
3	Green
4	Cyan
5	Blue
6	Magenta
7	Black/White

 The lines in my drawing plot too thick. Can I change this?

In Release 14, the pen widths default to .01. You may find this too faint or too thick. To change it, start the PLOT command and click Pen Assignments in the Print/Plot

Configuration dialog box. To select all the colors you use, you can do either of the following:

● Click at the top and drag down to the last color number you want to include.

● Click at the top, then press SHIFT while clicking the last color number you want to include.

In the Width text box at the right of the dialog box, type the new line weight and click OK.

When I use the HIDE command on a 3-D model, text in a TrueType font is not filled in. How can I get the text filled in properly?

There are a couple of workarounds to this problem, which is illustrated in Figure 4-24.

Note: *The text in Figure 4-24 was created using the View option of the UCS command so that the text would appear flat.*

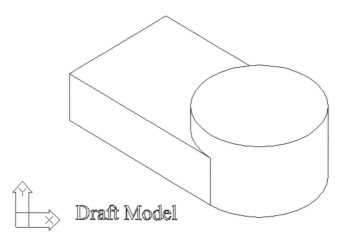

Figure 4-24 When you use the HIDE command, TrueType text loses its fill

For the first workaround, don't use the HIDE command. Instead, follow these steps:

1. Go into paper space and create a floating viewport for your model using the MVIEW command.

2. Use the MVIEW command again and choose the Hideplot option. Type **on** to turn on Hideplot.

3. At the "Select objects:" prompt, choose the viewport.

4. Start the PLOT command. In the Print/Plot Configuration dialog box, make sure Hide Lines is not checked.

5. Plot as usual.

Your TrueType text will be filled in, and the model gets hidden as well.

The second workaround is similar, as follows:

1. Remove the text from model space.

2. Create a floating viewport for your model using the MVIEW command.

3. In paper space, create the TrueType text.

4. Use the MVIEW command again and choose the Hideplot option. Type **on** to turn on Hideplot.

5. At the "Select objects:" prompt, choose the viewport.

6. Start the PLOT command. In the Print/Plot Configuration dialog box, make sure Hide Lines is not checked.

7. Plot as usual.

Your TrueType text will be properly filled in, as shown in Figure 4-25.

 When plotting 3-D models from paper space, can I hide lines in one floating viewport and not in another?

Yes, the technique is to uncheck Hide Lines in the Print/Plot Configuration dialog box and use the Hideplot option of the

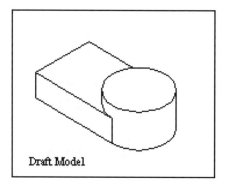

Draft Model

Figure 4-25 By placing either both the text and the model, or just the text, in paper space you can create filled-in TrueType text with a hidden 3-D model

MVIEW command, which hides hidden lines from the viewport or viewports you choose. To hide lines in one or more viewports, follow these steps:

1. Set up your viewports in paper space.

2. From paper space, choose View | Floating Viewports | Hideplot.

3. At the "ON/OFF/Hideplot/Fit/2/3/4/Restore/<First Point>: _h ON/OFF:" prompt, type **on** and press ENTER.

4. At the "Select objects:" prompt, pick one or more viewports. Note that if the viewport frames are on a frozen layer, you should unfreeze that layer so you can select the viewport. Press ENTER to end viewport selection. You won't see any difference on your screen.

 Tip: *You can use the LIST command and select the viewport to obtain the Hideplot setting.*

5. Start the PLOT command.

6. Make sure that Hide Lines is not checked.

7. Plot as usual.

Figure 4-26 shows a drawing where one viewport has hidden lines and the other does not.

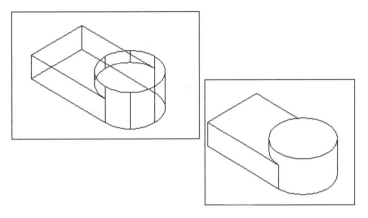

Figure 4-26 To hide lines in only some viewports, use the Hideplot option of the MVIEW command

To plot without hiding lines, use the same technique, and turn Hideplot off for the desired viewport.

 We do two kinds of plotting—draft plots on our printer and final plots on our plotter. Going from one to the other involves changing a lot of settings. Is there a shortcut?

Yes. Your plotting will soon be a lot easier! The answer is to create a plot configuration file. Release 14 introduces a new kind of plot configuration file, the PC2 file, which not only lets you specify which plotter or printer to use, but all the plotting parameters as well. When you are ready to print or plot, choose the plot configuration file that you have saved, and AutoCAD will automatically use all the settings you want. Here's how it works:

1. Click Print on the Standard toolbar to open the Print/Plot Configuration dialog box. Set all the options as you want them.

2. Click Device and Default Selection.

3. In the Device and Default Selection dialog box, shown in Figure 4-27, click Save under the heading Complete (PC2). Save the file in a folder that is in AutoCAD's support file search path, such as the \Support folder.

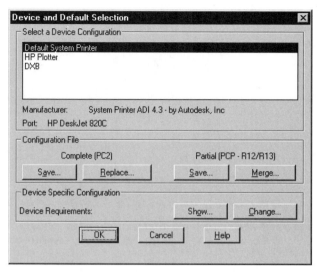

Figure 4-27 Use the Device and Default Selection dialog box to save configuration files

You can do this as many times as you need to, saving all your commonly used plotting configurations. To use a configuration file, follow these steps:

1. Click Device and Default Selection from the Print/Plot Configuration dialog box.

2. In the Configuration File section, under Complete (PC2), click Replace to open the Replace from PC2 File dialog box.

3. In the Replace from PC2 File dialog box, choose your configuration file and click Open.

4. AutoCAD asks you for a description in the Describe Device dialog box. Type a description and click OK.

AutoCAD uses the parameters in the configuration file to replace the current print/plot parameters.

 Note: *You can still use partial (PCP) configuration files to exchange drawings with people who use Release 12 or 13. Partial configuration files do not contain settings specific to your printer or plotter.*

Chapter 5

Managing Drawings

Answer Topics!

Managing Drawings @ a Glance

AutoCAD offers a number of ways to manage your drawings. For example, if you need to place a certain group of objects several times in your drawing, you can draw the group of objects once, save it as a *block,* and then insert it in any location, scale, and rotation. You can also save the block as a file so that you can insert it into other drawings, and automatically update the drawing when the block is updated.

You can attach placeholders for text (*attributes*) to blocks. You can then specify the text each time you insert the block. You can use attributes to track price information, for example. Another common use for attributes is to place text in a title block. If you are tracking price or other information, you can extract all the attributes to a text file that can be imported into a database management or spreadsheet program.

If you need to refer to other drawings, you can attach them to your drawing as external references (or xrefs). You can see xrefs and use their objects for object snaps, but you cannot change them. Release 14 offers a new xref manager that makes it much easier to keep track of xrefs.

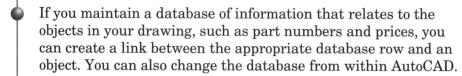

● If you maintain a database of information that relates to the objects in your drawing, such as part numbers and prices, you can create a link between the appropriate database row and an object. You can also change the database from within AutoCAD.

● Occasionally a drawing gets corrupted. AutoCAD has two commands, AUDIT and RECOVER, that try to repair these drawing files. AutoCAD also creates backup files by default, which are duplicates of your regular drawings. If the drawing gets corrupted, you may be able to use one of the backups. To control the size of drawings, you can purge unused layers, blocks, and other named symbols. If lists of layers or other symbols are not alphabetized, you can increase the value of the MAXSORT system variable.

● No program stands alone. You often need to import data into AutoCAD or export a drawing to another application. Release 14 offers increased support for bringing raster images—bitmap graphics—into your drawing. You can also import text from a word processor document into your drawing, or you can link the text so that your drawing always displays the most updated version of the word processor document. You can also place a drawing in a word processor document, including a 3-D view. And when you need to share drawings with colleagues who are using another CAD program, you can create a DXF file, an ASCII file that contains the data for your entire drawing.

● You can fax drawings using your fax software or the software that comes with Windows. Or, you can display drawings on a Web site by creating a DWF file. Anyone with the WHIP! viewer can view and print the drawing. If the actual drawing is in the same folder as the DWF file, viewers can access the actual drawing as well.

CREATING AND INSERTING BLOCKS

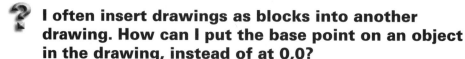 **I often insert drawings as blocks into another drawing. How can I put the base point on an object in the drawing, instead of at 0,0?**

The BASE command was created for just this situation. To change existing drawings, follow these steps:

1. Open the drawing you want to insert, type **base**, and press ENTER.

2. At the "Base point <0.0000,0.0000,0.0000>:" prompt, type or pick a new base point. You can use object snaps, of course.

3. Save the drawing.

Now when you insert that drawing, the base point will be on the new point you specified.

In the future, when you create drawings that you plan to insert as blocks, use the BASE command before saving the drawing.

✳ *Note:* *If you create a drawing file using the WBLOCK command, AutoCAD prompts you for an insertion base point. When you insert this file, it will always use that point as the base point. You only need to use the BASE command when you are inserting a drawing that was saved in the regular way, using the SAVE or QSAVE command.*

For more information on blocks, see the following box, "How to Create and Insert Blocks."

How to Create and Insert Blocks

A block is a collection of objects that you can insert and edit as one object. Blocks have many advantages compared to using individual objects:

● If you need many instances of the collection of objects, you don't need to create the objects each time. You create the objects once, save them as a block, and then insert the block as many times as you need to.

● Because your drawing only saves the block definition once, your drawing is smaller if you use blocks as compared to using individual objects. This reduces regeneration, open, and save time and uses up less space on your hard disk or network.

● You can insert blocks at any scale or rotation. You can even mirror them. As a result, blocks are very flexible.

● Blocks are treated as all one object. However, if you need to access the individual objects, you can explode the block.

● You can save blocks to a file, thus using blocks as a symbols or parts library.

● You can change all the instances of a block by redefining the block definition.

● You can attach attributes (block labels) to blocks. You can use attributes to create simple databases of information related to your drawing objects.

To create a block, follow these steps:

1. Create the objects you want to include in the block. To determine which layers to use for the objects, see "I'm confused about blocks and layers. How do I decide what layer the components of a block should be created on?," later in this chapter.

2. Choose Make Block from the Draw toolbar to open the Block Definition dialog box, shown here:

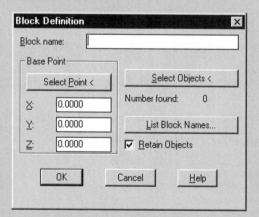

3. In the Block name text box, type a name for the block. The name cannot be more than 31 characters and cannot contain spaces.

4. Click Select Objects, and select all the objects you want to include in your block. Press ENTER to end object selection and AutoCAD returns you to the Block Definition dialog box.

Tip: *You can select the objects before choosing Make Block. The number of selected objects will be shown in the Block Definition dialog box under the Select Objects button.*

5. Click Select Point in the Base Point section of the dialog box. In your drawing, choose the base point for the block. AutoCAD returns you to the dialog box. (Or, if you know the exact coordinates, you can type them in the text boxes instead.)

6. Click OK.

AutoCAD creates the block, and by default the original objects remain as individual objects. If you uncheck Retain Objects in the Block Definition dialog box, however, AutoCAD erases the original objects. You can type **oops** and press ENTER to get them back.

To use the block, you need to insert it. Follow these steps:

1. Choose Insert Block from the Draw toolbar to open the Insert dialog box, shown here:

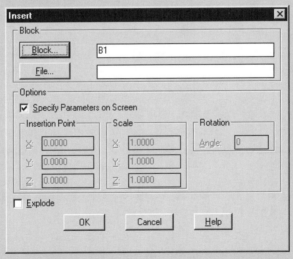

2. Choose the block or file you want to insert:

● If you want to insert a block from your current drawing, type its name in the Block text box or click Block to open a list of blocks in your drawing.

● If you want to insert a drawing file, type its name (including its path if it isn't in AutoCAD's support file search path) or click File to open a dialog box in which you can locate and select the file.

3. If Specify Parameters on Screen is checked, AutoCAD prompts you for the block's insertion point, scale, and rotation on the command line. To specify any of these parameters in advance, uncheck Specify Parameters on Screen and use the text boxes to specify the parameters in the dialog box. (This is the only way to specify a Z scale factor that is different from the X scale.) If you want to insert the block or file in exploded form, that is, as separate objects, click Explode. When you are done, click OK.

4. If Specify Parameters on Screen was checked, AutoCAD now prompts you for the insertion point. Specify a coordinate on your screen. Object snaps are ideal for this purpose.

5. Next, AutoCAD prompts you for the X scale factor. The default is one. Any number larger than one increases the size of the block and any number less than one decreases the size of the block.

6. AutoCAD now asks you for the Y scale factor. By default, this value is the same as the X scale factor you specified. By making the X and Y scale factors different, you can change the proportions of the block.

7. A negative X or Y scale factor creates a mirror image of the block. A negative X scale factor mirrors the block around the Y axis, and vice versa.

8. Finally, AutoCAD prompts you for the rotation angle. You can use a positive or negative angle. The default is zero.

What's the best way to organize all the standard parts or symbols that I use?

This is one of the top ten frequently asked AutoCAD questions. See question #7 in Chapter 1 for the answer.

I'm confused about blocks and layers. How do I decide what layer the components of a block should be created on?

You're not alone. You have four possibilities when creating components for a block. Table 5-1 explains these choices, their results, and some potential problems.

Component Properties	Result When Inserted	Potential Problems
On layer 0 (color and linetype set to ByBlock or ByLayer)	Block is inserted on current layer with that layer's color and linetype properties	None
On any layer except 0 with color and linetype set to ByLayer	Block keeps properties of layers of component objects	If the drawing doesn't contain the layer of the component objects, AutoCAD creates it. If the layer exists but has a different color and/or linetype, the block takes on that different color and/or linetype. If the current layer is different from the components' layer, the block looks like it is on the layer of the component objects, but the DDMODIFY command lists the block as being on the current layer, because it takes the block's layer from the insertion point.
On any layer except 0 with color and linetype set to ByBlock	Block is inserted on current layer with that layer's color and linetype properties	If the layer on which the components were created doesn't exist in the accepting drawing, AutoCAD creates the layer.
On any layer except 0 with color and linetype set specifically	Block keeps color and linetype that you set	If the layer on which the components were created doesn't exist in the accepting drawing, AutoCAD creates the layer.

Table 5-1   Results of Inserting Blocks by Properties of Component Objects

Creating the component objects on layer 0 gives you the most flexibility. You can get the block to look the way you want by inserting the block on a layer with the appropriate properties. However, this doesn't work if you have blocks with components that must have varying colors and/or linetypes. In that case, you may need to use one of the other options.

 When I insert a block, I don't see the usual image of the block moving with the cursor. Where did it go?

The image of an object when inserting a block or using editing commands, such as MOVE or COPY, is controlled by

the DRAGMODE command. DRAGMODE is set to Auto by default, which means that for any appropriate command, you will see an image of the object moving as you move the cursor, as shown here:

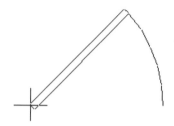

If someone, or perhaps an AutoLISP routine, changed the setting, you won't see the image. To turn the image back on, type **dragmode** at the command line and press ENTER. In parentheses, you can see the current setting.

● If the current setting is OFF, you never see the image.

● If the current setting is ON, you only see the image when you type **drag** during the command. (You don't need to use an apostrophe as you do with transparent commands.)

To see the image whenever possible, type **a** and press ENTER to return DRAGMODE to its default Auto mode.

Another reason you may not see the block is if its base point is widely separated from the objects in the block. The insertion point is on the screen but the block may not be. To check, do a ZOOM All, which works transparently, while inserting the block. You can also insert the block and do a ZOOM Extents afterward to see if the block appears.

 When I am inserting a block, I would like to see the dragged image at the scale and rotation I want to use. Is that possible?

Yes, it is. Seeing the dragged image at a suitable scale or rotation can certainly help you decide if you've specified the correct parameters. AutoCAD offers some little-known options that you can use at the "Insertion point:" prompt to preset the scale and/or rotation. These presets are shown in Table 5-2.

Preset Option	Description
Scale	Sets the X, Y, and Z scales.
Xscale	Sets the X scale only.
Yscale	Sets the Y scale only.
Zscale	Sets the Z scale only.
Rotate	Sets the rotation.
PScale	Preliminarily sets the X, Y, and Z scales but prompts you again for the scale after you pick the insertion point.
PXscale	Preliminarily sets the X scale only but prompts you again for the scale after you pick the insertion point.
PYscale	Preliminarily sets the Y scale only but prompts you again for the scale after you pick the insertion point.
PZscale	Preliminarily sets the Z scale only but prompts you again for the scale after you pick the insertion point.
PRotate	Preliminarily sets the rotation but prompts you again for the rotation after you pick the insertion point.

Table 5-2 Block Parameter Preset Options

When you use any one of these preset options, the dragged image of the block appears according to the scale or rotation you specify. If you used the preliminary options (the ones starting with a "P"), AutoCAD prompts you for the parameter again, after you pick an insertion point, so you can change preliminary settings. Otherwise, AutoCAD inserts the block with the parameter you specified. The following illustration shows a block being inserted with the Rotate option, which was specified at 45 degrees:

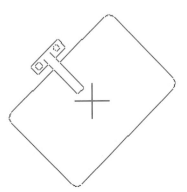

To use the presets, you only need to type the letter or letters that are in uppercase in Table 5-2. You can also use more than one preset. To use a second preset, type the first preset at the "Insertion point:" prompt, then when the prompt reappears, type the second preset.

Use of the presets can make inserting blocks more accurate and efficient, eliminating the need to subsequently scale or rotate the block.

 ## Is there any way I can control what layer objects end up on when I explode a block?

The XPLODE command can help. This command lets you specify the color, layer, and/or linetype of objects in the block. You can use XPLODE on more than one block at a time and set the object properties globally for all the blocks at once. Here's how to use XPLODE:

1. Start the XPLODE command. If you installed the Bonus commands, choose Bonus | Modify | Extended Explode. Otherwise, type **xplode** at the command line.

2. AutoCAD prompts you to select objects. Select the blocks you want to explode.

3. If you selected more than one block, AutoCAD displays the "XPlode Individually/<Globally>:" prompt. Press ENTER to accept the Globally default or type **I** and press ENTER to specify properties for one block at a time. AutoCAD then highlights the individual blocks, one after another, so that you know which block you are setting properties for.

4. At the "All/Color/LAyer/LType/Inherit from parent block/<Explode>:" prompt, choose an option. All lets you specify color, layer, and linetype. Inherit from parent block applies to blocks that were created on layer 0 and whose color and linetype were set to ByBlock. The Inherit from parent block option then lets these objects retain their color and linetype after you explode them. The Explode option works like the regular EXPLODE command.

5. Depending on which option you chose, AutoCAD prompts you to specify that property. For example, if you chose the LAyer option, you will see the "XPlode onto what layer? <0>:" prompt. Note that you have to know the name of the layer.

AutoCAD explodes the block using the properties you specified.

 ## Can I display only part of a block?

Yes! It is a little-known fact that you can clip blocks using the XCLIP command. With XCLIP, you can create rectangular or polygonal boundaries that hide any part of the block outside the boundary. For example, you may find that attribute text is distracting while you are drawing. You can XCLIP it out. For details, see the question, "How can I display only a portion of an xref?" in the section on incorporating external references, later in this chapter.

 ## How can I update the blocks in my drawing?

There are two ways to update blocks. Your choice of method depends on your needs. The first method is to use xrefs instead of drawings. The second is to use block substitution.

Using Xrefs

If your blocks change very often and you need to have the latest version every time you open your drawing, you may want to use external references instead of blocks. These are more fully explained later in this chapter. Stated briefly, however, when you use an external reference, what looks like a block in your drawing is actually an image of another drawing. Whenever you open your drawing, the other drawing is reloaded, giving you the latest version.

Using Block Substitution

If your blocks change only once in a while, you can do a block substitution to substitute each instance of a block with another drawing that contains the updated version.

Here are some reasons to substitute blocks:

● Your company switches to a new part and you want to replace all the old parts with the new parts in your drawing.

● You want to create two versions of a drawing, perhaps to present to a client. For example, you could show a house with two different types of doors.

● You have a very large drawing with many complex blocks, and opening, regenerating, and saving is slow. You can substitute a simple rectangle for the blocks to simplify the drawing until you're ready to plot. Then substitute back again.

Here's how to substitute blocks:

1. From the Draw toolbar, choose Insert Block.

2. Click File, locate the file you want to use, and click Open.

3. In the Block text box, type the name of the block you want to replace. If you try to click Block and choose it, AutoCAD automatically removes the File you have chosen, so you need to type the name of the block.

4. Click OK.

5. AutoCAD warns you that a block with this name already exists and asks if you want to redefine it, as shown here. Click OK.

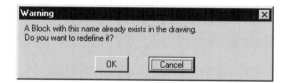

6. In your drawing, press ESC to avoid inserting a copy of the file. AutoCAD replaces all instances of the block with the file you specified. As well, the block definition is updated in the drawing.

 What's a good source for blocks that I can incorporate into my drawings (legally)?

The best place is the Internet. There are dozens of sites, some more general and others quite specific to various disciplines. Here are three of the best sites for blocks and block libraries:

- Autodesk, at www.autodesk.com, sells three block libraries—architectural, mechanical, and electronic. At the site, click Product + Solutions, then Autodesk Symbols.

- The AutoCAD Shareware Clearinghouse, found at www.cadalog.com, has a great library of files and blocks. Click Block Libs.

- CADsyst's Web site includes a huge library of blocks and other goodies. You can find it at www.cadsyst.com. Figure 5-1 shows CADsyst's front page. Click Blocks & Utilities.

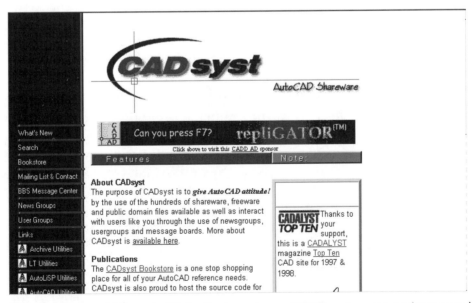

Figure 5-1 CADsyst's Web site (courtesy of CADsyst, www.cadsyst.com)

CREATING AND EXTRACTING BLOCK ATTRIBUTES

 I've gone over the DDATTDEF command to create attributes and the DDATTEXT command to extract them, but I still can't seem to put it all together. What am I missing?

Attributes are text objects that are attached to blocks. You can change the value of an attribute when you insert the block. This lets you use the attributes for variable information, such as purchase date, price, part number, and so on. Just understanding the two commands is not enough. Here's an overview of the entire process:

1. Draw the components of the block. If the block already exists, you must explode it.

2. Use the DDATTDEF command (choose Draw | Block | Attributes) to create the attributes in the Attribute Definition dialog box. In the Mode section, decide if you want the attributes to be invisible. In the Attribute section, create the tag (the name of the attribute), the prompt, and the value (to set a default). Use the Insertion Point section to specify the insertion point for the attribute and the Text Options section to define how the attribute will look. Click OK when you are done.

3. Repeat the command to create additional attributes for the same block. Check "Place below previous attribute" to line up these attributes under the first one.

4. Now use the BMAKE command (choose Make Block from the Draw toolbar). Select the block objects and the attributes to make up the block. When selecting the attributes, pick each attribute separately, in the order you would like the prompts to appear later when you insert the block.

 Note: *If you want to use the entire drawing as the block, as you might for a title block, you don't need to make a block. Just save the drawing. If you wish, use the BASE command to place the base point where you want it.*

5. To enter attributes in a dialog box, set the ATTDIA system variable to 1.

6. Now insert the block (or drawing file). AutoCAD automatically senses the attributes and prompts you for values. Continue to insert as many blocks as you need.

7. To extract the values of the attributes, you must create and save a *template file*. For more information, see the next box, "Creating a Template File."

! **_Caution:_** *Don't confuse attribute template files, which are for extracting attributes, with drawing templates, which store drawing settings.*

---

8. Start the DDATTEXT command to open the Attribute Extraction dialog box. Choose the type of file format you want to create. Then click Select Objects and select the blocks you want to include. Choose Template File to specify the template file you created. Finally, choose Output File to name and create the output file. Click OK when you are done. If the extraction is successful, AutoCAD displays a message saying how many records are in the extract file.

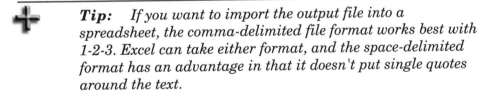 **_Tip:_** *If you want to import the output file into a spreadsheet, the comma-delimited file format works best with 1-2-3. Excel can take either format, and the space-delimited format has an advantage in that it doesn't put single quotes around the text.*

When I insert blocks with attributes, the dialog box I usually use to type in the data is missing. Where did it go?

The system variable ATTDIA determines whether the Enter Attributes dialog box, shown in Figure 5-2, appears when you insert a block with attributes. To see the dialog box, ATTDIA must be set to 1. Because the default of ATTDIA is 0, you

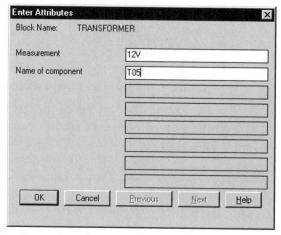

Figure 5-2 The Enter Attributes dialog box lets you enter attribute data. It appears only if ATTDIA is set to 1

may find that the dialog box does not appear when you expect it. For example, you may not be working in your usual template, or an AutoLISP routine may have set ATTDIA to 0 and not returned the setting to its original value.

To set ATTDIA to 1, type **attdia**, press ENTER, type **1**, and press ENTER again.

 How do I edit attributes?

There are three commands that you can use to edit attributes once you have placed them in a block. Each command has a different purpose, described in the next three sections.

Changing Attribute Values

Often you need to change the value of an attribute once you have inserted its block. Perhaps your company replaced a desk and you need to change the purchase date and price. For this purpose, you use DDATTE. To edit attribute values with DDATTE, follow these steps:

1. Choose Modify | Object | Attribute | Single, or type **ddatte** on the command line.

Creating a Template File

The template file is an ASCII (text only) file in two columns. It cannot include tabs, and each line, including the last line, must end with one return. Make sure not to have any added space characters at the end of any line. You must include at least one attribute tag but no duplicate rows. The following illustration shows an example of a short template file, including a space saver field:

```
BL:NAME   C009000
PART_NO   N004000
SPACE     C002000
SVC_DATE  C008000
```

In addition to extracting attribute information, you can extract some information about blocks, listed in the following table. The Syntax column shows how to format the second column of the template file, as follows:

- The first position specifies the type of data: C specifies character data, and N specifies numeric data

- w indicates the maximum width of the field (including the decimal point and any places after the decimal point)

- d indicates the precision, that is, how many places after the decimal point. Integers and character data always use 000 as the precision, as shown in the table.

Field	Syntax	Description
BL:NAME	Cwww000	Block name
BL:LEVEL	Nwww000	Block nesting level
BL:X	Nwwwddd	x coordinate of insertion point
BL:Y	Nwwwddd	y coordinate of insertion point
BL:Z	Nwwwddd	z coordinate of insertion point
BL:NUMBER	Nwww000	Block counter (AutoCAD counts the number of blocks you select when extracting attributes)
BL:HANDLE	Cwww000	Block handle

Field	Syntax	Description
BL:LAYER	Cwww000	Block layer name
BL:ORIENT	Nwwwddd	Block rotation
BL:XSCALE	Nwwwddd	X scale
BL:YSCALE	Nwwwddd	Y scale
BL:ZSCALE	Nwwwddd	Z scale
BL:XEXTRUDE	Nwwwddd	x component of extrusion direction
BL:YEXTRUDE	Nwwwddd	y component of extrusion direction
BL:ZEXTRUDE	Nwwwddd	z component of extrusion direction

2. Select one block that has attributes. AutoCAD opens the Edit Attributes dialog box, shown in Figure 5-3.

3. The Edit Attributes dialog box clearly lays out all the attributes for the block you selected and their values. Type new values as needed and click OK.

Changing Attribute Display and Global Values

The ATTEDIT command lets you make global changes in attribute values, a great help when your company decides to rename its part numbers and you need to change the part

Figure 5-3   The Edit Attributes dialog box

number in every instance of that block. To make global changes, follow these steps:

1. Choose Modify | Object | Attribute | Global, or type **attedit** on the command line.

2. At the "Edit attributes one at a time? <Y>:" prompt, type **n** and press ENTER to allow global editing.

3. At the "Edit only attributes visible on screen? <Y>:" prompt, type **n** and press ENTER if you want to include invisible attributes. However, you must know the text you want to change (even though you can't see it). To edit only visible attributes, press ENTER.

4. At the "Block name specification <*>:" prompt, you can limit the changes to a single block by typing its name. At the next prompt you will get a chance to select attributes and to limit the changes to specific attributes, but if you have overlapping blocks or a complex drawing, limiting the block here can help make attribute selection easier. If you don't need or want to limit the changes to one block, press ENTER.

5. At the "Attribute tag specification <*>:" prompt, you can limit the changes to one attribute tag by typing its name or press ENTER.

6. At the "Attribute value specification <*>:" prompt, you can limit the changes to one attribute value by typing its name or press ENTER.

7. If you are editing only visible attributes, AutoCAD asks you to select attributes. You can pick the attributes individually. To use a window to select attributes, you must first type **w** (for a regular selection window) or **c** (for a crossing window). When you have selected the attributes you want to change, press ENTER.

8. At the "String to change:" prompt, type the old text you want to change. For example, if you have a set of part numbers that all start with 13 and you want to change all the instances of 13 to 27, type **13** and press ENTER.

9. At the "New string:" prompt, type the new string. In the above example, you would type **27** and press ENTER.

AutoCAD replaces all the instances of the old string with the new string. You can see how useful this command can be when you need to make global changes to a large number of attributes.

The ATTEDIT command has a second purpose—to let you change the following properties of attributes, one at a time:

Value (the same as using the DDATTE command)
Position
Height
Angle
Text style
Layer
Color

To change attribute display properties, follow these steps:

1. Start the ATTEDIT command.

2. At the "Edit attributes one at a time? <Y>:" prompt, press ENTER to disallow global editing.

3. At the "Block name specification <*>:" prompt, type the name of a block if you want to limit changes to that block, or press ENTER to change more than one block.

4. At the "Attribute tag specification <*>:" prompt, you can limit the changes to one attribute tag or press ENTER.

5. At the "Attribute value specification <*>:" prompt, you can limit the changes to one attribute value or press ENTER.

6. At the "Select Attributes:" prompt, select the attributes you want to change. To use a window to select attributes, you must first type **w** (for a regular selection window) or **c** (for a crossing window). When you have selected the attributes you want to change, press ENTER.

7. At the "Value/Position/Height/Angle/Style/Layer/Color/ Next <N>:" prompt, AutoCAD highlights one of the attributes. Type the first letter of the property you want to change for that attribute.

8. AutoCAD prompts you for a new property value. For example, if you choose Layer, AutoCAD asks you for a

new layer. If you choose Value, AutoCAD lets you either change a specific text string (in which case it asks for the new string) or replace the entire text of the attribute.

9. AutoCAD repeats the prompt. You can either change another property of the same attribute or press ENTER to go to the next attribute. Continue changing properties and moving to the next attribute until you are finished.

10. Press ENTER to end the command.

Redefining Attributes

If you need to add or remove attributes, you need to redefine them using the ATTREDEF command. See the next question for more information on using this command.

How can I add or subtract attributes for blocks without losing all the values of the remaining attributes?

When you want to change the number of attributes or other attribute properties, you need to redefine the attributes using the ATTREDEF command. AutoCAD keeps the values for any remaining attributes. Here's how to redefine attributes:

1. Explode one of the blocks that contains the attributes.

2. To add new attributes, use DDATTDEF to define them (as explained earlier in this chapter).

3. Start the ATTREDEF command at the command line.

4. AutoCAD displays the "Name of Block you wish to redefine:" prompt. Type the name of the block.

5. AutoCAD prompts you to select the objects for the block. Select the objects and the attributes you wish to include. Omit those you wish to delete.

6. Specify the base point for the block at the "Insertion base point of new Block:" prompt.

AutoCAD re-creates the block with any new attributes you have created. The attributes are listed with their default values. Use the DDATTE command to change their values.

 How do I get my attribute data into Excel or 1-2-3?

Once you have an extraction file, you can import the data into Excel or 1-2-3. Here are the instructions for importing to Microsoft Excel 7.0, using a space-delimited format:

1. Open Excel and choose File | Open.
2. In the Open dialog box, choose Text files from the Files of type drop-down list. Locate and choose your extraction file. Click Open.
3. In the Text Import Wizard, Excel senses that your file is *fixed width* and displays a preview of the file. Click Next.
4. In the next screen, format the columns. You can add or delete columns as necessary.
5. In the next screen, set the format for the data. General, the default, is an all-purpose format that often works.
6. Click Finish and Excel imports the data.

Here are instructions for Lotus 1-2-3, using a comma-delimited file.

1. Open 1-2-3 and choose File | Open.
2. In the Files of type drop-down list, choose Text.
3. Locate and choose your extraction file. Click Open.
4. In the File Options dialog box, choose the "Select a new column at each" option.
5. Choose Comma from the drop-down list.
6. Click OK. 1-2-3 creates a new workbook with the information from your extraction file.

INCORPORATING EXTERNAL REFERENCES (XREFS)

 What's new in Release 14 for xrefs?

Release 14 introduces an updated dialog box for managing xrefs. Choose Insert | External Reference to open the

External Reference dialog box, shown in Figure 5-4. You can use this dialog box to attach, detach, bind, and list xrefs.

A new binding option works like the INSERT command and uses existing layers when possible, reducing the number of layers in the drawing. Another new feature is the ability to unload xrefs while you don't need to use them. AutoCAD retains the xref name and path information, but you get improved performance. You can then quickly reload the xref when you need it again.

There is a new tree view that shows you clearly how xrefs are nested and their relationship to the current drawing. To view the tree view, click the Tree View button at the top of the External Reference dialog box. Figure 5-5 shows a sample tree view. In this drawing, an office layout, COMPUTER.DWG is an external reference in DESK.DWG, which is an external reference in the current drawing, NORTH OFFICE.DWG.

There is a new command, XCLIP, that makes it easier to *clip* an xref. When you clip an xref, only the portion of the xref inside the clipping boundary is displayed. You can use polygonal clipping to create almost any shape boundary you want.

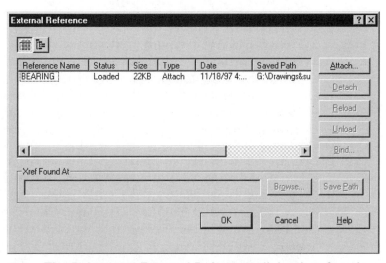

Figure 5-4 The Release 14 External Reference dialog box functions as a complete xref manager

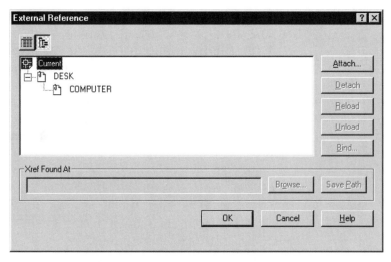

Figure 5-5 The new Tree View lets you see the relationships between xrefs and your drawing

Finally, Release 14 has added demand loading and special indices to speed up the display of large xrefs. For more information, see the next question.

 ### Is there any way to speed up the display of very large xrefs in my drawing?

Release 14 includes a new feature, *demand loading,* which lets AutoCAD load only that part of the xref—either in terms of area or layers—that you need to display. It is ideal for very large xrefs, such as maps or 3-D drawings. You can turn demand loading on or off at any time. Once it's on, in order to use it, the xref must have either a spatial or a layer index. To use demand loading, follow these steps:

1. Turn on demand loading. Choose Tools | Preferences and go to the Performance tab. In the "External reference file demand load" drop-down list, choose Enabled or Enabled with copy. Choose Enabled with copy to allow another user on a network to work on the xref while you are using it. AutoCAD makes a copy of the xref for displaying in your drawing. This copy is deleted when you close your drawing.

2. Open the drawing that you want to use as an xref. Save the drawing with either a spatial index, a layer index, or both. Choose File | Save As. In the Save Drawing As dialog box, choose Options. From the Index type drop-down list, choose Layer, Spatial, or Layer & Spatial, as shown here:

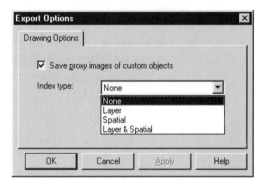

3. Click OK to return to the File | Save As dialog box. Here you can save the drawing or click Cancel. (You don't have to save the drawing to add the index.)

4. When you insert the drawing as an xref (choose Insert | External Reference), either clip it (for a spatial index) or freeze or turn off layers (for a layer index).

Once you have completed these steps, you gain the benefit of demand loading.

You can turn off demand loading when you don't need it anymore. To turn off the indices, choose File | Save As again and then click Options. From the Index type drop-down list, choose None. Click OK, then Cancel to return to your drawing.

 ### How can I display only a portion of an xref?

The XCLIP command lets you create a rectangular or polygonal boundary around an xref and visually clips off any part of the xref outside the boundary. This is great when you have an xref of an entire city block but you need only one house. To clip an xref, Choose Modify | Object | Clip. There is also an External Reference Clip button on the Reference toolbar that you may want to display when working with xrefs.

At the "Select objects:" prompt, select an xref or a block. At the "ON/OFF/Clipdepth/Delete/generate Polyline/<New boundary>:" prompt, choose one of the available options:

- **ON** Turns on a boundary that you previously turned off.

- **OFF** Turns off a boundary and you see the entire xref or block again. However, AutoCAD remembers the boundary so that you can turn it on again without re-creating it.

- **Clipdepth** In 3-D models, sets front and back clipping planes parallel to the clipping boundary. There is a Remove suboption to remove the clipping planes.

- **Delete** Deletes the clipping boundary.

- **generate Polyline** Uses the clipping boundary to create a polyline. The advantage is that you can use the PEDIT command to edit the polyline and use that polyline to define a new clipping boundary with the Select polyline suboption of the New boundary option.

- **New boundary** The default. Press ENTER for the suboptions. You can select an existing polyline, pick two corners of a rectangular boundary, or specify a polygonal area. If you create a polygonal area, AutoCAD prompts you for points on the polygon, which can be any irregular shape. Press ENTER to close the polygonal boundary.

 Note: *The XCLIPFRAME system variable turns on and off the visibility of the clipping boundary.*

How can I get my drawing to keep the layer settings of xrefs?

You can change the layer settings of xref layers, freezing them, turning them off, and so on. You can even change their properties, such as their color and linetype. However, by default, every time you open the drawing and load the xref, the original layer settings are reloaded as well. Sometimes you may wish to keep the changes you made. To do so, set the VISRETAIN system variable to 1. Now, when you load the

xref, your current layer settings will take precedence over the settings in the xref.

Can I turn my xrefs into blocks?

Certainly, this is called *binding*. If you want to make your xrefs a permanent part of your drawing, follow these steps:

1. Choose Insert | External Reference to open the External Reference dialog box.

2. Choose the xref that you want to bind.

3. Click Bind. AutoCAD opens the Xref Bind dialog box, shown here:

You can choose one of two methods of binding: Bind and Insert.

● **Bind**   The Bind option keeps layer names, text and dimension style names, and other named properties—called *symbols*—separate from those of your original drawing. When you have an xref in a drawing, AutoCAD assigns names to these symbols using the format *drawing name | symbol name*. For example, if the external reference is named no_bldg and a text style is named Planned, the text style in your drawing becomes no_bldg | planned. When you use the Bind option to change the xref to a block, AutoCAD changes the pipe symbol (|) to $#$, where the # is usually 0, but uses 1, 2, and so on if there are duplicates. So in the example, the text style would become no_bldg0planned. In this way, you always know that the planned text style came from the no_bldg

external reference. Also, there will not be any conflict with existing symbols in your drawing. All new symbols have unique, new names.

● **Insert** The Insert option removes the portion of symbol names that identify the original xref. If a symbol with that name exists (in our example, if your drawing already contains a text style called Planned), then text using that style adopts the properties of the Planned text style. If no symbol with that name exists, a new one is created. This system integrates the xref into the drawing more simply and completely.

Choose the option you want and click OK. Your xref is now a block. You can explode it if you wish.

I open a file that contains externally referenced files from my network and I get a message that the xrefs are "read only." What does this mean?

This message means that someone else on the network is using the xrefs. You can still reference the drawing, but you can't make any changes to it. That might be just fine, since you xref a drawing just to refer to it, not to change it. However, if you need to edit the drawing that you are referencing, you will have to wait until the other person is finished using it. By using the Enabled with copy option of demand loading, you can display an xref in your drawing even though someone else is working on it. For more information on demand loading, see the earlier question, "Is there any way to speed up the display of very large xrefs in my drawing?"

To access demand loading choose Tools | Preferences and click the Performance tab. In the Demand Load section, choose the Enabled with copy option to turn on demand loading for the drawing. Now you can open and edit the xref file because AutoCAD makes you a copy of the xref file that is separate from the original xref.

If you work on a network, you should set a standard for the demand loading option and save your template files with

the option you choose. In this way, you can ensure easy access to drawings that are often used as xrefs.

WORKING WITH OUTSIDE DATABASES

 ## What's new in Release 14 for ASE?

Using ASE is much, much easier because Release 14 has done away with the ASE.INI file that you had to manually edit in Release 13. Changes are now saved in the Windows Registry, and you configure an outside database using dialog boxes. To start defining the database environment, use the External Database Configuration program. Choose Start | Programs | AutoCAD | External Database Configuration. The External Database Configuration dialog box, shown in Figure 5-6, has a help button that can help you through the process.

ASE is not part of a typical installation, so you need to do a full or custom installation to gain access to this feature. You can add it at any time by starting Setup, choosing Add, and installing the External Db option.

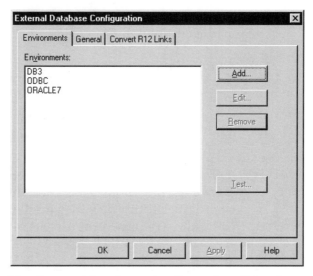

Figure 5-6 The External Database Configuration dialog box

 What can I do with ASE?

AutoCAD SQL Environment (ASE) is a means of accessing outside databases from within AutoCAD. You can view and edit the database, and you can also create a link between a row in a database and an object or group of objects in your drawing. For example, if you have a drawing of an engine that is comprised of many parts that you have listed in your database, you can link each part of the engine with the row of the database that provides details about that part, such as the part number, the weight, etc.

Once you have attached objects to database rows, you can find which object or objects relate to a row you specify.

You can also create *Displayable Attributes,* which display data from your database in your drawing. While these cannot be extracted like regular attributes, they provide visible information about the object within your drawing.

You can use ASE with dBASE III, ODBC databases (such as Excel, Access, and FoxPro), and Oracle 7.

 What is a schema?

There are several terms that you need to understand in order to get the most from ASE. A schema is one of four database objects used in ASE. They form a hierarchy because each object is contained in the next.

● *A table is a layout of data in rows and columns, and this is where your actual data resides.* It is usually contained in a database file. For example, you may have a table named Part_Nos containing part numbers and a table named Manuf containing information about the manufacturer of the parts.

● *A schema is a set of tables.* You may want to work with more than one table. You name the schema by the folder where the actual table files are located. For example, if your data are in several files in the \Assembly folder, your schema is called Assembly.

● *A catalog is a set of schemas.* You may have two schemas, one called Assembly and the other called Personnel. The

catalog's name is the same as the folder that contains the schemas.

● *An environment is the entire database system.* It includes not only the tables, schemas, and catalogs, but also the database management system (DBMS) and the drivers AutoCAD uses to communicate with the DBMS.

 ## What's the simplest way to access my Excel spreadsheet from AutoCAD?

It depends on how comfortable you are with ASE. If you don't want to bother setting up your own configuration using the ODBC driver and creating the information schema Excel worksheet, you can save your Excel worksheet in .DBF format by choosing File | Save As and choosing DBF 3 (dBASE III) (*.DBF) from the Save as type drop-down list. You can then use AutoCAD's default configuration, DB3, which is already set up for you.

If you want to use the ODBC driver, you need to install the ODBC Administrator. To check if you have it, choose Start | Settings | Control Panel in Windows and look for the 32-bit ODBC driver icon, shown here:

If you don't have the 32-bit ODBC driver, or you have an older 16-bit driver, you need to download the latest version from Microsoft at www.microsoft.com. As of the writing of this book, the latest version was called ODBC Driver Pack 3.0. On the Web site, choose Products and then do a search for ODBC. It's free and comes with installation instructions. Once you've installed the ODBC driver, here are the basic steps for adding the Excel driver:

1. First create your *information schema*. For more information, see the next question, "How do I create the information schema for using ASE with Excel?"

2. In the Control Panel, double-click the 32-bit ODBC icon.

3. In the Data Sources dialog box choose the Excel driver. Click Add.

4. In the Add Data Source dialog box, choose Microsoft Excel Driver (*.XLS), as shown here, and click OK.

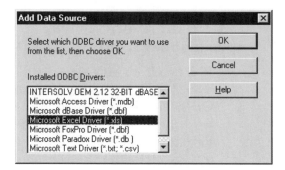

5. ODBC opens the ODBC Microsoft Excel Setup dialog box. Type a data source name and, if you want, a description. A simple name, such as Excel or ODBC_Excel is fine. Remember the name, because you will need it when you use AutoCAD's External Database Configuration program.

6. Click the Select Workbook button and find the information schema you created. It should be named INFSCH.XLS. Click OK twice.

7. Close the Data Sources dialog box and the Control Panel.

You are now ready to configure the database using AutoCAD's External Database Configuration program.

 ### How do I create the information schema for using ASE with Excel?

The information schema used with ODBC databases is a mechanism to tell AutoCAD's ASE feature the location and structure of the database. Here is a sample information schema created in Microsoft Excel:

	A	B	C	D
1	catalog_name	schema_name		
2	NULL	c:\databases\excel\part_nos		
3				
4	table_catalog	table_schema	table_name	table_type
5	NULL	c:\databases\excel\part_nos	parts	Base Table
6				

Here's how you change it to work with your Excel worksheets:

● Cells B2 and B5 should contain the location of the worksheet file you want to work with.

● C5 should contain the range name of the table in the worksheet you want to work with. Then go into your worksheet, select all the data, and name the range the same as shown in C5. You create a range name by selecting all the cells in the database and entering a range name in the name box at the left end of the formula bar. (A named range of cells in Excel is equivalent to a table database object in other DBMSs.)

● Name cells A1:B2 with the range name "schemata."

● Name cells A4:B5 with the range name "tables."

● Name the worksheet INFSCH.XLS (for information schema). It must be located in the same location as the files listed in B2 and B5.

Everything else remains the same.

CONTROLLING DRAWINGS

 Can I delete files with an .AC$ extension?

Yes, these are leftover temporary files. Usually they are automatically deleted when you exit AutoCAD, but whenever AutoCAD crashes, they are left on your hard drive, taking up space. To locate these files, choose Tools | Preferences. On the Files tab, click the plus next to Temporary Drawing File

Location. (You may have to scroll down to see this item.) You now see the location for AutoCAD's temporary files. You can change this location if you wish.

To delete the files, follow these steps:

1. Close AutoCAD.

 Caution: *It is important to close AutoCAD to make sure you don't accidentally delete current temporary files and crash AutoCAD.*

2. Use Windows Explorer to locate the folder containing your temporary files.

3. Highlight all the files ending with .AC$. (You may want to delete other temporary files as well.)

4. Press DELETE.

 Tip: *To make sure you don't accidentally delete temporary files that are in use, click the Modified column heading in Explorer to sort the files by date. Don't delete any files with today's date.*

 ## What can I do to lessen the chance of AutoCAD crashing?

Get more memory! While AutoCAD Release 14 requires a minimum of 16MB of RAM, you'll have a better experience with more. Another technique that sometimes helps is to move the Windows swap file to a drive that is faster or has more room, if you have one. (A partitioned drive works fine.) The swap drive grows and contracts automatically to use your hard drive when there is not enough memory. Here's how to move the swap drive:

1. Close all applications.

2. Choose Start | Settings | Control Panel.

3. Double-click System and choose the Performance tab in the System Properties dialog box.

4. Click Virtual Memory. In the Virtual Memory dialog box, shown in Figure 5-7, choose "Let me specify my own virtual memory settings."

5. Click the Hard disk drop-down list. Choose a hard drive that is faster or has more free space. Click OK. A warning message appears, asking if you are sure you want to do this.

6. Click OK. You cannot do any damage by moving the swap file. However, if by mistake you move it to a drive with very little free space, you will get out-of-memory messages, slow processing, or crashes. Just move it back to its original location.

7. Click OK. Click the Close box to close the Control Panel.

My drawing doesn't open at all. What can I do?

First, rename the .BAK file to give it a .DWG extension and a unique filename, and try to open it.

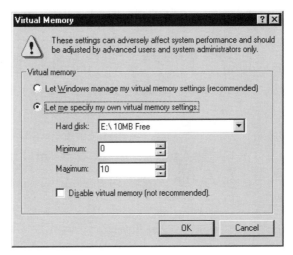

Figure 5-7 The Virtual Memory dialog box lets you specify where the swap file resides

 Note: *If Windows Explorer doesn't display filename extensions, choose View | Options and uncheck Hide MS-DOS file extensions for file types that are registered.*

If that doesn't work, and you crashed, try to find the . AC$ (temporary) drawing, which is generally in your \Windows\ Temp folder. Rename it to a .DWG file with a unique filename, and try to open it.

It's also a good idea to run ScanDisk and Defrag, which are Windows accessories that clean up the hard drive.

 Tip: *To find your temporary drawings, choose Tools | Preferences and on the Files tab click the plus sign next to Temporary Drawing File Location.*

If the above techniques don't work, the RECOVER command should come to the rescue. Open a new drawing in AutoCAD and choose File | Drawing Utilities | Recover. In the dialog box, choose the drawing you couldn't open, and click Open. AutoCAD tries to recover the drawing.

 ### Is there an easy way to purge all the unused blocks and layers I sometimes have in my drawings?

Purging deletes unused symbols—blocks, dimension styles, layers, linetypes, shapes, text styles, and multiline styles—from your drawing. Your drawing gets smaller and runs more quickly. Release 14 has a great new feature that doesn't require you to individually approve every item before it is purged. Here's how it works.

1. Type **purge** on the command line.

2. At the "Purge unused Blocks/Dimstyles/LAyers/LTypes/ SHapes/STyles/Mlinestyles/All:" prompt, type **a** to purge all unused symbols or choose one of the individual options, and press ENTER.

3. At the "Names to purge <*>:" prompt, press ENTER to purge all unused symbols in the category you specified in the previous prompt.

4. Here's the new feature. At the "Verify each name to be purged? <Y>:" prompt, type **n** to automatically purge all unused symbols without asking your permission for each one. Press ENTER if you want to be sure and verify each item.

5. If you choose to verify each item, AutoCAD lists each one. Type **y** for each one to accept its removal.

If you have trouble purging unused symbols, see the following box, "When Purging Doesn't Work."

When Purging Doesn't Work

Occasionally, you may have the experience that purging doesn't work. Although you think a block or layer is unused, it is not listed as you purge objects or, if you are purging without verifying individual symbols, it simply isn't purged. There can be several reasons for this problem.

● If the layer you want to purge is frozen, you may have objects on that layer. Unfreeze the layer and erase all objects on it.

● There may be tiny objects on a layer that you can't see. To be certain that there are no objects on a layer, freeze all other layers and use the ERASE command. At the "Select objects:" prompt, type **all** and press ENTER.

● The Incremental save % option may prevent a complete purge. Try purging a second time. If this doesn't work, choose Tools | Preferences and click the Performance tab. Set the incremental save option to zero. Another option is to save your drawing, reopen it, and immediately use PURGE.

● You may have blocks whose component objects are on a layer you want to purge. If you don't need the blocks, erase them and then purge the blocks. Then you can purge the layer. Or explode the blocks, change the layers of the component objects, create a new block of the same objects using the same name, and answer Yes when AutoCAD asks if you want to redefine the block.

One of the above solutions should let you purge all your unused symbols.

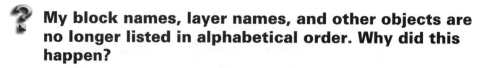 **My block names, layer names, and other objects are no longer listed in alphabetical order. Why did this happen?**

This means that the maximum number of sorted symbols has been reached. AutoCAD stores this maximum in the MAXSORT system variable and in the Windows Registry. Increase this value to let AutoCAD sort a greater number of items. To do so, choose Tools | Preferences and click the General tab, shown in Figure 5-8.

Increase the number in the Maximum number sorted symbols text box and click OK. (Note that higher numbers use more memory.)

When I open a drawing from the network, I get a message that says the file is 'read only.' How can I edit the file?

This is one of the top ten frequently asked AutoCAD questions. See question #5 in Chapter 1 for the answer.

How do I limit access to my drawings by other users?

This is one of the top ten fequently asked AutoCAD questions. See question #6 in Chapter 1 for the answer.

INTERFACING WITH OTHER APPLICATIONS

I want to import a graphic logo but I don't want to use the entire graphic. Is there some way to display only what I want?

You can clip raster images in the same way you can clip xrefs. Here's how to clip an image:

1. Attach the entire image. Choose Insert | Raster Image and click Attach.

2. Choose Modify | Object | Image Clip.

3. Select the image. Note that you need to pick the image on an outer border.

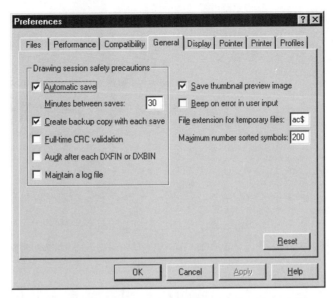

Figure 5-8   On the General tab of the Preferences dialog box, you can change the maximum number of items that AutoCAD can sort

4. Press ENTER to create a new boundary.

5. To create a rectangular boundary, press ENTER and pick two opposite points to create the rectangle.

6. To create a polygonal boundary, type **p** and pick points until you have defined the boundary. Use the Close option to complete the boundary. Figure 5-9 shows the process of creating a polygonal boundary.

AutoCAD displays only the portion of the image within the boundary. For the sake of good looks, you usually want to turn off an image's frame, as shown here:

Figure 5-9 Creating a polygonal boundary to clip a raster image

This would certainly be true for a logo. Choose Modify | Object | Image | Frame to start the IMAGEFRAME command. Type **off** and press ENTER to turn off the frame.

Caution: *With the frame off, you cannot select the image. Turn on the frame if you need to select the image to move, resize, or delete it.*

Note: *Alternatively, a number of graphics programs can clip images. You could use one of them to save the clipped image, and then import it to AutoCAD as is.*

I pasted a big Excel spreadsheet into my drawing, but part of the spreadsheet was cut off. How can I get the entire spreadsheet into my drawing?

This is one of the top ten frequently asked AutoCAD questions. See question #1 in Chapter 1 for the answer.

When I paste an image, an Excel spreadsheet, or another object into AutoCAD, it shows up fine onscreen, but doesn't plot or print. Why?

This is one of the top ten frequently asked AutoCAD questions. See question #3 in Chapter 1 for the answer.

 How can I get text from the Text Window into a word processor document?

Authors who write books on AutoCAD use this trick all the time to place AutoCAD prompts into their word processor documents. Here's how it works:

1. Press F2 to open up the AutoCAD Text Window.

2. Highlight the text you want to bring into your word processor document.

3. Right-click anywhere in the Text Window. In the shortcut menu, choose Copy. This copies the highlighted text to the Windows clipboard.

4. Go to your word processor document, place the cursor in the desired location, and press CTRL+V to paste the text.

Note: *You can also choose Copy History to copy contents of the entire text window for a drawing session to the clipboard.*

What's the quickest way to bring a word processor document into my drawing?

It depends on whether you want to bring in only some of the text or the whole document. It also depends on what results you want in AutoCAD. Here are four options:

● Probably the quickest way to bring some (or all) of the text into AutoCAD is to use drag-and-drop. Have both the word processor document and the drawing open. Select the text, press CTRL and click the selected data. Holding down the mouse button, drag the cursor to the AutoCAD button on the taskbar and wait until your drawing appears. Drag the data to the desired location in your drawing. This method creates an OLE object, meaning that you can double-click it to open the word processing program and edit the text. After editing the file in the word processor, choose File | Close and Return to *Name-of-Drawing* to return to AutoCAD. After a second, your text is updated in AutoCAD. This method does not create a link to the original document, so the text in your document is not updated when the original document is changed.

 Tip: *You can also drag an entire file into AutoCAD. Open Windows Explorer and locate the file. Size the Explorer window so you can see part of your drawing. Drag the file into your drawing.*

- Another quick way to bring text into AutoCAD is to open the word processor document, select the text you want to import into AutoCAD, click Copy on the Standard toolbar, go to AutoCAD (click its button on the taskbar or open it), and click Paste on the Standard toolbar. Your text comes into AutoCAD as an OLE object.

- If you want to be able to format the text in AutoCAD, again open the word processor document, select the text, and copy it to the clipboard. However, when you go to AutoCAD, choose Edit | Paste Special to open the Paste Special dialog box, shown in Figure 5-10. Choose AutoCAD Entities and click OK. Your text is now regular AutoCAD text and you can format it as you wish.

- Another option that lets you format the text in AutoCAD is to select the text in your word processor and copy it to the clipboard. Return to AutoCAD and start the MTEXT command by choosing Multiline Text from the Draw toolbar. Pick the two corners of the text area. AutoCAD opens the Multiline Text Editor. Press CTRL+V to paste the text directly into the editor. You can now format the text using the tools in the Multiline Text Editor.

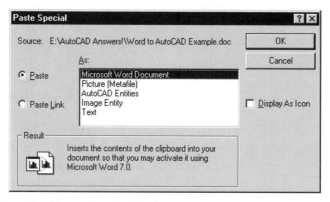

Figure 5-10 The Paste Special dialog box

 Can I link text in AutoCAD to the original document so it is always up to date?

Yes, you can link data in AutoCAD just as you can in other Windows applications. To link text, follow these steps:

1. In your word processor, select the text you want to import into AutoCAD with a link.

2. Press CTRL+C to copy the text to the clipboard.

3. In your drawing, choose Edit | Paste Special.

4. In the Paste Special dialog box, choose the option that pastes the text as a document of your word processor. For example, the option might say Microsoft Word Document. Only this option lets you create a link.

5. Click the Paste Link radio button.

6. Click OK.

Now, whenever your drawing is open and the source text changes, the text will automatically be updated in your drawing as well. In addition, when you open the drawing, you always have the current version of the text. For more information about linking data, see the following box, "Managing Links."

Managing Links

By default, a link is updated automatically. Whenever you open a drawing, AutoCAD loads the most recent form of the linked data. While the drawing is open, the link is updated almost immediately. Try linking some text from your word processor to an AutoCAD drawing. Keep both the word processor document and the AutoCAD drawing open at the same time. In the word processor, change the linked text. Now use the Windows taskbar to go to your drawing. Watch the text in your drawing. It changes within a couple of seconds.

You need to be aware of the link in your drawing. For example, if you rename or move either the source data or your drawing, the link may be broken. Here's how to reestablish the link:

1. In your drawing, select the linked object. You will see handles at its corners and sides.

2. Choose Edit | OLE Links to open the Links dialog box, shown in the following illustration. The OLE Links menu item is only available if there is a link in your drawing.

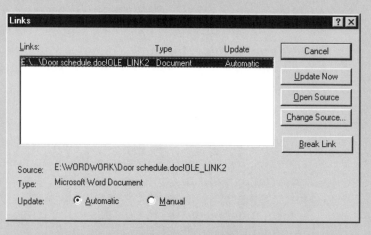

3. Choose the link that you want to reestablish.

4. In the Links dialog box, click Change Source.

5. In the Change Source dialog box, find the source file and click OK.

6. Click Close to close the Links dialog box.

Another Link management task is breaking a link. You may want to break a link once the drawing is finalized and ready to send to a client. This way, your drawing always contains the final result that you sent out. To break a link, open the Links dialog box, choose the link or links you want to break, and click Break Link. Click OK to confirm that you want to break the link. The information remains in your drawing but will no longer be updated if the source document changes.

Finally, you may want to change your link updating setting to manual. If someone else is working on the source document, you may find the traffic on the network to be too heavy, or you just may not want to see continual changes in your drawing. To change the updating to manual, open the Links dialog box and click the Manual radio button. Then, whenever you want to update the link, open the Links dialog box and click Update Now.

What's the quickest way to bring an AutoCAD drawing into my word processor document?

This is one of the top ten frequently asked AutoCAD questions. Look at question #9 in Chapter 1 for the answer.

What's the best way to bring a 3-D view of my drawing into a word processor document?

There are two methods you can use, described below. Both work better if the background in your drawing is the same color as the background in your word processor, usually white. To change the background color in AutoCAD, choose Tools | Preferences, click the Display tab, and click Color.

For both methods, first use the HIDE command on the view.

 Tip: *Turn DISPSILH on (to 1) to get a cleaner silhouette.*

The first and simplest method is to press CTRL+C and select the objects(s) to copy the view to the clipboard. Then go to your word processor and press CTRL+V to paste the view. This method produces the clearest image in your word processor.

If you want to permanently save the view, another option is to save it as an image file. Choose Tools | Display Image | Save to open the Save Image dialog box, shown in Figure 5-11. You can save the view in BMP, TGA, or TIFF formats. Check which formats your word processor accepts. Generally, all word processors can import BMP and TIFF files.

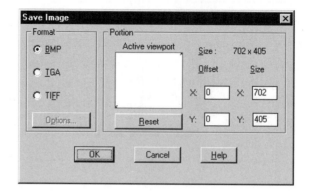

Figure 5-11   The Save Image dialog box lets you save a 3-D view as an
image file

The Portion section of the dialog box lets you crop the
image, but you'll probably find it easier to crop the image in
your word processor.

Caution: _Saving an image loads the Render module,
which can take a toll on your memory. To unload Render, type
arx on the command line and press ENTER. Choose the
Unload option. At the "Unload ARX file:" prompt, type **render**
and press ENTER._

Now, go into your word processor and import the image.
Figure 5-12 shows a sample result, using a BMP file.

Some of our clients use other CAD programs. How can we share drawings?

The most common way to share drawings between CAD
programs is through the use of drawing interchange format
(DXF) files. A DXF file is a text-only (ASCII) file that contains
all the data in your drawing. AutoCAD can export drawings
into DXF format and most other CAD programs can import
DXF files. AutoCAD can also import DXF files. Figure 5-13
shows a small excerpt of a DXF file—the Entities section. Here
you can see that the drawing contains a line. Each property of
the line is coupled with a code. For example, code 10
designates the x coordinate of the line's start point and code 20

Schedule of Brackets

9-inch bracket with four holes, shown below:

Figure 5-12   A BMP file inserted into Microsoft Word and shown in Print Preview mode

```
SECTION
  2
ENTITIES
  0
LINE
  5
4C
100
AcDbEntity
  8
0
100
AcDbLine
 10
3.258965
 20
5.544444
 30
0.0
 11
8.620129
 21
3.877778
 31
```

Figure 5-13   A portion of a DXF file

designates the y coordinate of the start point. Therefore, the line in this drawing starts at 3.258965,5.44444.

 Note: *Entities are defined using the same codes used in AutoLISP files.*

Most of the DXF file lists the values of system variables and other settings, so that these can also be translated into a drawing on another CAD program.

To create a DXF file, follow these steps:

1. Choose File | Export to open the Export Data dialog box, shown in Figure 5-14.

2. In the Save as type drop-down list, choose AutoCAD R14 DXF (*.DXF). Note that you can also save a drawing in R13 DXF format.

3. If you want to change the location and/or name, do so. By default, the file takes on the filename of the drawing, but with a .DXF extension.

4. Click Save.

AutoCAD creates the DXF file.

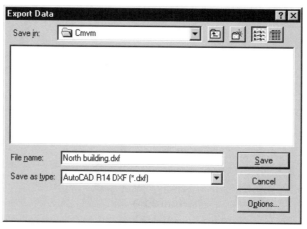

Figure 5-14   The Export Data dialog box

I can't import DXF files any more! I had no problem in Release 13. What's the problem?

Release 14 now requires that you start with a completely "clean" drawing before you import a DXF file. Follow these steps:

1. Start a new drawing using the Start from Scratch option.
2. Click Open from the Standard toolbar.
3. In the Select File dialog box, open the File of type drop-down list and choose DXF.
4. Find the DXF file and choose it. Click Open.

AutoCAD imports the DXF file.

If you need that file in a second drawing, save your drawing. Open the second drawing. You can now choose Insert | Block and click File to insert the drawing.

Note: *Release 14 only imports complete DXF files (not entity-only DXF files). There's a utility, HDRSUBST.EXE, on the Autodesk Web site (www.autodesk.com) that inserts a header in an entities-only DXF as a workaround.*

 Where do I specify the decimal place accuracy for my DXF file?

When you use DXFOUT on the command line, AutoCAD prompts you for the decimal accuracy of the file. However, you have probably been using the Export Data dialog box. To specify the decimal place accuracy in this dialog box, click Options to open the Export Options dialog box, shown in Figure 5-15. This dialog box changes according to the type of file you choose in the Save as type drop-down list.

You can also choose to make either an ASCII or a binary file. In most cases, ASCII files are used for sharing files between CAD programs. The dialog box also lets you choose to select objects so that you can create a DXF file containing only the selected objects. When you have specified the options you want, click OK to return to the Export Data dialog box and save the DXF file.

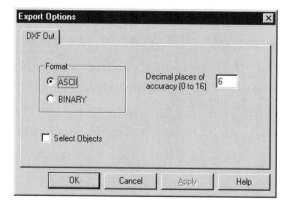

Figure 5-15 The Export Options dialog box lets you fine-tune your DXF file

Does exporting a drawing in DXF format export frozen layers?

Yes, when you create a DXF file, all objects are included, even those on frozen, off, or locked layers.

USING AUTOCAD ON THE INTERNET

Can I fax an AutoCAD drawing from my computer?

If you have a fax/modem card in your computer (you probably do), you can use your own fax software or Windows Exchange to fax a drawing. Here's how you can do it using Microsoft Exchange:

1. Open your drawing.
2. Choose File | Send. Exchange opens the Choose Profile dialog box. The listing depends on how you set up Exchange. Choose a profile and click OK.
3. In the New Message window, click the To button to open Address Book and choose a name or create a new name. Click OK.

4. In the New Message window, click Send (the first button on the top toolbar). AutoCAD opens the Print/Plot Configuration dialog box. Set the parameters as you want the fax to appear. Use the Scaled to Fit option to fit the drawing on the receiver's fax paper. Click OK.

5. Exchange prepares the fax format, dials the number, and faxes the drawing. In addition, AutoCAD actually prints or plots the drawing, useless though this may be.

What are DWF files?

A DWF file is a format for publishing and viewing drawings on the Internet. It has the following characteristics:

- It is a vector file, so you can zoom in and out without losing detail.

- It is a 2-D representation of your drawing, much like a plot. Viewers cannot access individual objects. The purpose of this feature is to prevent viewers from accessing all the details of your drawing.

- It can support URL links to other drawings or supporting files.

To create a DWF file you simply choose File | Export, choose DWF from the Save as type drop-down list, and choose Save.

Why can't I create a DWF file of a paper-space view?

The first versions of the WHIP! viewer, the program used to view DWF files, did not support paper space; however, WHIP! 3.0 does. You can download it free of charge from Autodesk's Web site, at www.autodesk.com. You can then look at a paper-space view that is saved in the DWF file.

Note: *Release 14 requires Release 2 or higher of the WHIP! viewer.*

 ## How do I create links for a DWF file?

One of the great advantages of DWF files is that you can attach links to objects and areas in the drawing. A link is a connection to a *uniform resource locator (URL),* which is an Internet address. When a viewer clicks on the object or area with the link, the information at the link address is displayed. There are a number of uses for attaching links to a drawing:

● You can refer viewers to a price list.

● You can transfer viewers to a more detailed drawing of an object or part.

● You can provide viewers with a list of specifications.

 Note: *Web browsers can only view certain types of file formats—generally text, HTML, or certain graphic file types. Therefore, the material you link to must be in one of these formats.*

When working with URLs, it's helpful to open the Internet Utilities toolbar, shown here:

To open the toolbar, right-click any toolbar and choose inet from the Menu Group drop-down list. Check Internet Utilities. If inet is not listed, your need to load it. At the command line, type **menuload** and press ENTER. Click Browse in the dialog box and locate INET.MNC, which should be in AutoCAD's \Support folder. Choose it and click Open. Click Load and close the dialog box. You can now choose inet from the Menu Group drop-down list.

To create a link, follow these steps:

1. Choose Attach URL from the Internet Utilities toolbar.

2. At the "URL by (Area/<Objects>):" prompt, press ENTER to attach the URL to an object or objects. Type **a** and press ENTER to attach the URL by area.

3. Either select objects or pick two corners of an area as prompted.

4. At the "Enter URL:" prompt, type the URL of the supporting data or files you want to link to.

Of course, you need to know the structure of the Web site where you will post the DWF drawing, and the links, in order to correctly type the URL.

How do I get a DWF file onto a Web site?

The DWF file is posted onto a Web site in the same way other files are posted onto the Web site. Your company's Web site administrator will know how to accomplish this.

Click Internet Help on the Internet Utilities toolbar and locate the topic, "Adding DWF Files to a Web Page," for more information, including specific HTML code.

Caution: *Before you can post a DWF file, your Internet server must recognize the DWF file type. The Web site administrator or Internet service provider must add the MIME type "drawing/x-dwg" to the server to register the drawing type with the server software.*

How do I view a DWF file on the Internet?

To view a DWF file on the Internet, you need one of the WHIP! viewers—either the WHIP! Plug-In, if you use Netscape Navigator, or WHIP! Control for ActiveX, if you use Microsoft Explorer. You can obtain either viewer from Autodesk's Web site at www.autodesk.com. The purpose of the WHIP! viewer is to let you zoom and pan, print, and use any embedded URLs.

Once you have installed WHIP!, go to a Web site with a DWF drawing. The drawing automatically appears. Figure 5-16 shows a DWF drawing in Microsoft Internet Explorer.

Right-click anywhere in the image to open the WHIP! menu, shown here:

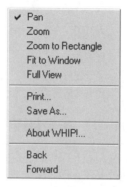

The menu lets you pan and zoom just like real-time pan and zoom in AutoCAD. There are also other zoom options

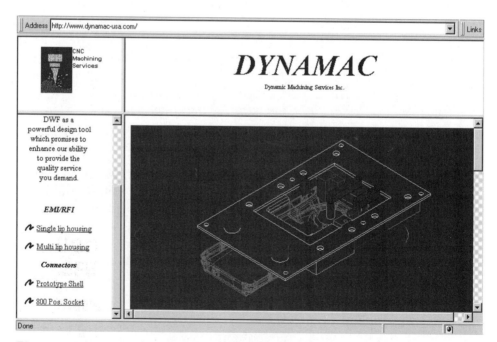

Figure 5-16 A DWF drawing on the Internet (courtesy of Dynamac Corp., www.dynamac-usa.com)

that work like ZOOM Window and ZOOM Extents. To print the image, choose Print from the menu.

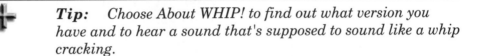

> ***Tip:*** *Choose About WHIP! to find out what version you have and to hear a sound that's supposed to sound like a whip cracking.*

If the DWF file contains URL links, the cursor changes to a pointing hand as it passes over the link and the name of the URL is displayed at the bottom-left corner of the screen. Click on it, and WHIP! transfers you to the link address.

I don't have a Web site. Can I still use DWF files?

Yes, you can, but you do need a Web browser, such as Microsoft Internet Explorer or Netscape Navigator. Your browser can view DWF files from your hard disk. The URL addresses can also be on your hard disk. You could use DWF files on your hard disk for a presentation or as part of an exhibit on a trade-show floor. Potential customers could view your DWF files and click on URLs for further information.

Is there a way to access actual drawings over the Internet?

Yes, you can now access drawings from any Web site. Your company might have an Intranet through which employees can access drawings of parts they can insert in their drawings. In other words, the parts library can be stored on the company's Web site.

To open an AutoCAD drawing from a Web site, choose Open from URL on the Internet Utilities toolbar. To insert a drawing into your drawing, choose Insert from URL. You can also access drawings using drag-and-drop. To insert using drag-and-drop, the actual drawing must be in the same folder as its DWF file. Follow these steps:

1. With the DWF file in view, press and hold down CTRL to insert a drawing or CTRL+SHIFT to open a drawing.

2. Click and drag the DWF image from your browser into AutoCAD. If AutoCAD is not in view, drag the image

onto the AutoCAD button on the taskbar, wait for AutoCAD's window to open, and continue to drag the image into the drawing area.

3. Release the mouse button, then release CTRL (or CTRL and SHIFT).

AutoCAD inserts or opens the actual drawing represented by the DWF file.

Chapter 6

Drawing and Editing in 3-D

Answer Topics!

Drawing and Editing in 3-D @ a Glance

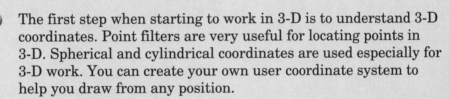

The first step when starting to work in 3-D is to understand 3-D coordinates. Point filters are very useful for locating points in 3-D. Spherical and cylindrical coordinates are used especially for 3-D work. You can create your own user coordinate system to help you draw from any position.

You can view your 3-D drawing from any angle or create a perspective view. You can also set several system variables to customize how 3-D models are displayed. To lay out your drawing for plotting, you can create 2-D displays of 3-D objects.

Surfaces are true 3-D objects but do not have volume. Surfaces are approximated using a mesh of planes defined by the vertices of the planes. AutoCAD has a number of commands that create basic shapes such as boxes and spheres. There are also commands that create surfaces from 2-D objects. This chapter discusses some special techniques for hiding text and working with irregular surfaces.

Solids are the most realistic type of 3-D object. You can combine and subtract solids to create complex objects. The commands for creating solids are similar to those for creating surfaces. You can create basic shapes and build solids from 2-D objects. There are a number of special commands to let you mirror, array, rotate, align, trim, and extend objects in 3-D space. You can also fillet and chamfer solids.

Rendering is the process of creating a photorealistic view of a 3-D drawing. Release 14 includes the capabilities of AutoVision, previously a separate Autodesk program, in its rendering feature. You can now add to your renderings shadows, transparency, and patterns mapped onto surfaces.

WORKING WITH 3-D COORDINATES AND COORDINATE SYSTEMS

Can you use tracking in 3-D?

No, tracking is strictly for 2-D, although you can use it in a 3-D drawing if the points you need to specify are all in one plane. For most 3-D work, you need to use point filters instead. For more information about point filters, see the box, "Locating Points in Three Dimensions."

Locating Points in Three Dimensions

Locating points is harder in 3-D than in 2-D because you can't always be sure of the depth of the point. Although AutoCAD understands the drawing in 3-D, your screen is still two-dimensional. For most 3-D drawing, you should use object snaps whenever possible. First, find a viewpoint that clearly displays the points you want. Then set running object snaps as needed. The new Release 14 SnapTip feature makes it easier than ever to be sure you are picking the point you want.

Tip: *You can cycle through object snaps that are close together. At any prompt that requires a coordinate, place the cursor near the object snap you want. Now press TAB until the object snap displays the Marker you want, and click to use it.*

But what do you do when the point you want isn't on an existing object? If you know the distance from an existing object to the point you want, you can use the From feature. To use From, at any prompt where you can specify a coordinate, choose Snap From on the Object Snap flyout (or type **from** on the command line). At the "Base point:" prompt, specify the point on the existing object, generally with an object snap. At the "<Offset>:" prompt, type the distance of the desired coordinate from the base point, using relative coordinates, for example, **@3,4**.

Point filters are another method of specifying points, and they are indispensable for 3-D drawing. You use point filters to locate a point based on the x, y, or z coordinates of existing points. For example, if the point you want has the same x coordinate as one line endpoint and the same y coordinate as another line endpoint, and you know the z coordinate, you can construct the new point using point filters.

Following is a solid box:

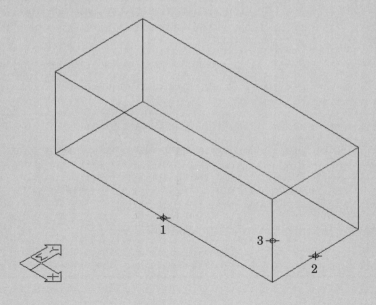

Let's say you want to draw a sphere whose center is the center of the box. You can locate the box's center using the following steps:

1. Set a running object snap for midpoints, and turn OSNAP on by double-clicking the OSNAP button on the status bar.

2. Start the SPHERE command.

3. At the "Center of sphere <0,0,0>:" prompt, type **.x** and press ENTER. Don't forget the period before the x, which tells AutoCAD you are creating a point filter.

4. At the "of" prompt, pick the midpoint object snap at 1 in the preceding illustration.

5. At the "(need YZ):" prompt, type **.y** and press ENTER. With this prompt, AutoCAD is informing you that it has the x coordinate but still needs the y and z coordinates.

6. At the "of" prompt, pick the midpoint object snap at 2 in the preceding illustration.

7. At the "(need Z):" prompt, pick the midpoint object snap at 3 in the preceding illustration.

8. At the "Diameter/<Radius> of sphere:" prompt, type or pick a radius. To draw the largest sphere that is entirely enclosed by the box, you need to find the center of the bottom (or top) plane of the box, and you can again use point filters. To do so, type **.x** and press ENTER.

9. At the "of" prompt, pick the midpoint object snap at 1 in the preceding illustration.

10. At the "(need YZ):" prompt, type **.y** and press ENTER.

11. At the "of" prompt, pick the midpoint object snap at 2 in the preceding illustration.

12. At the "(need Z):" prompt, type **end,** and press ENTER to start an endpoint object snap.

13. At the "of" prompt, pick the endpoint object snap of any of the bottom corners of the box.

The result is shown here:

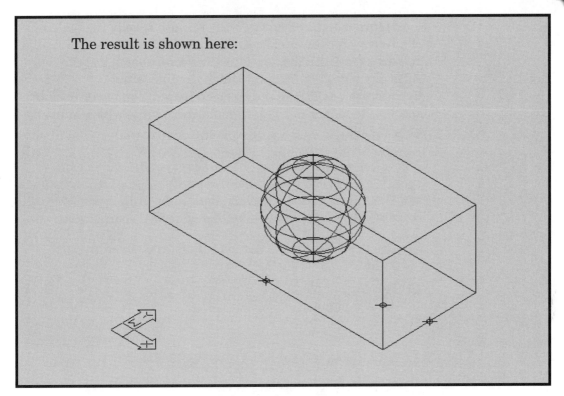

? What is the difference between cylindrical and spherical coordinates?

Cylindrical coordinates use the syntax *distance<angle, distance*. Add @ before the coordinate to make it relative. You can specify a cylindrical coordinate by specifying the location in the XY plane and in the Z direction. Here's how to build a cylindrical coordinate:

- The first distance is the number of units in the XY plane.
- The angle is the number of degrees from the X axis in the XY plane.
- The second distance is the number of units in the Z direction.

Figure 6-1 shows how @2<20,4 would specify the endpoint of a line with cylindrical coordinates. As you can see, although you are creating a diagonal line, the coordinates use the two sides of a right triangle—of which the line is the hypotenuse—to define the line's endpoint. You never need to specify the length of the line you are drawing, which happens to be 4.4721.

Spherical coordinates use the syntax *distance<angle<angle*. Add @ before the coordinate to make it relative. You can specify a spherical coordinate by specifying the actual distance and the angles in the XY plane and in the Z direction respectively. Here's how to build a spherical coordinate:

- The first distance is the actual distance from the last point.

- The first angle is the number of degrees from the X axis in the XY plane.

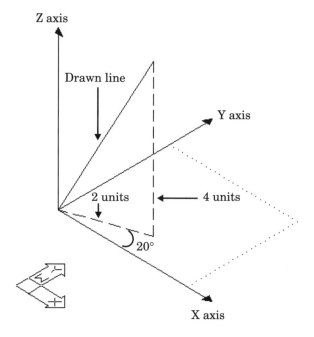

Figure 6-1 Drawing a line with cylindrical coordinates. The endpoint is specified as @2<20,4

● The second angle is the number of degrees from the XY plane in the Z direction.

Figure 6-2 shows how @3<20<45 would specify the endpoint of a line with spherical coordinates. As you can see, the line is actually 3 units long, and its endpoint is further defined by the two angles.

You choose which type of coordinate to draw based on the information you have available. Sometimes you know the distances in the XY plane and the Z direction but don't know the actual length of the object—then you need to use cylindrical coordinates. If you know the actual length of the object and its angles in the XY plane and the Z direction, use spherical coordinates.

In 3-D, I find it hard to remember in which direction the X and Y axes are. How can I tell?

Make sure the UCS icon is displayed. You may have gotten used to working without the UCS icon in 2-D drawings but in 3-D drawings it is essential for getting your bearings. Choose View | Display | UCS icon | On. The On item is a toggle; it's checked when the UCS icon is on and not checked when it's off.

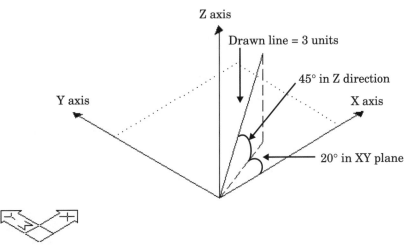

Figure 6-2 Drawing a line using spherical coordinates. The endpoint is specified as @2<20<45

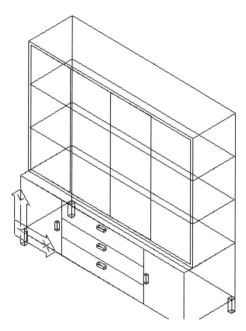

Figure 6-3 The UCS icon is shown at the origin of the current UCS

The Origin item in the same menu lets you specify that the UCS icon should be shown at the origin of the current UCS, as shown in Figure 6-3. Placing the UCS icon at the origin helps you get oriented when you are switching from one UCS to another.

However, if there is no room to place the UCS icon at the origin—for example, if the origin in not displayed on the screen—the UCS icon appears in its regular location at the lower-left corner of your drawing.

 ## Why can't I specify z coordinates when I draw an arc?

You can, but only for the first point on the arc. Because ARC is a 2-D command, the other points must be on the same z coordinate at the first point, so AutoCAD rejects any coordinate with a z value. The same is true of a rectangle, polyline, and an ellipse. A circle can accept a 3-D coordinate for its center, but the rest of the circle will all be on the same plane, parallel to the XY plane of your UCS. However, the

LINE command can accept 3-D coordinates at any time. To create 3-D polylines, use the 3DPOLY command. However, 3-D polylines cannot include arcs, have a width, or use a noncontinuous linetype.

What does the broken pencil icon mean?

The broken pencil icon means that you are looking at an object from a viewpoint that will make it hard for you to draw and edit your drawing. Whenever you view a drawing on edge, you see the broken pencil, as shown in Figure 6-4. In this view, you are looking at the same wall unit as shown in Figure 6-3. You can see that much of the drawing is not visible.

When this happens, try one of the isometric views available from the Viewpoint flyout. The isometric views look at your drawing from a diagonal view, letting you see most of your drawing clearly. The Viewpoint flyout offers a number of preset viewpoints that are quick and easy to use. The Viewpoint flyout is shown in Figure 6-5.

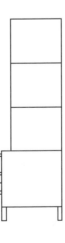

Figure 6-4 When you view a drawing on edge, AutoCAD displays the broken pencil icon at the lower-left corner to let you know that you may not be seeing most of the drawing

Figure 6-5 The Viewpoint flyout offers preset viewpoints that you can use for your 3-D drawings

What's the difference between a UCS and a viewpoint?

This is a common question from new 3-D users. A viewpoint looks at your drawing from a different direction. Nothing else changes. Figure 6-6 shows a 3-D model from three different viewpoints—top, front, and SE Isometric.

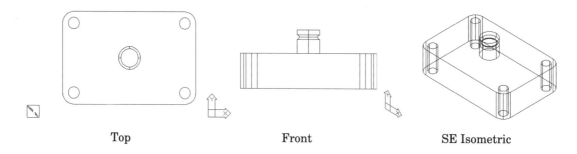

Top   Front   SE Isometric

Figure 6-6 Looking at a model from the top, the front, and the SE Isometric viewpoints

You change a viewpoint so that you can see your drawing from a better vantage point. In 3-D, sometimes two objects obscure each other and it is difficult to specify the object you want. Or, you may find it easier to conceptualize what's on your screen from a different viewpoint.

A user coordinate system (UCS) is a setting for the origin—point 0,0,0—and the direction of the X, Y, and Z axes. When you change the UCS, the coordinates change. For example, a point that was 0,0,0 could now be 5,4,-2 or anything else, depending on how you change the UCS. For more information on how to create a UCS, see the box, "Creating a User Coordinate System (UCS)."

You need to change your UCS when you can't draw in the current UCS—or can't draw easily. For example, if you need to draw a circle or other 2-D object, you can set the UCS so that your XY plane is on the plane where the circle needs to be. Now you can draw the circle.

Creating a User Coordinate System (UCS)

A UCS is defined by its origin and the direction of the X and Y axes. The X and Y axes define the XY plane. All the options of the UCS command (choose Tools | UCS) are different ways of specifying the location of the origin and the direction of the axes. The various ways you can define a UCS are listed here:

Option	Description
Object	Aligns the UCS with an object you specify. The result is not always obvious.
View	AutoCAD arbitrarily sets the origin and aligns the XY plane with the current view. Useful for applying annotation to a 3-D view.
Origin	You specify a new origin. The XY plane is parallel to the current UCS.
Z Axis Vector	You define the origin as the first point on the Z axis, then specify another point to define the direction of the Z axis. The XY plane is automatically perpendicular to the Z axis you have defined.

Option	Description
3 Point	The first point you define is the origin. Then you define the positive direction of the X axis and the positive direction of the Y axis.
X Axis Rotate	Retains the current origin and rotates the Y and Z axes around the X axis by an angle you specify.
Y Axis Rotate	Retains the current origin and rotates the X and Z axes around the Y axis by an angle you specify.
Z Axis Rotate	Retains the current origin and rotates the X and Y axes around the Z axis by an angle you specify.

Once you have created a UCS, you should save it for future use. Use the Save option and give the UCS a name. Use the Restore option to restore the UCS. You can use the Named option to choose one of the UCSs you have saved from a dialog box. The Preset option lets you choose from several preset UCSs.

If you are drawing a window in a pitched roof, it may be possible to draw it in the world coordinate system (WCS) but would be much easier if your UCS were aligned with the angle of the roof. Then the roof becomes your XY plane, and specifying coordinates is much easier.

VIEWING 3-D OBJECTS

Whenever I change to another UCS, I find myself using the PLAN command to return to plan view. Is there any shortcut?

Certainly. The UCSFOLLOW system variable determines whether AutoCAD returns to plan view whenever you change the UCS. By default it is off (0). Turn it on (1) and AutoCAD will return you to plan view each time you change the UCS.

When I hide a 3-D model, how do I get rid of the ugly lines AutoCAD uses? I just want nice, clean lines.

Ordinarily, AutoCAD uses the mesh lines to fully display curves on a 3-D model, as shown in the bushing in Figure 6-7.

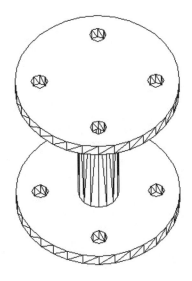

Figure 6-7 By default, AutoCAD uses mesh lines to display curves on a hidden 3-D model

While the mesh lines can help reveal errors, they don't look very pretty. You can hide them by changing the DISPSILH system variable to 1. DISPSILH, which stands for Display Silhouette, creates a simple silhouette without mesh lines, as shown in Figure 6-8.

 How do I create a custom viewpoint?

Probably the easiest method is to use the Viewpoint Presets dialog box, which despite its name, does not offer you preset viewpoints but lets you create your own. To open the Viewpoint Presets dialog box, shown in Figure 6-9, choose View | 3D Viewpoint | Select.

The dialog box is divided into two halves:

● The large box on the left side of the dialog box represents the XY plane. Imagine yourself walking around your model, or object, looking at it while maintaining the same height. The 0 degree setting represents the X axis, so if you use a 0 degree setting, you are looking at the your model from the right side. As you walk around the object,

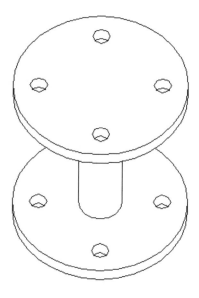

Figure 6-8 With DISPSILH on, AutoCAD omits the mesh lines when you hide a curved 3-D model

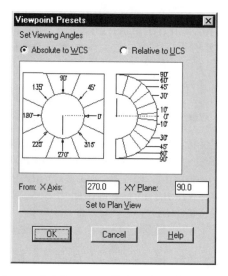

Figure 6-9 The Viewpoint Presets dialog box lets you create custom viewpoints

the angle changes, so that a 90-degree setting gives you a back view, a 180-degree setting gives you the left view, and a 270-degree setting gives you the front view. The text box for this setting is called From X Axis because 0 represents the X axis and other angles are relative to the X axis.

● The semicircle on the right side of the dialog box represents the angle in the Z direction. Any setting above zero means you are above the object, and any setting below zero means you are looking at the object from below. A setting of 90 degrees represents plan view, the view from above. Plan view is the view you usually use in 2-D drawings. In an architectural drawing, plan view shows the layout of the house or building as if you were hovering above it. The text box for this setting is called XY Plane because it measures the angle from the XY plane into the Z positive or negative direction.

Both the box and the semi-circle have a black needle that indicates the current angle. When you change the angle, the black needle moves to the new angle but a red needle appears at the current angle for reference purposes.

To set the angle in the XY plane, click inside any segment to set the angle as marked in that segment. If you click inside the inner circle, you get the exact angle based on your click, which is usually an unusual number such as 271.3. You can also type the angle you want in the From: X Axis text box.

To set the angle for the Z direction, click in any segment to set the angle as marked in that segment. If you click inside the inner semi-circle, you generally get an unusual number calculated from your exact click location, such as 32.1. You can also type the angle you want in the XY Plane text box.

At the top of the dialog box, you can choose to have your setting absolute to the world coordinate system (WCS) or relative to a UCS you have created. By default, AutoCAD creates the viewpoint absolute to the WCS. The WCS is the default coordinate system. Click Relative to UCS only if you have created your own UCS and you want the viewpoint to

use that UCS as its basis. The angles you specify will be based on the XY plane and z coordinate as you defined them in your UCS.

At the bottom of the dialog box is a Set to Plan View button, which quickly sets the viewpoint to plan view—270 degrees in the XY plane and 90 degrees in the Z direction.

Tip: *After using this dialog box, if you like the results, save a named view with the DDVIEW command. Choose View | Named Views.*

 ## How do I create a perspective view?

You can create a perspective view using the DVIEW command with the Direction option. A perspective view creates an effect of depth. Lines that are parallel in real life—and in your drawing—merge as the distance from the viewer increases. The purpose of DVIEW is to let you or a client view a drawing from a more realistic perspective. You can't draw in DVIEW.

Caution: *Once you create a perspective view you like, you should immediately save the view. DVIEW is a difficult command and it is difficult to reproduce your results exactly.*

To use DVIEW, choose View | 3D Dynamic View. At the "Select objects:" prompt, select only the objects you wish to include in the view, to save regeneration time.

After you select objects, you have the options shown in Table 6-1. Use these options to create the view.

Figure 6-10 shows an SE Isometric view before using DVIEW. Notice that the outer brackets diverge in the distance.

Figure 6-11 shows a perspective view created with DVIEW. This view is from the same angle as in Figure 6-10 but you can see that the outside brackets approach each other in the distance.

Option	Description
Camera	DVIEW uses a camera/target metaphor. The camera is the viewer's location and for this option you define the camera's angle in the XY plane and from the XY plane (in the Z direction). At the first prompt, type the angle from the XY plane, that is, the angle in the Z direction, or move the cursor to see the results in real time, and then click. Then type **t** and press ENTER to toggle to the "Enter angle in XY plane from X axis" prompt. Type an angle or move the cursor to see the results, and click when you like what you see. You may need to hold the cursor for a couple of seconds, while AutoCAD regenerates the new view, to see the result.
Target	The target is the object you are viewing. For this option you use the same suboptions as for the Camera option.
Distance	The Distance option turns on perspective mode. Without using this option, your view remains in parallel mode. AutoCAD displays a special Perspective mode icon at the lower-left corner of the drawing area. You can use the slider bar at the top of the screen to specify the difference as a zoom percentage. A zoom of 1x leaves the zoom unchanged. To zoom out, drag the cursor to the right of the slider bar. You can also type a distance in units, from the camera to the target, on the command line.
Points	The Points option lets you define the camera and target by coordinates. You should use object snaps or point filters to locate the point in 3-D.
Pan	DVIEW has its own pan mode, which works like the old displacement point PAN command.
Zoom	DVIEW has its own zoom mode. If you have turned on perspective mode (by using the Distance option), you define the zoom in terms of a lens length. A longer length, such as 70 mm, zooms in; a shorter length, such as 35 mm, zooms out. If you are in parallel mode, you specify the zoom by a zoom factor, as in the Distance option.
Twist	The Twist option twists the view in a circle, parallel to the current view. You can move the cursor or type an angle.
Clip	The Clip option creates front and back clipping planes that hide anything in front of the front plane and behind the back plane. Clipping planes are always parallel to the current view, you just set their distance from the target. With this option, as with others, you can use a slider bar or type a distance.
Hide	Hides hidden lines, like the HIDE command.
Off	Turns off perspective mode, letting you draw again when you exit the DVIEW command.
Undo	Undoes the effect of the most recently used option. You can do multiple undoes.
eXit	Exits DVIEW.

Table 6-1   DVIEW Options

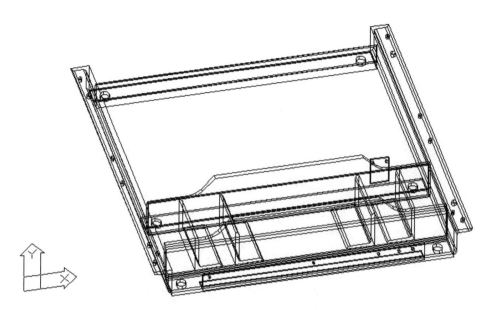

Figure 6-10 In a parallel view, parallel lines diverge as the distance from the viewer increases

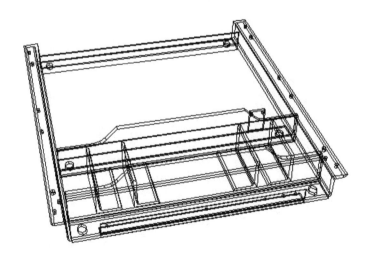

Figure 6-11 In a perspective view, parallel lines approach each other as the distance from the viewer increases, similar to your experience in real life

 I have a 3-D drawing that I want to save with lines hidden and send as a DXF file to a client who has only 2-D capabilities. Is there a way to do this?

You can turn a 3-D drawing into a 2-D drawing by creating a DXB file. A DXB file is a binary file that converts plotting instructions to vector data. You can then import this file back into AutoCAD as a 2-D drawing. Finally, you can create a DXF file of the 2-D drawing to send to your client. Simple! To create a DXB file, follow these steps:

1. Create the view you want to show.

2. Choose Tools | Preferences and click the Printer tab.

3. Click New.

4. In the Add a Printer dialog box, choose AutoCAD DXB file format. If you wish, type a description. Then click OK.

5. At the prompts in the AutoCAD Text Window, accept the defaults for size and printer steps.

6. Next, AutoCAD lists the current plot parameters and asks if you want to change anything. Type **y** and press ENTER. Go through the individual plot parameters, accepting or changing the defaults as needed until the question about hidden lines.

7. At the "Remove hidden lines? <N>:" prompt, type **y** and press ENTER. AutoCAD now lists AutoCAD DXB file on your list of printers, as shown in Figure 6-12.

8. Start the PLOT command.

9. In the Print/Plot Configuration dialog box, click Device and Default Selection.

10. Choose AutoCAD DXB file and click OK. AutoCAD automatically configures the plot according to the parameters you chose when adding the DXB printer. For example, the Hide Lines box is checked.

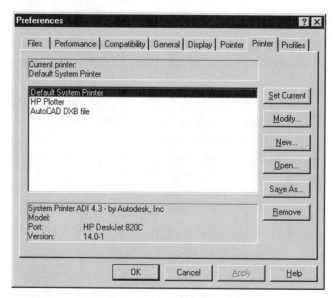

Figure 6-12   You can add AutoCAD DXB file to your list of printers to create 2-D drawings from 3-D drawings

Tip: *You can do a full plot preview to see the results and make changes to the plot parameters as required. For example, you might discover that you need to rotate the plot. You can also click File Name to change the name and / or location of the DXB file that will be created. Omit the filename extension; AutoCAD automatically gives the file a DXB extension.*

11. Click OK to plot. AutoCAD automatically plots to a file with the same name as your drawing and gives it a .DXB extension.

12. Open a new drawing using the Start from Scratch option.

13. Choose Insert | Drawing Exchange Binary to start the DXBIN command. In the Select DXB File dialog box, choose the DXB file and click Open. AutoCAD imports the file.

Figure 6-13 shows an imported DXB file, created from the perspective view in Figure 6-11.

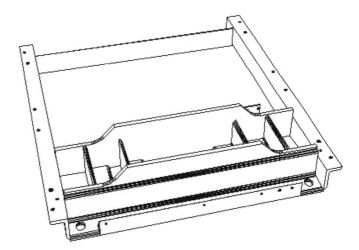

Figure 6-13 A 2-D drawing created from a 3-D perspective view using AutoCAD's DXB printer

You can now create a DXF file from this new drawing and send it to your client. The drawing is made up completely of lines. Objects that were curves in the 3-D drawing are now represented by many short lines. All objects have a Z coordinate of 0. What you are seeing is a 2-D representation of your 3-D drawing. This type of drawing is ideal for illustration purposes. You can easily add text or remove unwanted lines. A common trick is to create a DXB drawing of a house, and then add 2-D clip art, such as trees and people.

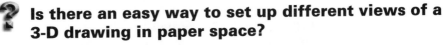

! *Caution:* *All colored lines become black when you export to DXB format.*

Is there an easy way to set up different views of a 3-D drawing in paper space?

AutoCAD provides three commands—SOLVIEW, SOLDRAW, and SOLPROF—to help you lay out 3-D drawings. They are not exactly easy to use, but once you get used to them, they can speed up your work considerably. These commands are described in the next three subsections.

SOLVIEW

SOLVIEW creates floating viewports and orthogonal views, which are typical in mechanical drawings. You can find SOLVIEW on the Solids toolbar. Here are the options:

● UCS starts you off by letting you choose a UCS and setting the scale, center, and clipping corners (diagonal corners) of a floating viewport. You can always change the scale later. The center specifies the location of the viewport's center on your screen, and the clipping corners define the viewport's boundaries. SOLVIEW lets you continue to specify view centers until you get what you like. Press ENTER to go to the next prompt. SOLVIEW prompts you for a view name, which should describe the point of view, such as top or right.

● Ortho creates orthogonal views, which are based on the first viewport you created with the UCS option. At the "Pick side of viewport to project:" prompt, pick one of the borders of the existing viewport. SOLVIEW prompts you for a view center (keep picking until you like the result), clipping corners, and a name.

● Auxiliary creates inclined views. At the "Inclined Plane's 1st point:" prompt, pick a point in one of the viewports, then pick another point in the same viewport to define the inclined plane. SOLVIEW prompts you for a side to view from. Then specify a view center, clipping corners, and a name.

● Section creates cross-section views. The option prompts you for two points of the cutting plane, which you specify in one of the viewports. Specify a side to view from, the view scale, a view center, clipping corners, and a name.

Type **x** to exit the command. You can reuse the command to create more viewports, or use regular commands in model and paper space to adjust the results.

SOLDRAW

After you have used SOLVIEW, use SOLDRAW to create hatching and hidden lines for sectional views. When prompted to select objects, pick one or more floating

viewports. SOLDRAW automatically creates the views. Hatching is drawn using current defaults, but you can use HATCHEDIT to change the hatch.

Figure 6-14 shows a layout created with SOLVIEW and SOLDRAW.

SOLPROF

The SOLPROF command creates clean-looking profiles (somewhat like SOLDRAW, but it works on its own). To use SOLPROF, follow these steps:

1. First create a floating viewport in paper space, and switch to model space (double-click PAPER on the status bar).

2. SOLPROF asks you if you want hidden profile lines on a separate layer. Choose **Y** to create separate layers for lines that would be visible and hidden. You can then freeze or turn off the layers of the hidden lines to create a clearer display, or change the color and/or linetype of the hidden layer.

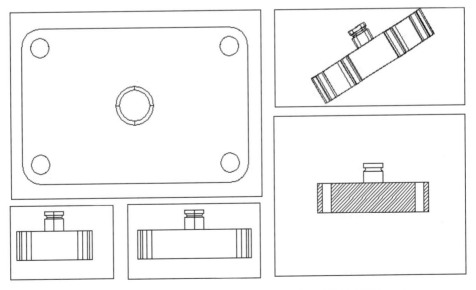

Figure 6-14   A paper space layout created using SOLVIEW and SOLDRAW

3. You can then choose to project profile lines onto a plane. Choose **Y** to create 2-D objects instead of 3-D objects. Visually, the profile looks the same either way.

4. When asked if you want to delete tangential edges, choose **Y** or **N**. Most drafting conventions do not require you to show tangential edges—where two contiguous faces meet—and the default is to delete these edges.

AutoCAD creates the profile. Figure 6-15 shows a profile created with SOLPROF. SOLPROF creates the profile on top of the original object; therefore, the layer of the original object has been turned off. Also, the hidden layer, which always starts with Pv, has been given a different color and a dashed linetype. You could also freeze this layer.

When I create a cylinder, it appears with so few lines that I can't visualize the curve. Is there any way to adjust this setting?

You are probably referring to the *isolines* that AutoCAD uses to represent curves in 3-D. By default, the number of isolines is set to 4, which doesn't represent a curve very precisely, although it does save regeneration time.

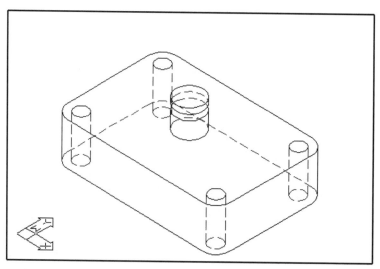

Figure 6-15   A profile created with SOLPROF

Here you see a cylinder with four isolines:

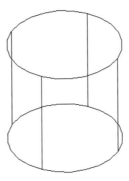

You can change the ISOLINES system variable by typing **isolines** and specifying a new number. Here you see the same cylinder with eight isolines. You can see that the curvature of the cylinder is much more apparent.

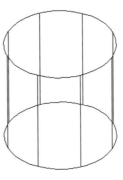

Note: *After changing the number of isolines, type* **regen** *and press ENTER to change the display of existing objects.*

You can also change the isolines in the Preferences dialog box. Choose Tools | Preferences and click the Performance tab. Change the number in the Contour lines per surface text box.

I created a revolved surface, but it has so few facets that it doesn't look curved. Can I adjust the display?

Several types of 3-D surfaces use tabulation lines to represent the surface mesh. You can change the number of lines AutoCAD uses with the SURFTAB1 and SURFTAB2 system variables. Here's how to use these system variables.

For ruled surfaces (surfaces created with RULESURF) and tabulated surfaces (surfaces created with TABSURF), SURFTAB1 sets the number of tabulations. These surfaces only have tabulation lines going in one direction.

For revolved surfaces (surfaces created with REVSURF), SURFTAB1 sets the number of lines in the direction of revolution. SURFTAB2 sets the number of lines along the path curve that you revolved. Here you see a revolved surface with a SURFTAB1 of 16 and a SURFTAB2 of 4.

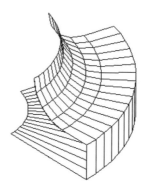

For edge surfaces (surfaces created with EDGESURF), SURFTAB1 sets the number of lines in the direction of the edge created by the first two pick points, and SURFTAB2 sets the number of lines in the direction of the adjoining edge.

DRAWING AND EDITING SURFACES

 What's the simplest way to get started drawing 3-D objects?

If you're just starting out with 3-D drawings, you should know about 2½-D, which is like 3-D but simpler. You can create almost any 2-D object and give it a thickness, thereby adding a third dimension. Because the third dimension that you add is very simple—always a straight side perpendicular to the 2-D object and always one thickness throughout, it's sometimes called 2½-D. Adding thickness to a 2-D object creates the 3-D AutoCAD object called a surface. It's not solid inside and you cannot calculate volume/mass or inertia properties. But surfaces can be hidden and rendered to look just as real as solids and are sometimes more flexible to edit.

Perhaps the best way to start playing with 3-D is to use the new options of the RECTANG command, which let you give a rectangle thickness on the fly—as you are creating the rectangle. These options are fully described in Chapter 4 in the "Drawing Basic Objects" section under the question, "The RECTANG command has lots of new options in Release 14. What do they mean?"

There are two ways to add thickness to other 2-D objects. First, you can set the current thickness. When you set the current thickness to any value other than zero, all objects that you subsequently create (that can accept thickness) have the new thickness. To change the current thickness, type **elev** on the command line. At the "New current elevation <0.0000>:" prompt, press ENTER if you want your objects to be drawn at a z coordinate of 0, the default. At the "New current thickness <0.0000>:" prompt, type the thickness you want and press ENTER.

Tip: *The current thickness is stored in the THICKNESS system variable, so you can just type **thickness** and type the desired current thickness.*

Because it's easy to forget that all the objects you are drawing now have this new thickness, many users prefer to draw a 2-D object at zero thickness and change the thickness afterward. To change an object's thickness, select the object and click Properties on the Object Properties toolbar. In the dialog box, type a new value in the Thickness text box. If the Thickness text box is not available, you cannot give that type of object a thickness.

The following objects cannot have a thickness:

● Ellipse
● Xline
● Ray
● Multiline
● Spline
● 3-D Polyline
● Multiline text

Single-line text created with DTEXT or TEXT, and block attributes, are always created with no thickness, regardless of the current thickness. However, you can give them thickness by clicking Properties on the Object Properties toolbar and changing the value in the Thickness text box.

Elevation refers to how many units a 2-D object is placed from the XY plane. Objects with a positive elevation are above the XY plane and objects with a negative elevation are below it. You can set the current elevation using the ELEV command. All subsequent objects that you create are placed on that elevation.

The easiest way to change the elevation is to move the object up or down in the Z direction. For example, to change an object's elevation from 0 to 2, start the MOVE command and select the object. At the "Base point or displacement:" prompt, type **0,0,2** and press ENTER twice to end the command.

 When I add a thickness to 2-D objects, some have tops and bottoms and others don't. What's going on?

AutoCAD puts tops and bottoms on some objects with thickness but not on others. Here is a list of some objects and whether they end up with tops and bottoms when you give them thickness.

Circle	Yes
Polyline with width	Yes
Closed polyline without width	No
Closed line segments	No
Solid (2-D command)	Yes

Figure 6-16 shows you some surfaces created by adding thickness to 2-D objects.

 How can I get AutoCAD to hide text when I use the HIDE command?

The way to hide text is to give it a thickness. The thickness can be very small, so that it is hardly noticeable. When text has no thickness, the HIDE command ignores it.

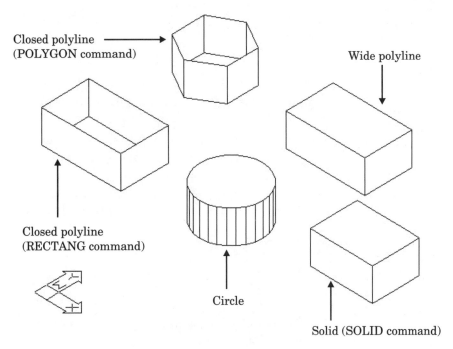

Closed polyline
(POLYGON command)

Wide polyline

Closed polyline
(RECTANG command)

Circle

Solid (SOLID command)

Figure 6-16 When you add thickness to 2-D objects, some resulting surfaces have tops and bottoms, others don't. You can tell the difference after using the HIDE command

Tip: *If you want to give a thickness to multiline text, you can explode it to convert it to Text objects. Then you can give it a thickness.*

What's the best way to create an irregular topological surface from surveyor's data?

The 3DMESH command lets you create a surface from individual coordinates. The surveyor's data will provide you with each measured location, including the elevation, which becomes the z coordinate. Some surveyors can provide you with a 3-D drawing in which the measurements are points at their actual locations. The polygon mesh that 3DMESH creates can also be smoothed using the PEDIT command to create a smoother, more realistic topology.

 Tip: *You can use the Bonus tool, ASCPOINT.LSP, to import point data from an ASCII file to generate meshes. To use this command, type* **ascpoint** *on the command line.*

To use 3DMESH, you need to create a grid of points. Start by counting the number of measurements and assigning them a place in a grid of rows and columns. Then start the 3DMESH command and respond to the prompts asking for the M and N mesh size. M and N are the two directions of the grid.

AutoCAD now prompts you for each vertex by number, based on the M and N size you specified. The numbers start with zero, so that a mesh of 3 by 5 has a last vertex of (2,4).

 Tip: *You may be able to attach a surveyor's drawing as an xref and pick the points on the screen using the xref as a guide. You can then edit the mesh vertices with grips, stretching each grip to its proper height. To move a vertex 54.7 in the Z direction, for example, click the grip to make it hot, and type* **@0,0,54.7**.

 ### What's the difference between 3DFACE, PFACE, and 3DMESH? Don't they all make similar surfaces?

3DFACE, PFACE, and 3DMESH are similar in that they all create surface planes. However, they have a number of differences.

3DFACE creates flat planes. You cannot create curved surfaces with 3DFACE, nor can you give 3-D faces a thickness. Each plane can have three or four sides—no more—but you can continue to add planes to the first 3-D face to create many multisided planes. While AutoCAD adds a line separating each plane, a special command, EDGE, lets you make these lines invisible if you wish to create the effect of one large surface.

 Note: *You can set the SPLFRAME system variable to 1 and regenerate the drawing to see all 3-D face edges. Set SPLFRAME back to 0 and regen to return edges to their previous state.*

You can edit the vertices of a 3-D face using grips. Figure 6-17 shows a bookcase created with the 3DFACE command.

PFACE creates polyface meshes. Unlike 3-D faces, polyface meshes can have any number of sides, and sections on one plane do not show edges. You can assign each plane a different layer or color. Polyface meshes explode into 3-D faces.

The input of vertex coordinates is awkward, perhaps because PFACE was designed for automated entry of vertices, as in an AutoLISP routine. First you specify all the vertices, then AutoCAD prompts you for each vertex again by number (1, 2, 3, and so on) so that you can specify which vertex goes on which plane. Figure 6-18 shows a tabletop created using PFACE.

3DMESH is used for creating irregular surfaces. To create a 3-D mesh surface, specify the number of vertices in each direction, then specify each coordinate as prompted, keeping in mind that AutoCAD counts the vertices from zero. 3-D meshes can be edited with PEDIT. A common use of PEDIT with 3-D meshes is to use the Smooth option to create a more

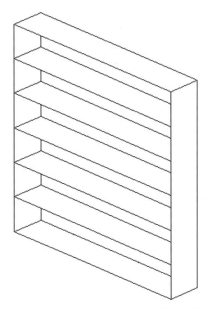

Figure 6-17   A bookcase created using the 3DFACE command, viewed after using the HIDE command

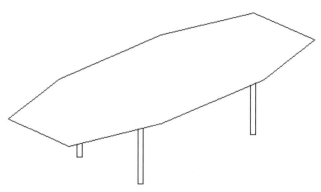

Figure 6-18 A conference table whose top was created using PFACE

naturally curved surface. Figure 6-19 shows a 3-D mesh after being smoothed with the PEDIT command.

The Surfaces toolbar contains buttons to create a box, a wedge, a pyramid, a cone, a sphere, a dome, a dish, and a torus (a doughnut-shaped surface). These commands are actually AutoLISP routines that use the 3DMESH command.

Besides adding thickness, how can I create 3-D surfaces from 2-D objects?

Adding thickness to a 2-D object creates a simple surface object with a uniform thickness throughout. To create complex surfaces, use one of the commands described next.

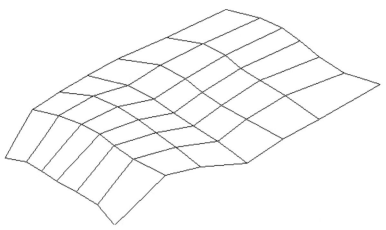

Figure 6-19 A 3-D mesh surface after being smoothed with the PEDIT command

REVSURF

The REVSURF command creates revolved surfaces. You start with a 2-D object—a line, circle, polyline, ellipse, or elliptical arc. This object is called a path curve, even though it may not be curved. The path curve can be open, like a line, or closed, like a circle. You then use another 2-D object, generally a line, to specify the axis of revolution. You can revolve the path curve any number of degrees, up to 360. A positive angle revolves the path curve counterclockwise. A negative angle revolves the path curve clockwise. (To understand more about the direction of revolution, see the next question.) Figure 6-20 shows a carafe created using REVSURF; to the left you see the original path curve and axis.

Tip: *REVSURF does not delete the original 2-D objects you use as a basis for the surface. Create them on a different layer in a different color so you can easily erase them if you wish.*

TABSURF

TABSURF creates tabulated surfaces, which are created by extruding a 2-D surface along a vector. (There is also an EXTRUDE command, which creates solids.) As with REVSURF, you start with a path curve. You also choose

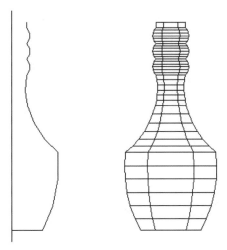

Figure 6-20 A carafe created using REVSURF. To the left are the path curve and axis line used to create the revolved surface

another object, usually a line, to represent the direction and length of the extrusion. This extrusion line is called a *vector* because it specifies length and direction. The vector should be in a different plane than the path curve, because you are using it to extrude the 2-D path curve into the third dimension.

If the extrusion is perpendicular to the path curve, the result is similar to adding a thickness to a 2-D object. However, TABSURF can extrude at any angle, making this command much more flexible than applying thickness values. Figure 6-21 shows a circle that was extruded along an angled vector. (The SURFTAB1 system variable is set to the default of 6, making the circle look like a hexagon.)

RULESURF

RULESURF creates ruled surfaces. A ruled surface extends between two objects, which can be lines, polylines, circles, ellipses, elliptical arcs, splines, or even points. You specify the two curves and AutoCAD creates the surface.

 Caution: *AutoCAD matches the pick points on the two curves. If you have two parallel lines and pick one side of the first line and the opposite side of the second line, the resulting surface intersects itself, usually an unwanted result.*

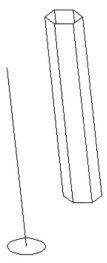

Figure 6-21 A circle extruded along an angle using TABSURF

Figure 6-22 shows a ruled surface created with RULESURF.

EDGESURF

An edge surface is created from four touching objects—any combination of lines, arcs, splines, or polylines. First create the 2-D objects. Then select them as prompted by the EDGESURF command. Figure 6-23 shows an edge surface created with EDGESURF.

Can you explain how to figure out which way an object will rotate in 3-D?

You use the *right-hand rule*. Make sure the UCS icon is displayed (choose View | Display | UCS Icon | On). Point the thumb of your right hand toward the positive direction of the X axis. Then point your index finger in the positive direction of the Y axis. The direction your other three fingers curl is the direction of rotation—the positive direction of the z coordinate.

When you are creating a revolved surface with REVSURF or a revolved solid with REVOLVE, you need to determine the positive direction of the axis of rotation, which may have no relation to any of the axes. For both commands, you

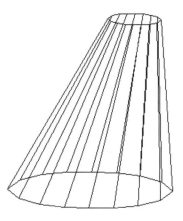

Figure 6-22 A ruled surface created from two ellipses with RULESURF

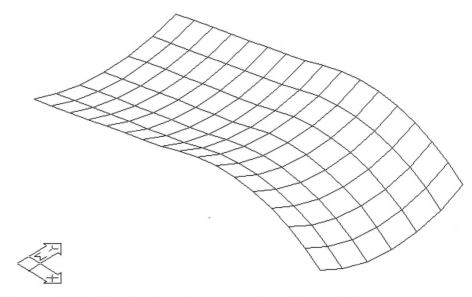

Figure 6-23 An edged surface created from four polylines

specify an axis of rotation, either by picking an object or specifying two points.

● If you pick an object, usually a line, the end of the line nearest your pick point is equivalent to 0,0,0. Point your thumb along the line toward the *opposite* endpoint.

● If you specify two points, the first point is equivalent to 0,0,0. Point your thumb along the line of the two points toward the second point.

Don't worry about your index finger. Just look at the direction your fingers curl to determine the direction of rotation.

DRAWING AND EDITING SOLIDS

How can I edit solids? Can I use grips?

Editing solids with grips is limited. You can only move or copy them. Otherwise, and unlike surfaces, solids are not directly editable with grips. While all commands that edit

objects as a whole can be used on solids—such as COPY, MOVE, ROTATE, and SCALE—to modify the solid itself, you need to use special commands. Table 6-2 lists the editing commands that you can use to modify solids.

What commands do I use to create solids?

AutoCAD offers a number of commands for creating solids. Some create standard shapes and two other commands create solids from 2-D objects. Use these commands to create the basic building blocks of the models you create. Then, you can use some of the editing commands, such as UNION and SUBTRACT, to create more complex shapes.

Tip: *When creating solids, display the Solids toolbar.*

Here is a list of the solids commands:

● BOX creates a box, specified by its corner, length, width, and height. You can also specify the center instead of the corner.

● SPHERE creates a sphere, specified by its center and diameter or radius.

Command	Description
CHAMFER	Chamfers the edges of solids.
FILLET	Fillets the edges of solids.
EXPLODE	Explodes solids into regions and bodies.
UNION	Combines two or more solids into one solid.
SUBTRACT	Subtracts one solid from another, leaving the remainder.
INTERSECT	Creates a new solid from the volume that two solids share. The original solids are transformed into the new solid.
INTERFERE	Creates a new solid from the volume that two solids share, leaving the original solids intact. This command also compares sets of solids so that you can see where their volumes interfere.
SLICE	Cuts a solid into two solids along a plane.

Table 6-2 Commands Used to Modify Solids

- CYLINDER creates a cylinder. The cylinder can have either a circular or elliptical base. You can define the height for a cylinder that rises perpendicularly, or specify the center of the top to create a slanted cylinder.

- CONE creates a cone with a circular or elliptical base. You can specify either the height of the top or the apex.

- WEDGE creates a wedge, which is a box cut in half diagonally. You specify a wedge in the same way you specify a box.

- TORUS creates a torus, a 3-D doughnut. You specify the center, the radius of the entire torus (from the center of the hole to the edge), and the radius of the tube.

- EXTRUDE extrudes a 2-D object, such as a polyline, circle, ellipse, closed spline, donut, or region, to create a 3-D solid object.

- REVOLVE revolves a 2-D closed object, such as a closed polyline, circle, ellipse, closed spline, or region. For the axis of revolution, you can use a line, the X or Y axes, or select points.

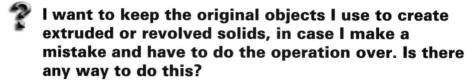 **I want to keep the original objects I use to create extruded or revolved solids, in case I make a mistake and have to do the operation over. Is there any way to do this?**

The DELOBJ system variable determines whether the original objects that you use to create solids are deleted. By default, DELOBJ is set to 1, which deletes the original objects. To keep the original objects, set DELOBJ to 0.

 Tip: Place the original objects on another layer with a different color than the layer you want to use to create the solid. Then switch back to the layer you want for the solid, before using commands such as EXTRUDE or REVOLVE. You can then freeze the layer of the original objects. They won't be visible, but will be there in case you need to revise the objects and recreate the solid.

Can I extrude a 2-D object along an arc?

Yes, the path used for extrusion can be a line, circle, arc, ellipse, elliptical arc, polyline, or spline. The extrusion path must be in a different plane from the object you are extruding. However, AutoCAD will have difficulty extruding the object along the path if the path is too close to the object's plane, is too complex, or is too tightly curved for the object's size. Figure 6-24 shows a circle extruded along an arc.

Is there any way to see the inside of a 3-D solid model?

There are two commands that can help you. The SECTION command leaves the original object unchanged but creates a region object along the plane you specify to represent the section. You can then move that region and examine it separately from the object. You'll find it easier to manipulate and view the region if you create it on a layer whose color is different than the original solid.

The SLICE command slices your solid into two solids along the plane that you specify. You can choose to delete one of the solids or keep both. If you slice a symmetrical solid in half, you can delete one half, view the inside of your model,

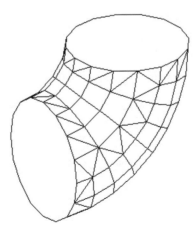

Figure 6-24   A circle extruded along an arc, shown after a hide

mirror the model to get back the other half, and use UNION to reunite the two halves. You can also simply undo the SLICE operation once you are satisfied that the inside of your model is accurate.

How do I get a hole inside a cylinder?

Creating a hole is probably the most common use for the SUBTRACT command. To create a cylinder with a hole, create two cylinders, one inside the other. Then use the SUBTRACT command to subtract the inner cylinder from the outer cylinder. Now you have a cylinder with a hole inside.

Can I trim a solid?

You can't use the TRIM command on a solid, but the INTERSECT and SUBTRACT commands create a similar result. The trick is to place a second solid so that it cuts through your first solid. You can even trim the solid along a curved object.

The INTERSECT command creates a solid from the volume the two solids share. The result is that the first solid is trimmed where the second solid cuts through it. Here you see the side view of a sphere that cuts through a box:

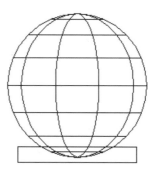

Now look at the two solids from a different viewpoint, so you can see them as three-dimensional. Here you can also see that the sphere dips into the box:

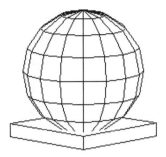

By subtracting the sphere from the box, you can create a box with the dish shaped interior scooped out, as shown here after a hide:

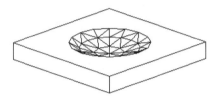

On the other hand, by subtracting the box from the sphere, you create a sphere with a flat bottom, as shown here after a hide. Because the box has a flat top, the result is more like the traditional concept of trimming, except that you are trimming along a plane instead of along a cutting edge.

Yet another option is to use the INTERSECT command to create a solid made up of only the volume that the two solids had in common, as shown here:

 I drew a chair, but it's lying down on its back compared to the rest of the house in my drawing. How can I get it in plan view?

A number of 3-D commands require you to work in more than one plane. For example, to extrude a 2-D object, you need a 2-D object in one plane and an extrusion path in another plane. It can be hard to visualize the final result and you may find that you need to rotate the final object. Also, sometimes a complex shape is easier to draw on the XY plane even though you later want that direction to be perpendicular to the XY plane. And sometimes you might think you need to change the UCS or the viewpoint when you simply need to rotate the object in 3-D space. In these situations, ROTATE3D is the right command.

To rotate an object in 3-D space, you need to define the axis of rotation and the rotation angle. ROTATE3D has seven options that you can use to define the plane:

● Object lets you choose an object as the axis of rotation. When determining the direction of rotation, the positive axis direction goes from your pick point to the opposite end of the object. When you choose a circle or arc, AutoCAD uses the center as the first pick point and a line perpendicular to the circle or arc as the axis.

● Last specifies the most recently defined axis.

● View creates an axis parallel to the current view, through the point you specify.

● Xaxis rotates around an axis parallel to the X axis, through the point you specify.

● Yaxis rotates around an axis parallel to the Y axis, through the point you specify.

● Zaxis rotates around an axis parallel to the Z axis, through the point you specify.

● 2points, the default, lets you specify the axis by picking two points. The first point is equivalent to 0,0 and the second point determines the positive direction of the rotation axis.

Use the right-hand rule to determine the direction of rotation. For more information on the right-hand rule, see the question "Can you explain how to figure out which way an object will rotate in 3-D?," earlier in this chapter.

How can I move one solid so its edges match up with those of another solid?

A common task is to both move and rotate an object at the same time so that it aligns with another object. For this purpose, you can use the ALIGN command. This command is also useful in 2-D drawing. You can find ALIGN on the menu by choosing Modify | 3D Operation | Align.

Aligning an object involves determining which points on the object you want to align—called *source points*—and which points on the second object you want to move to—called *destination points*.

In other words, aligning an object involves choosing points on the object that is to be aligned (the source points) and matching them with points on the second object (the destination points). ALIGN then moves the source points to the destination points—moving and/or rotating the object to be aligned as necessary. ALIGN asks for up to three sets of source and destination points. If you stop after one set, you just rotate the object in 2-D space. If you stop after two sets, you move and rotate the object, still within one plane. By specifying three sets of points, you can rotate the object in the third dimension.

Note: *The source and destination points don't have to be an exact match. For example, one object might be longer than the other and therefore the endpoints might not match. By choosing the closest endpoints for the last set of points, AutoCAD will still align the first object correctly.*

Can I trim lines in 3-D space?

Yes, you can use the TRIM command in 3-D space, but only on 2-D objects. The TRIM command has a Project option that is specifically for use in 3-D. To use this option, start the TRIM

command, select the cutting edge or edges, type **p,** and press ENTER. Then choose one of the following three suboptions:

- **None**   Use this to trim only objects that actually intersect or could intersect in 3-D space.

- **UCS**   Use this suboption, the default, to project objects onto the XY plane of the current UCS. The result is like changing the z coordinate of all the involved objects to 0. You can therefore trim objects when the objects and the cutting edges are on different z coordinates.

- **View**   Use this to project objects parallel to the current view. This is similar to using the UCS command's View option. You can trim objects if the cutting edges look like they intersect from your viewpoint.

 Caution: *Take some time to make sure you use the right suboption. Each suboption creates a very different result.*

Can I fillet solids?

Yes, you can. When you select a solid after starting the FILLET command, AutoCAD senses that you have selected a solid and displays different prompts than it displays when you select other objects. To fillet a solid, follow these steps:

1. Choose Fillet from the Modify toolbar.

2. At the prompt, select the edge of the solid that you want to fillet.

3. AutoCAD prompts you for a radius. Type the radius that you want to use.

4. At the "Chain/Radius/<Select edge>:" prompt, you can select any additional edge or press ENTER to complete the command. You can also use the Chain option to create a chain of attached filleted edges. If you use the Chain option, select contiguous edges and press ENTER when you are finished.

AutoCAD fillets the solid.

RENDERING 3-D OBJECTS

Is there any way to make rendering a little less daunting?

It depends on the results you want. You can do a simple rendering using the default lighting and no materials, but you probably won't be happy with the results. However, it might help to understand the components of the process. Then you can study the individual commands involved. Not all of these steps are always necessary, and you may sometimes choose to do them in a different order. Here they are:

1. Open the Render toolbar. It is very useful for rendering.

2. Set up the view of what you want to render, and save the view (DDVIEW).

3. Choose Render from the Render toolbar, and click Render. The resulting rendering lets you know what changes you need to make.

4. If you need to adjust the lighting—and you probably do—choose Lights from the Render toolbar. This is a complex command, letting you create three types of lights: point, spotlight, and distant. You can also set the ambient light, which is the overall lighting. Each light has a name and color. Depending on the type of light, you also need to specify the attenuation (how it loses intensity over distance), intensity, position, target, hotspot, and falloff (for spotlights only). For each type of light, you can turn shadows on or off. For an architectural drawing, set the North location if you want to create a distant light to mimic the sun—especially if you will create shadows.

5. Choose Scenes from the Render toolbar to create a scene. A scene is simply a named view with lights. The purpose of this command is to simplify the creation of various combinations of lights and views.

6. Choose Materials Library from the Render toolbar to import materials. AutoCAD comes with a large number of materials, but usually you need to create your own.

 Tip: *Don't create a material from scratch. In the Materials Library dialog box, import the material that is closest to your needs, and work from there to create your own.*

7. Choose Materials from the Render toolbar to create your own materials. Choose the materials you have imported, and click Modify to adjust them as you wish. There are four overall types of materials—standard, marble, granite, and wood. Once you choose the type, you specify the attributes—color/pattern, ambient, reflection, roughness, transparency, refraction, and bump map. You won't use all the attributes for every material.

8. From the Materials dialog box, attach your materials to objects in the drawing by object, color, or layer.

9. If you want, you can add a background. Choose Background from the Render toolbar. You can create solid or gradient backgrounds or use an image. You can also merge the rendering with the background currently on your screen.

10. Release 14 has added some landscape objects, such as trees and signs. If you want to use these, choose Landscape New from the Render toolbar.

11. Again choose Render from the toolbar. Choose the type of renderer you want to use. (For shadows you need to choose Photo Real or Photo Raytrace.) If you want shadows, check Shadows. Click Render.

Rendering usually involves some trial and error. You will probably have to go back and make some adjustments to lights and/or materials.

 ## How do I decide which type of renderer to use, now that AutoCAD offers three types?

The following table describes the three types of renderers and their characteristics. You will see the differences mostly in shadows, reflections, and refractive effects.

Type of Renderer	Characteristics
Render	No shadows, quickest results
Photo Real	Creates images line by line, displays bitmaps, can create transparent materials, creates volumetric and mapped shadows
Photo Raytrace	Creates images line by line, like Photo Real, but uses ray tracing to create reflections, refraction, and precise shadows

What are some of the new features of rendering in Release 14?

Autodesk previously sold a separate program called AutoVision, which was an advanced rendering product. The capabilities of AutoVision are now included in Release 14. Some of these new features are described next.

Shadows

You can now create shadows in your renderings. There are three types of shadows. Each type calculates the shadows in a different way and produces a somewhat different result. You may not care about these differences, in which case you can simply accept the defaults, but if you are particular, you have the choice.

To set the shadow type, start the LIGHT command. In the Lights dialog box, click New to create a new light. In the Shadows section of the dialog box, check Shadows On and click Shadow Options to open the Shadow Options dialog box, shown here:

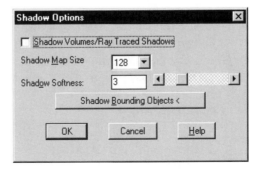

Volumetric shadows are based on the volume of space cast by the object's shadow. Volumetric shadows have hard edges with inexact outlines. These shadows are also affected by the color of transparent objects. You can create volumetric shadows with both the Photo Real and the Photo Raytrace renderers. If you want to use volumetric shadows, click Shadow Volumes/Ray Traced Shadows in the Shadow Options dialog box and use the Photo Real renderer.

Mapped shadows are based on a map size that you specify. The map size can be from 64 to 4,096 pixels. Larger maps provide greater accuracy but take longer to calculate. Mapped shadows have soft edges. You can adjust the level of softness using the Shadow Softness text box or the slider bar. The softness number represents the number of pixels that are blended. The most common settings are between 2 and 4, but you can set the softness from 1 to 10. Mapped shadows are not affected by the color of transparent objects. If you want to use mapped shadows, uncheck Shadow Volumes/Ray Traced Shadows and specify the map size and shadow softness.

Ray-traced shadows are calculated by tracing the path of rays from a light source. Ray-traced shadows have hard edges, accurate outlines, and are affected by the color of transparent objects. To create ray-traced shadows, check Shadow Volumes/Ray Traced Shadows in the Shadow Options dialog box and use the Photo Raytrace renderer.

To create shadows, you must first check Shadows On in the individual dialog boxes for each light. Then, in the Render dialog box, you must also choose either the Photo Real or the Photo Raytrace renderer and check Shadows.

Caution: *Adding shadows to renderings greatly increases rendering time. For trial renderings that don't require shadows, uncheck Shadows in the Render dialog box. Recheck Shadows for your final rendering.*

Transparency

Release 14 now supports the creation of transparent materials. AutoCAD includes a number of transparent materials in the materials library, such as BLUE GLASS and

GREEN GLASS. To create your own transparent material, follow these steps:

1. Choose Materials Library from the Render toolbar. Choose a material from the list and click Import.

2. Click OK.

3. Choose Materials from the Render toolbar. Choose the material you want to use. Click either Modify to modify the material or Duplicate to create a new material from the old one.

4. In the resulting dialog box, check the Transparency property. In the Value text, type a value from 0 to 1 or use the slider bar. A value of 1 means that the material is completely transparent. Figure 6-25 shows the Modify Standard Material dialog box with a material set to a transparency of 0.98.

5. Click OK.

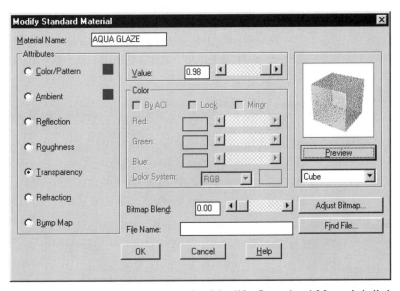

Figure 6-25 The Value setting in the Modify Standard Material dialog box lets you set the level of a material's transparency

Sun Angle Calculator

If you are creating architectural renderings and want to create a distant light that is accurate for a specific location, date, and time of day, use the new Sun Angle Calculator. In the New Distant Light dialog box, click Sun Angle Calculator to open the dialog box shown in Figure 6-26. Use this dialog box to set the latitude and longitude of the building's location, as well as the day and date.

If you don't know the location's latitude and longitude, click Geographic Location to open the Geographic Location dialog box, shown in Figure 6-27.

In this dialog box, you can choose any continent (except Antarctica!) from the drop-down list and either select any large city listed or click on the map to choose any location you need.

Backgrounds

Another major new feature of rendering in Release 14 is the ability to place backgrounds behind your renderings. To place a background, choose Background from the Render toolbar. In the Background dialog box, shown in Figure 6-28, choose the type of background: a solid color, a gradient of up to three colors, an image from a bitmap file, or a merge to combine a rendering and the current background.

Figure 6-29 shows a semi-transparent glass that casts a shadow on a table with a cloudy sky background.

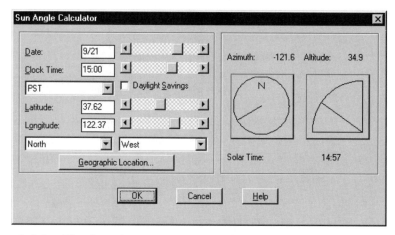

Figure 6-26 The Sun Angle Calculator dialog box

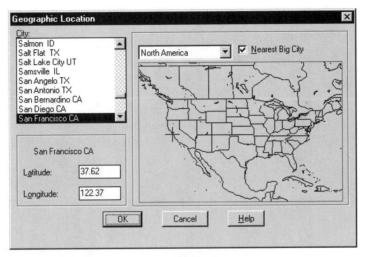

Figure 6-27   The Geographic Location dialog box

Mapping

Mapping means projecting a 2-D image on a 3-D object. Only the Photo Real and the Photo Raytrace renderers support mapping. AutoCAD comes with a large number of bitmaps in the TGA format that you can use for mapping. You need to do

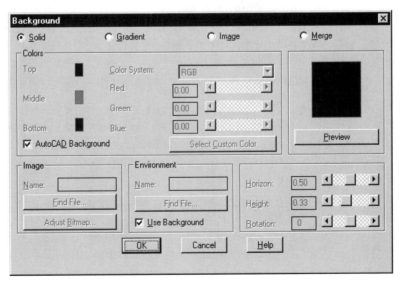

Figure 6-28   The Background dialog box

Figure 6-29 In this rendering, you can see the table showing through the semi-transparent glass, the shadow cast by the glass, and a background of sky and clouds

a complete installation to get them (they're called *textures*) or a custom installation specifically including the textures. To apply a mapped material, first create the material. In the dialog box you use to define the material (such as the Modify Standard Material dialog box), add a bitmap file to the Color/Pattern, Reflection, Transparency, or Bump Map attributes to create one of the following four types of maps:

● *Texture maps* project a pattern of colors onto an object. An example is AutoCAD's Checker texture, which adds a checkered pattern to an object's surface. To create a texture map, add a bitmap to the Color/Pattern attribute of a material.

● *Reflection maps* project a scene onto a reflective surface. Reflection maps give the impression of an image reflected on a shiny surface. To create a reflection map, add a bitmap to the Reflection attribute of a material.

- *Opacity maps* create areas of opacity and transparency. Adding a bitmap to the Transparency attribute of a material creates an opacity map.

- *Bump maps* create the effect of bumps. An example is AutoCAD's Bumpywhite stone material. To create a bump map, add a bitmap to the Bump Map attribute of a material.

If the Adjust Bitmap button is available, click it to set bitmap options, such as origin and scale. You can also choose to tile a bitmap so that it repeats to cover the object (the default) or crop it so that the bitmap is used only once.

In addition, you use the SETUV command to specify how the maps are projected onto the geometry of your models. This process is called assigning *mapping coordinates*. After you select objects, AutoCAD opens the Mapping dialog box, shown in Figure 6-30.

In this dialog box, you choose the shape that is closest to the model on which you are mapping an image: planar, cylindrical, spherical, or solid. If you already have an object with mapping coordinates, you can click Acquire From and choose the object whose mapping coordinates you want to use.

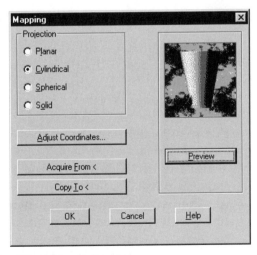

Figure 6-30 The Mapping dialog box

Then click Copy To to copy the coordinates to a new object or objects. Click the Preview box to see the results.

Is there an easy way to create materials with mapping?

Yes, use the mapped materials that come with AutoCAD. AutoCAD provides a number of TGA (Targa format) files in the \Textures subfolder of the AutoCAD folder (available if you do a Full installation or choose the texture maps in a Custom installation). The most commonly used types of mapping place a texture or a bumpy effect on the material. If you open the Materials Library dialog box and try out the materials that start with the word "bumpy," you'll see the bumpy effect. Try Eyeball Pattern or Clover Pattern for examples of texture maps. You can import these materials and then modify their color, reflective value, etc., to get the result you want.

Can I use my own graphics files to create backgrounds for my renderings?

You can use any bitmap file in TGA, BMP, TIFF, PCX, GIF, or JPG format for backgrounds or for mapping onto surfaces.

How can I render text?

In order to include text in your renderings, the text needs to be a surface or a bitmap file. If you can create text characters using the 3DFACE command, for example, you can attach materials to it and render it. You can also create a bitmap file containing the text, and map the bitmap onto the surface. Figure 6-31 shows an example of a bitmap of text mapped onto the surface of a glass. The text bitmap was created using MTEXT in AutoCAD and saved by choosing Tools | Display Image | Save.

Another idea is to use the Bonus tool, Explode Text, which converts text into line segments. You can then edit these line segments, by adding thickness, for example, into 3-D objects that you can render. Choose Bonus | Text | Explode Text on the menu.

Figure 6-31   A bitmap of text on a glass

Can a 2-D drawing be rendered?

You can render a 2-D drawing if it contains surfaces such as 3-D faces or regions.

How can I import my rendered image into a word processor document?

When you have rendered your drawing to your satisfaction on screen, choose Tools | Display Image | Save. In the Save Image dialog box, shown in Figure 6-32, choose one of the image types. Most word processors import the three types offered, but check the documentation of your word processor. If you choose TGA or TIFF, you can click Options to choose to compress the file.

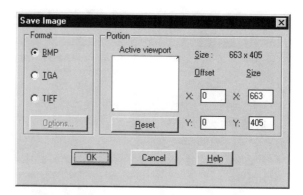

Figure 6-32   The Save Image dialog box

Tip: *You can crop the image in this dialog box, but you may find it easier to crop the image from within your word processor.*

Click OK to open the Image File dialog box. Choose a location and a name for your file, and click Save.

You can also choose to render to a Render window from the drop-down list in the Destination section of the Render dialog box. From the Render window, you can copy and paste into other applications.

How do I unload Render?

When you have finished rendering, it is wise to unload Render because it takes a toll on your computer's resources. To unload Render, type **arx** and press ENTER. At the prompt, choose the Unload option by typing **u** and pressing ENTER. At the "Unload ARX file:" prompt, type **render** and press ENTER.

Chapter 7

Customizing AutoCAD

Answer Topics!

Customizing AutoCAD @ a Glance

AutoCAD's famous *open architecture* provides a way for you to customize almost every aspect of AutoCAD. Many support files are simple text (ASCII) files that you can edit with any text editor. When you're working with these files, it helps to understand the standard customizing conventions, and also the command variations that enable you to avoid opening dialog boxes.

AutoCAD's menus and toolbars are fully customizable. The menu file includes sections for the mouse buttons, the pull-down menu at the top of the screen, the screen menu that used to appear at the right of the screen, the toolbars, and the tablet menu you use if you have a digitizing tablet. You can also create brief command descriptions that appear on the status bar, menus with image tiles, and keyboard shortcuts. Toolbars can also be customized directly, without editing the menu file, using the Customize Toolbars dialog box.

You can also create shortcuts for commands that you type on the command line, called *aliases*. For example, you can type **l** instead of **line** to start the LINE command. Also, most people are familiar with the concept of macros—sets of commands that you can execute all at once. AutoCAD calls these *scripts*, and you can make them by creating a file with the filename extension .SCR. Simply type the commands as you would type them on the command line. Script files can be executed from within AutoCAD and from the target expression used by Windows to load AutoCAD.

Customized linetypes are noncontinuous lines that you can assign to any layer. Simple linetypes contain dots, dashes, and spaces. Complex linetypes, in addition to dots, dashes, and spaces, also contain text and/or shapes. To create a customized linetype, you usually add its definition to ACAD.LIN, although you can create your own .LIN file. AutoCAD's linetype code lets you define the linetype's features.

Hatches are used to fill in closed areas in your drawing. AutoCAD comes with a large number of hatches, and you can easily adjust line spacing and angle. You can create complex hatches by creating families of lines that form distinct patterns, using AutoCAD's hatch code. You can add hatch definitions to ACAD.PAT or create a .PAT file for your hatch pattern.

Shapes are most often used to create fonts, but have other uses as well. For example, you can create a shape to place in a complex linetype. The shape code, while complicated, lets you create both lines and arcs.

PREPARING TO CUSTOMIZE

 What are the main customizable files and what are they for?

Here is a list of the most commonly customized files. Before starting to customize, copy these files to a diskette and keep it in a safe place, in case you need to get back the original file versions.

ACAD.LIN	Linetypes
ACAD.PAT	Hatch patterns
ACAD.PGP	Command aliases
ACAD.LSP	AutoLISP routines
ACADR14.LSP	AutoLISP routines
ACAD.MNU	Menu template file
ACAD.MNL	AutoLISP routines used by the menu file
ACAD.MNS	Source menu file that includes toolbar changes made onscreen

Another safety feature is to only use customization files with different names. For example, you can use Windows Explorer to make a copy of ACAD.MNU, then rename the copy MYACAD.MNU. Now, make your changes only in MYACAD.MNU. For details on how to load your new menu, see the box later in this chapter, "Loading a Complete Menu."

Each time you customize a file, make a backup copy of that file before you make changes. If you make a mistake or the file gets corrupted, you will always have your latest version available.

Can I use my word processor to customize AutoCAD files?

Yes, but before saving the file, be sure to change the Save as type drop-down list to Text only. Because it's easy to forget to specially save the file in text format, and because you don't need the formatting capabilities of a full-fledged word processor, it may be easier to use Notepad or WordPad, two programs that come with Windows 95. Notepad can handle most customization files except the menu files, which are too long. WordPad handles the menu files with no problem.

What characters are allowed in text-only files?

Generally, you should stick to characters on the keyboard, spaces, and returns. Tabs may not work, depending on the file, so it is best to avoid them.

Are there any standard conventions for customizing AutoCAD files?

Yes, there are, but each type of file has its own format. For guidelines, open the default file that comes with AutoCAD and take a look. For example, you will see that menu file commands all start with ^C^C. This represents a double ESC. The double ESC is only really necessary if a user is in the outdated dimensioning "Dim": prompt, a rare occurrence. But it remains a convention of menu files.

One important convention that you should comply with is placing comments in your customized files. Even you may

forget what you were doing when you look back at the file six months later. Comments are especially helpful if others use your customized files. In most customizable files, text preceded by a semicolon is ignored and is therefore used for comments. Some users place two semicolons before comments for clarity. In menu files, you use a slash (/) or a double slash before comments. Figure 7-1 shows AutoCAD's ACAD.PGP file. You can see the comments at the top of the figure, preceded by semicolons.

How do I deal with commands that open dialog boxes in scripts, AutoLISP routines, and menu files?

When you use commands that need to be automated or semiautomated in scripts, menus, and AutoLISP routines, you need to use a form of a command that doesn't open a dialog box. That's because scripts, AutoLISP routines, and menu files do not offer a way to specify preset values in a dialog box. Table 7-1 lists the command-line form or substitute, where available.

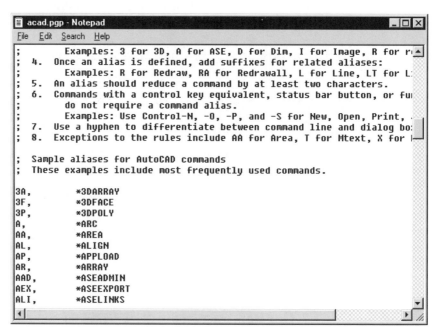

Figure 7-1 AutoCAD's ACAD.PGP file uses comments, preceded by semicolons, extensively

Command	Non-Dialog-Box Format
BHATCH	-BHATCH
BMAKE	BLOCK
BOUNDARY	-BOUNDARY
DDATTDEF	ATTDEF
DDATTE	ATTEDIT
DDATTEXT	ATTEXT
DDCHPROP	CHANGE/CHPROP
DDCOLOR	COLOR
DDGRIPS	System variables GRIPBLOCK, GRIPCOLOR, GRIPHOT, GRIPS, GRIPSIZE
DDINSERT	INSERT
DDMODIFY	CHANGE/CHPROP, COLOR, -LAYER, -LINETYPE, LTSCALE, and system variables CELTYPE, CELTSCALE
DDOSNAP	OSNAP
DDPTYPE	System variables PDMODE, PDSTYLE
DDRENAME	RENAME
DDRMODES	BLIPMODE, FILL, GRID, GROUP, ISOPLANE, ORTHO, and SNAP, and system variables HIGHLIGHT and PICKSTYLE
DDSELECT	System variables PICKADD, PICKAUTO, PICKBOX, PICKDRAG, PICKFIRST, SORTENTS, TREEDEPTH
DDSTYLE, STYLE	-STYLE
DDUCS, DDUCSP	UCS
DDUNITS	UNITS
DDVIEW	VIEW
DDVPOINT	VPOINT
EXPORT	DXFOUT, STLOUT, BMPOUT, PSOUT, ACISOUT, 3DSOUT, WMFOUT
GROUP	-GROUP
HATCHEDIT	-HATCHEDIT
IMAGE	-IMAGE
LAYER	-LAYER
LINETYPE	-LINETYPE
MTEXT	-MTEXT
TOOLBAR	-TOOLBAR
XREF	-XREF

Table 7-1   Non-Dialog-Box Command Forms

There are also three system variables that affect the display of dialog boxes. These system variables are widely used in customization.

● The FILEDIA system variable determines whether AutoCAD displays a dialog box for commands that require you to choose a file, such as the Open Drawing File dialog box. Set FILEDIA to 0 to force these commands to prompt for files on the command line.

● The CMDDIA system variable affects the PLOT command and the ASE commands, forcing them on the command line if set to 0.

● The ATTDIA system variable determines if a dialog box appears when you insert a block with attributes. The default is 0, which does not display a dialog box. Set it to 1 to use a dialog box.

If you set these system variables to 0, don't forget to set them back to 1 for normal use. It is very frustrating for a user to suddenly find that the Plot/Print Configuration dialog box is gone.

CUSTOMIZING MENUS AND TOOLBARS

 I'm confused about all the menu files. Is there a way to make sense of them?

The problem is that AutoCAD's menus are really text files at heart, but Windows requires the graphic user interface and direct onscreen customization, especially for toolbars. Keeping up two systems at once is complicated! Table 7-2 explains all the menu files and their purposes. The default menu files are all named ACAD with various extensions (such as ACAD.MNU and ACAD.MNS). When you create your own menus, you can use another filename.

File Extension	Purpose
.MNU	Template menu file. You use this file to customize the menu with a text editor. However, the template menu file doesn't contain direct changes you have made to toolbars onscreen. AutoCAD uses this menu to create the .MNS and .MNC files.
.MNS	Source menu file. This is also an ASCII file, based on the .MNU file but also containing any customization of toolbars you applied onscreen.
.MNC	Compiled menu file. This is a binary (not text) file, the one AutoCAD actually uses when you use the menu. AutoCAD automatically creates this file if you change either the .MNU or .MNS file.
.MNR	Resource menu file, containing bitmaps, such as slides for image tiles, used by the menu.
.MNL	AutoLISP menu file containing AutoLISP routines used by the menu.

Table 7-2   AutoCAD's Menu File Types

Note: *A new file type, .MND—a menu definition file, can be used to facilitate the process of creating menu files. A menu definition file has two main purposes: to contain macros for placing repeating text in menu files, and to easily place duplicate text in the tablet section of the menu when you want large menu boxes on the tablet. You use the menu compiler utility, MC.EXE, on the DOS command line to compile the .MND file.*

I created a custom menu, but now some of the regular AutoCAD commands, such as DDMODIFY and the Make Object's Layer Current button, don't work, and some dialog boxes don't appear. What happened?

The ACAD.MNL file contains AutoLISP routines that you often use as regular AutoCAD commands. You have no way of

knowing that these commands are actually AutoLISP routines when you use them. However, if you customize ACAD.MNU, change its name, and load it, AutoCAD does not automatically make a copy of the .MNL menu file for you. All you need to do is make a copy of ACAD.MNL and give it the same filename as your customized menu file. For example, if you called your menu file MYACAD.MNU, make a copy of ACAD.MNL, rename the copy MYACAD.MNL, and reload the menu. Now all the commands and dialog boxes will work.

 If I make toolbar changes onscreen and then customize a menu, AutoCAD warns me that loading the file will overwrite my toolbar changes. How do I customize my menus and keep my toolbar changes?

This is a good question. If you make toolbar changes onscreen, such as creating a new toolbar or adding a button to an existing toolbar, the customization gets saved to the .MNS file. If you then customize the menu by editing the .MNU file, AutoCAD creates a new .MNS (and .MNC) file, overwriting your toolbar changes! To keep your toolbar changes, follow these steps:

1. In WordPad or another text editor, open the .MNS file of your menu.

2. Locate the ***TOOLBARS section of the file. (In WordPad, choose Edit | Find to locate the section.)

3. Select the entire ***TOOLBARS section and copy it to the clipboard.

4. Close the .MNS file. You don't need to save it because you didn't change it.

5. Open the .MNU file that you are customizing.

6. Locate and select the entire ***TOOLBARS section.

7. Choose Edit | Paste (or press CTRL+V). The .MNS ***TOOLBARS section replaces the .MNU ***TOOLBARS section.

8. Save the .MNU file now or after making any other desired changes.

Now, your toolbar changes are in the .MNU file. When AutoCAD compiles the .MNU file to create new .MNS and .MNC menu files, your toolbar changes will be included. For a discussion of which menu file to customize, see the next question. For instructions on loading a complete menu, see the box, "Loading a Complete Menu."

 Which menu file should I customize—the .MNU file or the .MNS file?

Some people like to customize the .MNU file and others like to customize the .MNS file.

Loading a Complete Menu

To load a complete menu, either because you have made changes to your menu, or to switch menus, type **menu** on the command line. In the Select Menu File dialog box, shown here, locate and choose the menu you want to load.

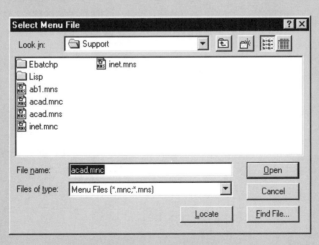

● To recompile a .MNU file that you have changed, choose Menu Template (*.MNU) from the Files of type drop-down list and then choose a .MNU file.

● To load a different menu that is already compiled, choose a .MNC or .MNS file.

Click Open in the dialog box to load the menu. If you have chosen a .MNU file, AutoCAD always warns you that loading the file will overwrite toolbar changes. See the question on toolbar changes, two questions back, for more information on saving your toolbar changes.

Caution: *Because loading an .MNU file overwrites toolbar changes, pay great attention to the type of file you are loading.*

There are advantages and disadvantages to each method. Many people customize the .MNU file out of habit from earlier releases, when the .MNS file didn't exist. The AutoCAD Help documentation assumes you will edit the .MNU file. The advantage to this is that you can create all the other menu files, including the .MNS file, from the .MNU file. You only work with the .MNU file and, by loading it, all the other files are taken care of. The disadvantage is that when you load an .MNU file, toolbar changes that you made onscreen are overwritten. The previous question provides the standard workaround to this problem—the answer provided in AutoCAD Help.

Many experts now recommend customizing the .MNS file. The advantage is that you never have to worry about overwriting your toolbar changes. The only disadvantage is that if you or anyone else ever loads the .MNU file of the same name, which is not customized, you lose all your customizations! The workaround for this problem is to copy the .MNS file to an .MNU file. That means, when you have customized the .MNS file, make a copy of it and rename the copy with the same name but with the .MNU extension. Now the .MNU and .MNS menu files are the same. However, you should remember to do this operation each time you change your .MNS menu. Another safety feature is to rename your menu file as something other than ACAD. Since the standard ACAD menu files are always available on the AutoCAD CD-ROM, you or someone else could inadvertently overwrite

your customizations when performing an install or upgrade. But if your menu has another name, you won't lose it.

Of course, it goes without saying that you should keep a backup of your menu.

 ## Is there a simple way to add a small pull-down menu with a few menu items to the regular menu?

Yes, you can create a *partial menu* and add it to your regular menu. To create a partial menu, you create a new *menugroup* definition that has a name that lets AutoCAD identify the partial menu. Open Notepad or another text editor and start the partial menu with the following three lines:

```
***MENUGROUP=menuname
***POP1
[label]
```

In these lines, *menuname* is the name you want to use for your partial menu; the second line creates the first (and perhaps only) pull-down menu of your partial menu; and the last line creates the label that actually appears at the top of the menu. It is helpful to keep *label* the same as *menuname*, but not necessary.

Tip: *To underline a letter of the label so that you can open the menu without the mouse (by pressing ALT and the underlined letter), put an ampersand (&) before the letter you want to underline.*

Type the commands you want to add to the menu. In the simplest format, put the label that will appear as the menu item in square brackets, and then type the command. Here is an example of a short partial menu named UnitSolids that creates single unit-sized solids:

```
***MENUGROUP=UnitSolids
***POP1
[UnitSolids]
[1X1Cyl]^C^C_cylinder \1 1
[1x1Box]^C^C_box \1 1 1
[1x1Cone]^C^C_cone \1 1
```

Place each menu item on a separate line. If a line is too long, add a plus sign (+) at the end of the line and continue on the next line. End the file with a return, and save it with the same name as the menu group name, and add a .MNU file extension.

Follow these steps to load the menu:

1. In AutoCAD, choose Tools | Customize Menus (the MENULOAD command).

2. On the Menu Groups tab of the Menu Customization dialog box, type the menu filename in the File Name text box or click Browse to locate the file.

3. Click Load.

 Note: *To reload a partial menu that you have edited, first choose the menu file in the Menu Groups box and click Unload. Then reload the file.*

4. Click the Menu Bar tab, shown in Figure 7-2.

5. From the Menu Group drop-down box, choose the menu group you want to load.

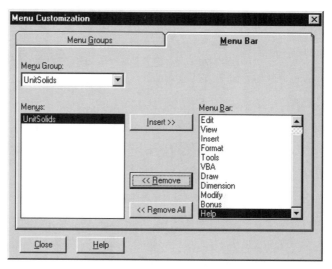

Figure 7-2   The Menu Bar tab of the Menu Customization dialog box lets you place a partial menu on the menu bar

6. From the Menu Bar list on the right, choose the placement of your partial menu by selecting the menu item that you want to place your partial menu to the left of.

7. From the Menus list on the left, choose the menu that you want to insert.

8. Click Insert.

9. Click Close to close the dialog box. AutoCAD places your partial menu in the location you specified.

Here's how the menu looks when loaded in AutoCAD.

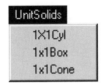

 How do I remove a button from a toolbar?

You can remove a button from one of the standard toolbars or from a custom toolbar that you created. Follow these steps:

1. Right-click any toolbar to open the Toolbars dialog box.

2. Click Customize. You must leave this dialog box onscreen, although it isn't used directly.

3. Drag the button off the toolbar itself, onto any part of the screen-pointing area. Release the mouse button.

AutoCAD removes the button from the toolbar. Figure 7-3 shows the process of dragging a button off a toolbar.

 I miss the arc flyout from Release 13. Is there any way I can get it back?

If you draw a lot of arcs, it sure would be nice to have the various arc options displayed all the time. Release 14 includes all the buttons from the Release 13 flyouts so that you can re-create them if you wish. Here's how:

1. Right-click any toolbar to open the Toolbars dialog box.

2. Click New.

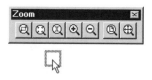

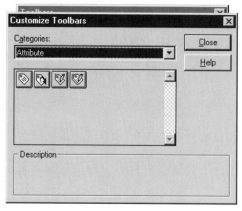

Figure 7-3 Dragging a button off a toolbar

3. Type a name for the toolbar and click OK. AutoCAD lists the new toolbar in the list of toolbars, and places a new toolbar on your screen. The new toolbar is quite small.

4. Click Customize in the Toolbars dialog box to open the Customize Toolbars dialog box, shown in Figure 7-4.

5. From the Categories drop-down list, choose Draw. You can now see all the Release 13 arc flyout buttons.

6. To determine what a button does, click it. You will see a description of the button in the Description box at the bottom of the dialog box.

7. When you find a button you want, drag it onto the new toolbar on your screen.

8. Continue to drag buttons to the toolbar, dropping each one to the right of the existing buttons.

 Note: *If you make a mistake, you can remove buttons by dragging them off the toolbar and dropping anywhere on the screen. You can also drag a button to a new position on the toolbar.*

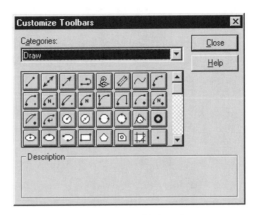

Figure 7-4 The Customize Toolbars dialog box

Here's how the new Arc toolbar might look:

 I created a new toolbar button and it looked fine, but now when I open AutoCAD the toolbar button just shows a little yellow smiley face. Why did this happen and where is the original button?

This is one of top ten frequently asked AutoCAD questions. See question #4 in Chapter 1 for the answer. For more information about creating toolbar buttons, see the following box, "Creating Toolbar Buttons."

Creating Toolbar Buttons

If you want to create your own toolbar from existing commands, you can drag existing buttons onto the toolbar, as explained two questions back in "I miss the arc flyout from Release 13. Is there any way I can get it back?" However, if you want to create your own command macro, you should also create a unique button to identify it. If you want to

start by creating a new toolbar, choose Tools | Customize Menus and click New. Give the toolbar a name and click OK. If you want to add the button to an existing toolbar, make sure the toolbar is displayed by checking it in the Toolbars dialog box. Whether you are starting with a new toolbar or adding a button to an existing toolbar, follow these steps:

1. Click Customize in the Toolbars dialog box.

2. From the Categories drop-down list, choose Custom. You will see the two blank buttons shown here:

3. If you want to create a regular button, drag the left-hand button onto the new or existing toolbar. Release the mouse button when the button is in the desired location. To create a flyout button, drag the right-hand button. These instructions assume you will create a regular button.

4. Right-click the blank button on your toolbar. AutoCAD opens the Button Properties dialog box, shown here:

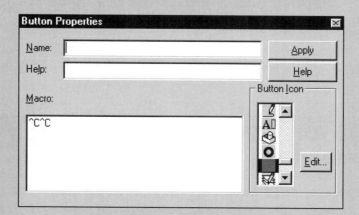

5. In the Name text box, type the name that will appear on the ToolTip when you place the cursor over the button.

6. In the Help text box, type the text you want to appear on the status line when you place the cursor over the button. The help text should briefly explain the function of the button.

7. In the Macro box, write the macro. AutoCAD automatically starts the macro with ^C^C, which is equivalent to pressing ESC twice to cancel any existing command. Use the same form you would use for customizing a menu.

8. In the Button Icon section of the dialog box, choose an existing button if you want to create a variation of the button.

Tip: *If the macro you want to create is similar to a regular AutoCAD command, you can use the button for that command and edit it. The advantage to this is that you don't have to create the button design from scratch.*

9. Click Edit to open the Button Editor, shown here:

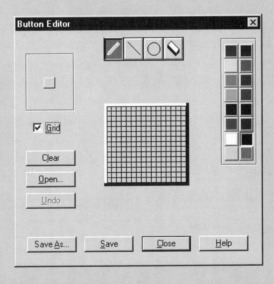

10. Modify the button you chose or create a button from scratch, using the Button Editor tools. The tools are described after these steps. The following illustration shows an example of a button that changes the color of all objects to Bylayer.

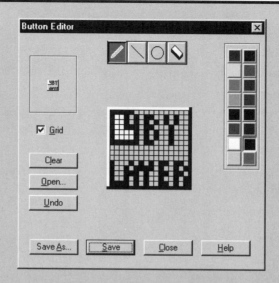

11. Click Save to save the icon button. If you want to choose the filename and location, choose Save As.

> ***Caution:*** *If you save the button in a location that is not in AutoCAD's support file search path, AutoCAD won't be able to find the button icon. The next time you open AutoCAD, you will see a small smiley face smiling at you instead of your button icon.*

12. Click Close.

13. In the Button Properties dialog box, your button now appears at the right, as shown here:

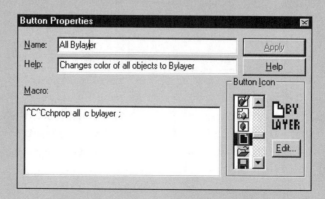

14. Click Apply. Your button appears on the toolbar. Click the Close box of the dialog box and close the other two dialog boxes to return to your drawing. The example button is shown here:

The Button Editor has the following tools:

- **Color swatches**   Click a color to draw in that color.
- **Grid**   Check to place a grid on the button drawing area.
- **Pencil**   Click to draw one grid square at a time or drag to draw lines.
- **Line**   Click and drag to draw lines.
- **Circle**   Click the center and drag out to the desired circumference.
- **Eraser**   Click to erase one grid square at a time or drag to erase lines.
- **Clear**   Click to clear the button drawing area.
- **Open**   Click to open a BMP file and place it in the button drawing area.
- **Undo**   Click to undo your last action.
- **Save As**   Click to choose a filename and location for the BMP icon file.
- **Save**   Click to save the BMP file under a name arbitrarily chosen by AutoCAD.
- **Close**   After you save the BMP file, click to close the dialog box.

How can I undo my toolbar changes?

Your toolbar changes are saved in the .MNS file but not in the .MNU file. Assuming you made the toolbar changes onscreen (not by editing the .MNU file), you can use the

.MNU to overwrite your toolbar changes. If you also customized your menu file, you need to be careful not to undo those changes as well. If you customized using the .MNU file, your .MNU file contains the menu customization you want without the unwanted toolbar changes. Before loading a new menu, back up your current menu, even though it has toolbar customizations that you don't want. To load the .MNU file, follow these steps:

1. Choose Tools | Customize Menus.

2. On the Menu Groups tab, choose ACAD as the Menu Group (or the Menu Group of the .MNU file you want to load).

3. Click Replace All so that AutoCAD will replace all the current menu items with the new menu items.

4. In the File name box, type the name of your .MNU file or click Browse to find it.

5. Click Load.

6. At the warning that you will lose your toolbar customization changes, click Yes.

7. Click Close. AutoCAD reloads the .MNU file and recompiles all the other menu files.

If you have been customizing your menu using the .MNS file, you can open the .MNU file, select the entire ***TOOLBARS section, copy it to the clipboard, open the .MNS file, select the entire ***TOOLBARS section there, and press CTRL+V. These steps paste the Toolbars section of the .MNU file into the .MNS file. Now reload the .MNS file.

Can I create keyboard shortcuts for commands?

You certainly can. Keyboard shortcuts are called *accelerators*. Your menu file has an ***ACCELERATORS section that you can customize to create keyboard shortcuts. Figure 7-5 shows the ***ACCELERATORS section of ACAD.MNU. Notice the use of comments preceded by the double slashes in the menu file.

```
//   Keyboard Accelerators
//
//   If a keyboard accelerator is preceded by an ID string that references a menu item
//   in a pull-down menu, then the keyboard accelerator will run the command referenced
//   by that menu item.
//
***ACCELERATORS
// Toggle PICKADD
[CONTROL+"K"]$M=$(if,$(and,$(getvar,pickadd),1),'_pickadd 0,'_pickadd 1)
// Toggle Orthomode
[CONTROL+"L"]^O
// Next Viewport
[CONTROL+"R"]^V
// ID_Spell     ["\"F7\""]
// ID_PanRealti ["\"F11\""]
// ID_ZoomRealt ["\"F12\""]
ID_Copyclip  [CONTROL+"C"]
ID_New       [CONTROL+"N"]
ID_Open      [CONTROL+"O"]
ID_Print     [CONTROL+"P"]
ID_Save      [CONTROL+"S"]
ID_Pasteclip [CONTROL+"V"]
ID_Cutclip   [CONTROL+"X"]
ID_Redo      [CONTROL+"Y"]
ID_U         [CONTROL+"Z"]
```

Figure 7-5   The ***ACCELERATORS section of ACAD.MNU

AutoCAD has a special format for designating the keyboard keys, shown in the following table. Notice that the CTRL and SHIFT keys don't require quotation marks; they are used only in combination with other keys.

CTRL key	CONTROL
SHIFT key	SHIFT
INSERT key	"INSERT"
DELETE key	"DELETE"
ESC key	"ESCAPE"
HOME key	"HOME"
END key	"END"
F1 through F12	"F1", "F2", and so on. F10 is not usable—it is reserved by Windows.
Arrow keys	"UP", "DOWN", "LEFT", "RIGHT"
Numeric pad keys	"NUMPAD0", "NUMPAD1", and so on

There are two types of formats for creating keyboard shortcuts. The first type starts with the shortcut in brackets. In Figure 7-5, look at the line that reads as follows:

```
[CONTROL+"L"]^O
```

The comment that precedes this line explains that this keyboard shortcut toggles Orthomode. The first part of the code defines the keyboard shortcut, in this case CTRL+L. The second part of the code defines the action that the shortcut will take, in this case CTRL+O, which toggles Orthomode. The next shortcut is similar; it switches you to the next active viewport.

The second type of shortcut format uses *ID Strings*, which are identifiers that you can place before pull-down menu items. They are used for accelerators and help strings. (Help strings are the text placed on the status bar when you place the cursor over a menu item.) In this second format, first type the ID String, exactly as it appears in front of the menu item you want to execute. Then type the keyboard shortcut in square brackets. Figure 7-5 shows several examples of this type of accelerator, most of which are standard Windows shortcuts. For example, the following line opens a new drawing, executing the NEW command:

```
ID_New     [CONTROL+"N"]
```

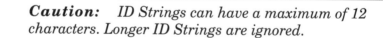

Caution: *ID Strings can have a maximum of 12 characters. Longer ID Strings are ignored.*

In Figure 7-5, you can see that the menu includes three accelerators that are preceded by double slashes and are therefore inactive—Spelling, Pan Realtime, and Zoom Realtime. You can activate them by removing the slashes and extra quotation marks, as in this example:

```
IC_Spell   ["F7"]
```

Be careful, though. I almost had my own technical question to solve. I found that the Pan Realtime item didn't work; the ID String for Pan Realtime, listed in the ***ACCELERATORS section as ID_PanRealti, was incorrect.

In the pull-down menu section of the menu, the item for Pan under the View menu was listed as ID_Pan. Correcting this ID String solved the problem. Here are two additional useful accelerators:

```
["DELETE"]   erase
["END"]      end
```

Adding the DELETE key as a shortcut for the ERASE command lets you select objects first and then press DELETE to erase them. This is the typical way of erasing data in other Windows programs and quickly becomes a habit. Now you can use this method in AutoCAD as well. The second accelerator lets you use the END key for the Endpoint object snap.

Note: *In order to create Accelerators, Priority for accelerator keys in the Preferences dialog box (choose Tools | Preferences) on the Compatibility tab must be set to Windows standards.*

What are the underscores before the commands in the menu file?

Placing an underscore before a command allows international versions of AutoCAD to translate the command into other languages. Only existing commands can be translated, not new commands that you create. Adding the underscore to commands when you create AutoLISP routines and menu macros makes your customization usable in other countries.

I customized the button menu for my mouse buttons, but it isn't working. What am I doing wrong?

Assuming that your menu macros are correct and you are loading the menu properly, you are probably customizing the wrong button menu. There are eight menu sections that customize buttons—four ***BUTTONS sections and four ***AUX sections. The Buttons sections are used for a digitizing puck or some other input device, but not for the system mouse that Windows uses. The Aux sections are for

the system mouse buttons. Therefore, if you want to customize the buttons for your mouse, you need to customize the Aux sections. Here are the four sections:

 ***AUX1 customizes the buttons on your system mouse when you simply click them. However, the first button is always the pick button, and the last button (or perhaps another button) is usually used for the Return button. Therefore, you should only use this section to customize the other buttons, if any, on your mouse.

 ***AUX2 customizes the buttons on your system mouse when you hold down SHIFT while clicking a button.

***AUX3 customizes the buttons on your system mouse when you hold down CTRL while clicking a button.

 ***AUX4 customizes the buttons on your system mouse when you hold down CTRL and SHIFT at the same time while clicking a button.

✳ ***Note:*** *The four Buttons sections work similarly to the Aux sections, each working for a different combination of puck buttons and keyboard keys.*

➕ ***Tip:*** *A useful button customization is to assign ^F, which turns OSNAP on and off, to one of the buttons, such as AUX3 (or BUTTONS3). Then you don't have to move the cursor down to the bottom of the screen to the OSNAP button, away from the object you want to pick.*

WORKING WITH ALIASES AND SCRIPTS

How do I create a script file that includes commands that open dialog boxes?

Since script files cannot provide a response to a dialog box, you must use the command-line format for all commands in your script files. Refer to Table 7-1 at the beginning of this chapter for a list of command-line equivalents for commands that ordinarily open dialog boxes.

As mentioned earlier, by setting the system variable CMDDIA to 0, you can use PLOT and the ASE commands at the command line. Set FILEDIA to 0 to use commands that request files on the command line.

 Is there a way to create a few new command aliases if I don't want to fool around with editing text files?

The bonus commands include a new Command Alias Editor to edit aliases (command shortcuts) in a dialog box. To get the Alias Editor, you need to do a full installation or a custom installation that includes the Bonus commands and the Batch Plotting Utility. Once you have the Bonus menu, choose Bonus | Tools | Command Alias Editor. The Alias Editor is shown in Figure 7-6.

The Alias Editor is easy to use, and if you have any questions about it, choose Help from its menu.

● To add an alias, click Add.

● To remove an alias, choose it and click Remove.

● To change an existing alias, choose it and click Edit.

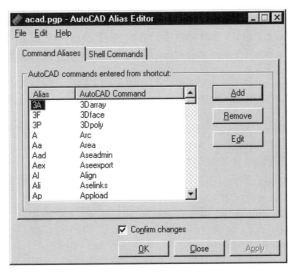

Figure 7-6 The Alias Editor

When you're done, click OK.

However, it's not that difficult to edit the actual ACAD.PGP file, which is shown at the beginning of this chapter in Figure 7-1. The format is simple:

```
shortcut, *command_name
```

To edit ACAD.PGP, open it in Notepad, make the desired changes, save the file, and close it. A safe way to start is to add a new shortcut without changing any existing ones.

You cannot use aliases for options of commands. For example, to start the ARC command with the Center option, you should create a toolbar button.

 Tip: *If you find it hard to remember your aliases, print out ACAD.PGP and tape it up next to your computer. After using the aliases for a while, you'll learn most of them by heart.*

Caution: *When creating scripts or menus, use the actual name of a command. Do not use command aliases.*

I changed ACAD.PGP and the changes didn't show up. But when I opened AutoCAD the next day, my changes worked. What happened?

AutoCAD only reads ACAD.PGP when you load a drawing, new or existing. To make your changes effective immediately, use the REINIT command. Type **reinit** and press ENTER. AutoCAD opens the Re-initialization dialog box, shown here. Check PGP File and click OK.

 Most times when I'm ready to plot, I freeze the floating viewport layer, save the drawing, and then plot. How can I automate these steps?

If you often use the same series of commands, a simple script file such as this one can speed up the process:

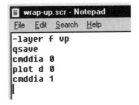

This script file does the following:

- Freezes a layer named vp (for viewport)
- Saves the drawing
- Changes the system variable CMDDIA to 0 so you can use the PLOT command on the command line
- Plots the current display using current defaults
- Changes CMDDIA back to 1

If you ever change plot parameters, you should include all the parameters you need in the script. Another alternative is to use a plot configuration file, which can be loaded during the plot process, on the command line.

Also remember that you can add comments to your script. For example, you could add the following comment before the first line:

```
;freezes the vp layer
```

 How do I run a script file that works on more than one drawing?

In order to run a script file that works on a series of drawings, you need to give AutoCAD the command to start the script at the same time as you start AutoCAD. In Windows, you do this by changing the target expression used to open AutoCAD. The easiest way to do this, especially if you

only want to run the script occasionally, is to create a shortcut to AutoCAD on your desktop.

To create a desktop shortcut, use Windows Explorer to find ACAD.EXE in your main AutoCAD folder. Right-click ACAD.EXE and choose Create Shortcut. Drag the shortcut, which is named SHORTCUT TO ACAD.EXE, to your desktop. Click it once and rename it as you wish.

To change the shortcut's target expressions, follow these steps:

1. Right-click the shortcut.

2. Choose Properties.

3. Choose the Shortcut tab.

4. Use the Target text box to add the following to the end of the command-line statement, where "*drawing name*" is the name of the first drawing you want to open and *scriptfile* is the name of the script file. If either the drawing name or the script filename include spaces, place quotation marks around the name.

    ```
    "drawing name" /b scriptfile
    ```

Note: *You must include the entire path (drive, folders, and filename) if either the drawing or the script file are not in AutoCAD's support file search path.*

5. Click OK.

To run the script file on all the drawings except the first, use the open command in the script file. Here is a sample script file that is started from a shortcut and then opens a second drawing to run the same commands:

```
filedia 0
zoom e
attedit n n desk part_no   3927
3928
qsave
open floor3
zoom e
attedit n n desk part_no   3927
3928
qsave
filedia 1
```

This script file changes all copies of a block attribute with the value 3927 to 3928. It could be used to run through a number of drawings in the same way.

How do I write a script file line that needs two returns at the end of the line?

For customization purposes, AutoCAD usually accepts a SPACEBAR space as the equivalent of a return. While you could type two spaces at the end of the line, some text editors don't register these trailing spaces. Instead, just type two returns. The result will be a space between the current line of the script file and the next line. The blank line is the second return.

CREATING LINETYPES

How do I use custom linetypes?

To use a custom linetype, you generally create a layer with the new linetype. Follow these steps:

1. Add the linetype definition to ACAD.LIN or create your own .LIN file using Notepad or another text editor. For more information on creating linetype definitions, see the box, "Creating Simple Custom Linetypes."

2. Save and close the file.

3. In AutoCAD, choose Layers from the Object Properties toolbar.

4. Choose New and name the new layer. Omit this step if you want to change an existing layer's linetype.

5. Click the word Continuous in the row of the new or existing layer. AutoCAD opens the Select Linetype dialog box.

6. Click Load.

7. In the Load or Reload Linetypes dialog box, if you didn't place the definition in ACAD.LIN, click File and choose your .LIN file. Click Open.

8. From the Available linetypes list, choose your custom linetype and click OK.

9. In the Select Linetype dialog box, choose your linetype again and click OK.

10. Click OK to return to your drawing. Any objects you draw with the layer now use your new linetype.

Creating Simple Custom Linetypes

It is not hard to create your own simple linetypes. AutoCAD's linetypes are contained in the support file ACAD.LIN, which is in AutoCAD's \Support folder. You can simply add your linetypes to the end of this text file or you can create your own file with the extension .LIN.

Each linetype contains two lines of text. Here's the syntax for the first line:

```
*linetypename, description
```

Remember the following three points:

● All linetype definitions start with an asterisk.

● The description is optional, but you must precede it with a comma if you include one.

● The description can be up to 47 characters.

The second line of the linetype format defines the linetype. Each line starts with the letter A and all portions of the linetype definition are separated by commas with no spaces. The second line can be up to 80 characters. Here's the code:

● A positive number defines a dash's length in units.

● A negative number defines a space's length in units.

● A zero defines a dot.

Here's the definition for a linetype that contains two dashes and a dot. The dashes are .5 units each and the dashes and dots are separated by spaces of .25 units.

```
*twoandone, two dashes and a dot
A,.5,-.25,.5,-.25,0,-.25
```

Here you see the result. Note that AutoCAD lengthens the end dashes when the length of the line doesn't allow for another complete repetition of the linetype pattern.

Is there a quick way to create a linetype?

Yes, you can create a linetype on the fly using the command-line format of the LINETYPE command (-LINETYPE). See the question, "Is there a quick way to create a custom linetype without opening up a text file and learning all about customization?" in the "Using Layers, Colors, and Linetypes" section in Chapter 3.

I created a complex linetype with a shape, but when I use the linetype, the shape is much too large. Can I scale the shape?

Yes, you can scale, displace, and rotate a shape in a complex linetype. To create a complex linetype, you use the same definition syntax as for simple linetypes, adding the specifications for the shape or text in brackets. Within the brackets, the format for shapes is as follows:

```
[shapename, filename, details]
```

The *shapename* is the name of the shape as defined in the definition of the .SHP file. The *filename* is the name of the .SHX file.

The details let you rotate, scale, and displace both shapes and text. Table 7-3 lists these details.

In the complex linetype definition shown here, the shape is scaled to 10 percent (.1) of its original size and is displaced .1 unit downward.

```
*hedge, dash & bush shape
A,.5,-.25,[BUSH,BUSH.SHX,S=.1,Y=-.1],-.5
```

Here is the linetype. You can see that the shape would be huge without scaling:

How can I place text in a custom linetype?

The overall format for creating complex linetypes with text is the same as that for shapes. For more information, see the

Detail	Description
Relative rotation	Rotates the shape or text relative to the angle of the line. For example, R=90 would rotate the shape 90 degrees relative to the direction of the line.
Absolute rotation	Rotates the shape or text relative to the world coordinate system. The default is zero, which keeps text facing upright regardless of the direction of the line. A=180 would always create upside-down text (or an upside-down shape).
Scale	Scales the shape or text. A number less than one scales down, and a number greater than one scales up. For text, this number is multiplied by the height of the text in the text style. Use a height of 0 to allow this scale to determine the height of the text. S=.25 scales the shape or text down to one-quarter size.
X offset	Displaces the shape or text relative to the direction of the line. A positive X offset moves the shape or text toward the line's endpoint; a negative X offset moves the shape or text toward the line's start point.
Y offset	Displaces the shape or text perpendicular to the direction of the line. In a line drawn from left to right, a positive Y offset moves the shape or text upward.

Table 7-3 Details for Complex Linetype Definitions

previous question and the earlier box, "Creating Simple Custom Linetypes." The format for text in the second line of the definition is as follows:

```
["text string",text_style,details]
```

The *text string* is the text you want to display in the linetype. Place it in quotation marks. The details are explained in the answer to the previous question.

Note: *The text style must have been added to the drawing before you load the linetype.*

The linetype definition shown here includes the word "Hedge" between dashes. The text appears using the default Standard text style. The scale is set to .2. The Y offset moves the text down, centering it relative to the dashes.

```
*hedgetext, dash & hedge text
A,.5,-.25,["Hedge",STANDARD,S=.2,Y=-.1],-1.1
```

Here is a sample of the Hedgetext linetype:

———— Hedge —— Hedge —— Hedge —— Hedge ————

Note that the space after the word "Hedge" is defined as 1.1 units, while the space before the word is only .25 units. This larger space after the word is necessary to leave room for the length of the word. Getting this second space length right is a matter of trial and error.

CREATING HATCHES

Can I create a crosshatch pattern that creates checks instead of just parallel lines?

Easily, but you need to create a user-defined hatch. Follow these steps:

1. Choose Hatch from the Draw toolbar to open the Boundary Hatch dialog box, shown in Figure 7-7.

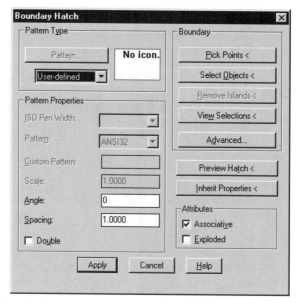

Figure 7-7 The Boundary Hatch dialog box

2. In the Pattern Type section of the dialog box, choose User-defined from the drop-down list.

3. In the Pattern Properties section of the dialog box, type an angle for the first set of parallel lines in the Angle text box.

4. In the Spacing text box, type the spacing between the lines, in units.

5. Check Double. This option is only available when you choose a User-defined hatch.

6. Choose Pick Points or Select Objects to specify the area to hatch. Press ENTER to return to the dialog box.

7. If you want to see the results before you apply the hatch, click Preview Hatch and then click Continue to return to the dialog box.

8. Click Apply to apply the hatch and close the dialog box.

AutoCAD adds a second set of lines perpendicular to the lines you defined in your user-defined hatch, as shown here:

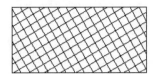

How do I use my own hatch patterns?

To use a hatch pattern that you have defined, follow these steps:

1. Save the definition in ACAD.PAT or your own file. If you use your own file, the name of the file must match the pattern name, and the extension must be .PAT. Save the file in a folder in AutoCAD's support file search path.
2. Choose Hatch from the Draw toolbar.
3. In the Boundary Hatch dialog box, choose Custom from the drop-down list in the Pattern Type section.
4. In the Pattern Properties section, type the name of the hatch pattern in the Custom Pattern text box.
5. Continue to apply the hatch as you would for any other hatch pattern.

For more information on creating hatch patterns, see the next box, "Hatch Pattern Codes."

How do I create a hatch pattern that looks like a shape?

You add additional lines to the hatch pattern definition. The relationship of these definitions can create a hatch pattern that looks like a shape.

Here's an example of a hatch pattern with two definition lines:

```
*corner, corner-shaped pattern
0, 0,0, 0,.5, .5, -.5
90, .5,0, 0,1, .25, -.25
```

Hatch Pattern Codes

Hatch patterns are a little more complex than simple linetypes, but with a little practice you can create your own useful patterns. Hatch pattern definitions have two or more lines. The syntax of the first line is as follows:

*pattern_name, description

All hatch definitions start with an asterisk. The pattern name cannot have spaces. The description is optional, but if you include it, precede it with a comma. The first line cannot exceed 80 characters.

Here's the syntax for the second line. You can add additional definition lines; they have the same syntax. End the last line with a return.

angle, x-origin,y-origin, delta-x,delta-y, dash1, dash2, …

This line must also be 80 characters or less.

Notice the spaces in the definition line. These are added for readability. By putting the x and y origins together and separating them from the delta x and y specifications, you can more easily understand the code.

Here's what the parts of the definition line mean:

- *Angle* defines the angle of the hatch lines.

- *X-origin* means the starting x coordinate of the hatch pattern. You always use 0,0 as the base point for a hatch pattern, even though the actual pattern may never be used near 0,0 in your drawing. If you want a line's starting point to be offset from the 0,0 base point, you would indicate the offset using the X-origin specification.

- *Y-origin* means the starting y coordinate of the hatch pattern. You always use 0,0 as the base point for a hatch pattern, even though the actual pattern may never be used near 0,0 in your drawing.

- *Delta-x* is the offset in units of succeeding lines from the first one. It only applies to dashed lines. The resulting effect is to stagger the dashed lines of the hatch pattern so that they don't line up.

- *Delta-y* is the distance in units between the lines of the hatch pattern. It applies to all hatch patterns. This is the same as setting the Spacing parameter in the Boundary Hatch dialog box when creating user-defined hatch patterns.

- The dash specifications are optional. You use them only if you want the hatch lines to have noncontinuous lines. The codes for the dash specifications are the same as those for linetypes. (See the box "Creating Simple Custom Linetypes," earlier in this chapter.)

Here is what this hatch pattern looks like:

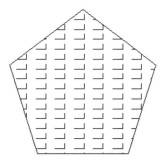

DRAWING SHAPES AND FONTS

 How do I insert shapes in a drawing?

To use a shape, follow these steps:

1. Type the shape definition in Notepad or another text editor. Add a return at the end of the definition and save the file under any name with a .SHP extension in a folder in AutoCAD's support file search path.

2. In AutoCAD, type **compile** and press ENTER.

3. Choose your file in the Select Shape or Font File dialog box and click Open. AutoCAD automatically compiles the shape (or issues you a message if there was an error in the file) and creates a corresponding .SHX file. You only

have to compile a shape once; it is then ready to load and use in all your drawings.

4. Type **load** and enter the name of the compiled shape file, or choose Browse to find it. Click Open.

5. Type **shape** and press ENTER.

6. At the "Shape name (or ?):" prompt, type the name of the shape, or type **?** and press ENTER to get a list of loaded shapes.

7. At the "Starting point:" prompt specify the insertion point for the shape.

8. At the "Height <1.0000>:" prompt, type a scale factor, or press ENTER to accept the default of 1.

9. At the "Rotation angle <0>:" prompt, type a rotation angle, or press ENTER to accept the default of 0.

AutoCAD inserts the shape. For more information on creating shapes, see the following box, "Creating Simple Shapes."

Creating Simple Shapes

The codes for shapes are much more complex than those for linetypes and hatch patterns because they give you the flexibility to create almost any shape. If you can stick to using only line segments, it's not too hard to create shapes. These instructions do not apply to shapes that you use for fonts.

A shape definition has two lines. Here's the syntax for the first line.

```
*shapenumber, numberofspecs, SHAPENAME
```

Start the definition with an asterisk. The *shapenumber* is any number between 1 and 255. The *numberofspecs* is the number of items in the second line of the definition, including the last zero. The *SHAPENAME* is the name you use to insert the shape. It should be in uppercase letters only.

The second line lists the specifications for the shape. Each line segment is separated from the others by commas, and there are no spaces. The last specification must be zero.

Both lines can have a maximum of 128 characters. Specifications are usually entered in hexadecimal format, which can define numbers up to 15. Each specification contains three numbers, as follows:

● The first number is zero, to indicate that you are using hexadecimal format.

● The second number is the length of the line segment in units.

● The third number is the direction of the line segment using the direction codes shown here:

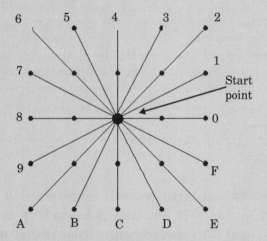

For each line segment, imagine that the start point of the line segment is at the center dot in the diagram. The endpoint of that line segment is then defined by the length and direction codes.

The confusing thing about the direction codes is that they do not represent equidistant angles around a center; instead, they are X and Y displacements. For example, direction 1 is two units in the positive X direction and one unit in the positive Y direction—or a multiple thereof. As a result, the length part of the specification is not exact if you are using any of the diagonal directions, because the line segment's endpoint "snaps" to the nearest point on the imaginary grid shown in the preceding illustration.

You cannot create lengths of less than one unit. However, you can always scale down the shape when you insert it.

Here's the code for a simple shape:

```
*5,6,ARROW
041,002,01F,019,028,0
```

The resulting shape inserted at various angles and scales is shown here:

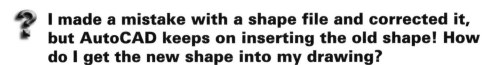

? I made a mistake with a shape file and corrected it, but AutoCAD keeps on inserting the old shape! How do I get the new shape into my drawing?

Once you use the Load command, a shape is stored in the drawing database. To update an existing shape you need to follow these steps:

1. Erase all instances of the shape in your drawing.

2. Use the PURGE command with the SH option to delete the shape from the drawing's database.

3. Recompile the .SHP file using the COMPILE command.

4. Load the new .SHX file using the LOAD command.

5. Use the SHAPE command to reinsert the shape. You will now see the new version.

How do I create a font?

Font files are created using the same codes as are shape files. However, there are some special features for shape files that define fonts:

● While a shape file may contain one shape, a font file must, of course, contain shape definitions for the entire alphabet, uppercase and lowercase, and numbers. Use one file per font.

● You start the entire file with two lines that define the font as a whole in the format shown at the end of this point. The first two codes of the first line are always as shown here. The font name is the same as the filename. *Above* defines how far above the baseline (in units) uppercase letters extend. *Below* defines how far below the baseline lowercase letters such as g or j extend. The sum of the above and below values define the total height of the font. Of course, when you use the font and provide a height, AutoCAD scales the font accordingly. *Modes* can contain only two codes—0 for a horizontal font or 2 for a font that can be used both horizontally and vertically.

```
*0,4,font_name
above,below,modes,0
```

Here's an example of the font definition lines for a font called myfont. It extends 14 units above the baseline and 7 below the baseline:

```
*0,4,myfont
14,7,0,0
```

● If you are creating a font for the Latin (English) alphabet, the *shapenumber* must correspond to the decimal (or hexadecimal) ASCII code for the character. For example, a lowercase "a" has the decimal code 97.

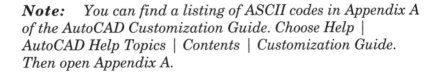

Note: *You can find a listing of ASCII codes in Appendix A of the AutoCAD Customization Guide. Choose Help | AutoCAD Help Topics | Contents | Customization Guide. Then open Appendix A.*

- The *shapename* specification is lowercase. Use it to label the character. AutoCAD's convention is "uca" for an uppercase "A" and "lca" for a lowercase "a", continuing similarly throughout the alphabet. The format for defining shapes is explained in the previous box, "Creating Simple Shapes."

- In order to be able to place lines of text one beneath the other, the linefeed character is defined as ASCII code 10.

- You need to create a space after each letter and number so that AutoCAD puts a space between characters. To do this, you need to use the *Special Codes*. Look in Chapter 3 of the AutoCAD Customization Guide under Shape Definition Files. Then choose the Shape Descriptions Topic. At the bottom of the page, choose Special Codes. Here you will find a listing of the special codes you need to use for fonts, including the pen-up and pen-down codes that let you "raise" the pen and move it to create a space after a character.

Tip: *You can find AutoCAD's SHP files for all of the fonts on the AutoCAD CD-ROM. Look in the Acad\Bonus\Fonts subfolder. Don't look in the Fonts folder. It contains only the TrueType fonts.*

Do you have any tips for creating fonts?

Sure. Draw each letter first in an AutoCAD drawing, using a 1×1 grid. Turn SNAP on with one-unit spacing. Draw the letters big enough so that no line is less than one unit long. Once you have all the letters (and numbers and other symbols that you may want) drawn, creating the shape codes is much easier. Finally, open the .TXT and Simplex .SHP files in a text editor for examples.

Chapter 8

Using AutoLISP and VBA

Answer Topics!

Using AutoLISP and VBA @ a Glance

AutoCAD supports AutoLISP, a variation of the LISP programming language. AutoLISP lets you incorporate sophisticated programs to help automate your work. AutoLISP routines must be contained in ASCII files that have a file extension of .LSP. You can find AutoLISP routines on the Internet or write your own. If you use these programs regularly, you can place them on a menu item or toolbar button for easy access, or you can set them to load and run automatically when you open a drawing.

You can also use simple AutoLISP expressions on the command line. For example, you can create a variable that will let you reuse a number or text string whenever you want in that drawing without having to retype it. You can also perform calculations when you are asked for input.

You can create your own commands using AutoLISP. They can be as simple or as detailed as you want. AutoLISP contains a special function called S::STARTUP that automatically runs whenever you start a new drawing. You can include in this function all the commands that you use to set up a drawing.

Release 14 introduced support for VBA (Visual Basic for Applications). VBA is a Microsoft programming language that lets you add programming to applications, including visual features such as dialog boxes. VBA includes an editor in which you type the code, so you don't have to use an external text editor. The great advantage of VBA is that you can use it to integrate other applications with AutoCAD. The most often used example is Microsoft Excel, which has supported VBA for several years.

LOADING AND USING AUTOLISP ROUTINES

 Where can I find good AutoLISP routines?

Lots of places! There are two magazines that specialize in AutoCAD and they usually contain AutoLISP routines. In addition, their Web sites contain vast libraries of AutoLISP routines.

● CADENCE at 800-289-0484 or www.cadence-mag.com

● CADalyst at 800-346-0085 ext. 477 or www.cadonline.com

In addition, there is an AutoCAD forum on CompuServe at GO ACAD. This forum has a large library of AutoLISP routines that you can download. Here are some of the more extensive Web sites:

Autodesk	www.autodesk.com
AutoCAD Shareware Clearinghouse	www.cadalog.com
CADsyst	www.buildingweb.com/cadsyst
CAD Shack	www.cadshack.com/support.htm
Digital Business Media	www.dbm.com.au

 Where should I put my AutoLISP routines?

You have several choices:

● You can keep them in separate .LSP files and place them in any folder in AutoCAD's support file search path. You must load each file when you want to use its routine.

● You can put them in the ACAD.LSP file, which comes with AutoCAD as an empty file. (If it doesn't exist, you create it.) AutoCAD loads ACAD.LSP automatically whenever you open a new or existing drawing.

● You can create your own "holding" .LSP file for commonly used AutoLISP routines. When you load this file, all your routines in the file are loaded at one time. This .LSP file must be in AutoCAD's support file search path.

There is another file, ACADR14.LSP, which contains some AutoCAD commands, such as BMAKE (to make blocks), DDMODIFY, DDINSERT, MVSETUP, and others. You could place routines in this file as well, because it is automatically loaded when you open a drawing. However, it makes sense to keep your own files separate from the ones that come with AutoCAD. Staying out of ACADR14.LSP ensures that you don't erase necessary AutoLISP commands!

Keep ACAD.LSP or your own .LSP file somewhere safe on a floppy disk in case you have to reinstall AutoCAD. You can then copy this file back onto your hard drive. This technique also works when you upgrade to the next release of AutoCAD.

I found an AutoLISP routine on the Internet that I hope will solve all my problems. Now, how do I use it?

This is one of the top ten frequently asked AutoCAD questions. See question #10 in Chapter 1 for the answer.

Since I upgraded from Release 13 to Release 14, my ACAD.LSP file doesn't load automatically anymore. What is the problem?

Your ACAD.LSP file is probably not in AutoCAD's support file search path. Either move it to the \Support folder in your AutoCAD folder or add the folder containing ACAD.LSP to AutoCAD's support file search path.

Note: *To add a folder to AutoCAD's support file search path, choose Tools | Preferences. On the Files tab, click the plus next to Support File Search Path. Click Add, then Browse, then locate and choose your folder.*

Can I load an AutoLISP file that is not in AutoCAD's support file search path?

Yes, you can, but you need to specify the entire path. If you type it in on the command line, there is a special format, because the backslash (\), which is usually used when specifying paths, has another meaning in AutoLISP—it tells

AutoLISP to interpret the character following the backslash literally. Therefore, you should either use a forward slash or two backslashes, as in the following examples:

```
(load "c:/lisp/repeat")
(load "c:\\lisp\\repeat")
```

Both these lines would load a file called REPEAT.LSP in the \Lisp folder on the C: hard drive.

If you use APPLOAD, you can load a file from any location using the dialog box File option.

How can I get a routine to run automatically when I start a drawing?

A special function, S::STARTUP, automatically executes whenever you open a drawing. You can combine several AutoLISP routines within this function if you want. You usually place S::STARTUP in ACAD.LSP so that it automatically loads and runs when you start a new drawing. You can use S::STARTUP to automate setting up a new drawing. Here's a sample S::STARTUP routine.

```
(defun s::startup ()
  (princ "Title block name: ")
  (setq tb (getstring))
  (command "_insert" tb "0,0" "1" "1" "0" pause pause
   pause pause)
)
```

Whenever you open a new drawing, this routine prompts you for the title block you want to insert. The routine sets the program variable *tb* to the name of the title block that you typed. It then starts the INSERT command and provides the required responses to the INSERT command's prompts, inserting the title block at 0,0 with X and Y scales of 1 and a rotation of 0. The title block was saved with four attributes: Name of drawing, Scale, Date, and Initials of drafter. Each pause prompts you for an attribute. Presumably, the values of these attributes would change with each drawing. Once you have specified the values, AutoCAD inserts the title block with the attribute text already in place. The result is shown in Figure 8-1.

Figure 8-1   This title block was automatically inserted with the attribute text in place using the S::STARTUP function of AutoLISP, placed in ACAD.LSP

As you can see, you can use the S::STARTUP function to make your drawing much more efficient.

USING AUTOLISP ON THE COMMAND LINE

 I use some hard-to-type numbers repeatedly in my drawings. Can I use AutoLISP to help?

Sure. Let's say you need to create a circle with a radius of 3.01487 and several lines of the same length. By creating a variable, you can avoid typing that long number more than once, increase your accuracy, and save time as well. A *variable* is a name that stores information that you can work with over and over.

Create the variable using the SETQ function. Let's say you want to call it "n1" (for number 1). You type the following on the command line:

```
(setq n1 3.01487)
```

AutoLISP will then repeat n1's value on the command line. To use a variable on the command line, precede it with an exclamation point. Here are some ways you can use the n1 variable:

● Start the CIRCLE command and specify the center point. At the "Diameter/<Radius>:" prompt, type **!n1** and press ENTER. AutoCAD creates a circle with a radius of 3.01487.

● Start the LINE command and specify the start point. At the "To point:" prompt, you can use Direct Distance Entry (if appropriate for your situation) and simply type **!n1** and press ENTER. AutoCAD creates a line 3.01487 units long in the direction you moved the cursor.

● Draw an object and then start the SCALE command. Specify a base point. At the "<Scale factor>/Reference:" prompt, type **!n1** and press ENTER. AutoCAD scales the object by 3.01487.

 Note: *You cannot use a variable within an expression such as a relative coordinate.*

 I sometimes need to calculate the sum of two numbers and use the result for a radius or line length. How can I do this?

You can use AutoLISP expressions wherever AutoCAD requires input. AutoLISP's syntax puts the operator (in this case the plus sign) first. Let's say you want to add 34.87 and 49.95. If you're drawing a circle, at the "Diameter/<Radius>:" prompt you can type **(+ 34.87 49.95)** and press ENTER. Don't forget the spaces between the three parts of the expression. AutoCAD creates a circle with a radius of the sum of the two numbers.

You can also use AutoLISP as a calculator. Type **(+ 34.87 49.95)** at the command line and AutoCAD displays the answer, 84.82.

 Note: *You can also use the CAL command to do calculations.*

? Can I use AutoLISP to insert text?

Under certain circumstances you can. Let's say you are approving drawing changes and need to mark certain edits with your approval, initials, and the date. Each time, you need to place "Approved EF 2/22/98" next to objects that have been edited. You can create a variable equal to that text and use it any number of times to save yourself from typing the same text over and over.

To use a variable for text, you need to use the TEXTEVAL system variable. Because text can begin with an exclamation mark or an open parenthesis, like an AutoLISP expression, you need to tell AutoCAD to evaluate the variable as an AutoLISP expression, not as text. By default, AutoCAD evaluates text literally, so that if you type **!t1** at a text prompt, AutoCAD draws the text "!t1", just as you typed it. However, if you set TEXTEVAL to 1, AutoCAD evaluates text starting with an exclamation point or an open parenthesis as an AutoLISP expression.

TEXTEVAL only works for the TEXT and ATTDEF commands. You cannot use it for the DTEXT or MTEXT commands.

Here are the steps:

1. Set TEXTEVAL to 1.

2. Create the variable. For example, you could type the following:

   ```
   (setq t1 "APPROVED EF 2/22/98")
   ```

3. Start the TEXT command.

4. Specify the insertion point, height, and rotation angle.

5. At the "Text:" prompt, type the variable preceded by an exclamation. In this example you would type the following and then press ENTER:

   ```
   !t1
   ```

AutoCAD places the entire text that is represented by the variable.

! ***Caution:*** *Don't forget to set TEXTEVAL back to 0. Most users would find it very frustrating not to be able to type text starting with an open parenthesis and would have a hard time figuring out why AutoCAD was not accepting the text.*

CREATING YOUR OWN COMMANDS

? How do I create my own AutoCAD commands with AutoLISP?

You can create your own AutoCAD commands that you can use on the command line like any other command. You can also place these commands on a menu or a toolbar button. Here's a simple example:

```
(defun c:arc-csa ()
  (command "_arc" "_c" pause pause "_a")
)
```

This code creates a command called ARC-CSA, which stands for ARC Center Start Angle. Note that it uses the underscore before the commands and options for translation into other language versions of AutoCAD. It does the following:

● Executes the ARC command

● Provides the Center option

● Pauses for you to specify the center point

● Pauses for you to specify the start point

● Provides the Angle option and lets you specify the angle

Here are some guidelines for creating your own commands:

● AutoLISP expressions are always enclosed in parentheses.

● The DEFUN function creates commands. It stands for define function.

● When you place a C: before the command's name, you can use the command on the command line in the same way you would use any other AutoCAD command.

- The two parentheses after the command name define a place where you can put variables or arguments. This routine has no variables or arguments, so there is nothing between the parentheses. However, the parentheses are required.

- Use the COMMAND function to access AutoCAD commands.

- When you use the COMMAND function, the syntax is similar to that of script files; you type out all of the command-line entry as you would if you were typing on the command line, and include spaces to replace the times you would normally press ENTER. The COMMAND function is enclosed in its own set of parentheses.

- Any text that you would type needs to be enclosed in quotation marks. Otherwise, AutoLISP assumes the text is meant to be a variable.

- When you are specifying a response to a command prompt, a double quotation mark is equivalent to entering a space or pressing the ENTER key.

- To pause for user entry within the command function, use the PAUSE function.

- When you use the DEFUN command, you enclose the rest of the routine that defines the command in parentheses. Therefore, don't forget to close the parentheses at the end of the command definition. Also, note that placing the closing parenthesis on its own line at the end of the routine is a programming convention that helps the reader more easily see that the opening and closing parentheses are a matching pair, and that one isn't missing.

I often draw red lines to mark revisions and queries. How can I automate this process?

Here's a simple AutoLISP routine that changes the current color to red, prompts you for start and end points of a line, and changes the current color back to Bylayer. You can place

short routines like this in a partial menu and draw red lines
easily whenever you need them.

```
(command "color" "red")
(command "line" pause pause "")
(command "color" "bylayer")
```

Here is a partial menu that includes these three
AutoLISP lines in a menu item. To create a red line, you
simply choose Rev Line from the UnitSolids menu. (The Rev
Line routine is contained in the last two lines of the menu.)

```
***MENUGROUP=UnitSolids
***POP1
[UnitSolids]
[1X1Cyl]^C^C_cylinder \1 1
[1x1Box]^C^C_box \1 1 1 1
[1x1Cone]^C^C_cone \1 1
[Rev Line]^C^C(command "color" "red") +
(command "line" pause pause "")(command "color" "bylayer")
```

It's best to put more complex routines in the ACAD.LSP
file, because the longer text is difficult to fit into the menu
format. To make it easy to use, you could create a new
AutoCAD command by entering (**defun c:revline** () before
the three lines shown previously for the menu, and ending
the entire routine with a closing parenthesis as shown here:

```
(defun c:revline ()
  (command "color" "red")
  (command "line" pause pause "")
  (command "color" "bylayer")
)
```

As with any other AutoLISP routine, you can place it in
its own file and load it, or add it to ACAD.LSP. You can also
place a routine that defines a command in the .MNL file. For
more information, see the box, "Putting AutoLISP Routines
in the .MNL File."

 **I use a script file to do some cleanup editing before I
plot. Can I use an AutoLISP routine instead?**

Yes, certainly. One advantage to this is that you can put a
simple routine in a menu or on a toolbar. You can also include

Putting AutoLISP Routines in the .MNL File

If you create a command using the DEFUN function with AutoLISP and want to put it on the menu, you can add it to the .MNL file that has the same name as your menu. The ACAD menu (ACAD.MNU, ACAD.MNS, ACAD.MNC) has a corresponding ACAD.MNL file. The purpose of an .MNL file is to contain AutoLISP routines for that menu. You can therefore edit the menu file to include an item with the command name you have created and include the routine in the .MNL file.

If you want to add the menu item to ACAD.MNU, add the routine to ACAD.MNL (back up ACAD.MNL first). If you want to add the menu item to a partial menu, include the menu item in the .MNU file, and create an .MNL file with the same name as the partial menu. Place the routine in the .MNL file.

The following illustration shows a partial menu that includes an AutoLISP command:

```
UnitSolids.mnu - Notepad
File   Edit   Search   Help
***MENUGROUP=UnitSolids
***POP1
[UnitSolids]
[1x1Cyl]^C^C_cylinder \1 1
[1x1Box]^C^C_box \1 1 1 1
[1x1Cone]^C^C_cone \1 1
[Rev Line]^C^Crevline
```

Here you see the corresponding .MNL file that includes the AutoLISP routine that defines the AutoLISP command:

```
UnitSolids.mnl - Notepad
File   Edit   Search   Help
(defun c:revline ()
  (command "color" "red")
  (command "line" pause pause "")
  (command "color" "bylayer")
)
```

it in ACAD.LSP so that it loads automatically. Then you can simply type the routine's command on the command line. Here's a simple example:

```
(defun c:pp ()
  (command "_chprop" "_all" "" "_c" "bylayer" "")
  (command "_-layer" "_s" "0" "_f" "approval" "")
)
```

This routine creates a command, PP (which stands for pre-plot). It uses the CHPROP command to change the color of all objects to Bylayer. It then uses the LAYER command in its command-line form (with the hyphen preceding the command) to set the current layer to 0 and to freeze the Approval layer.

When I use one of my AutoLISP routines, AutoCAD always prints nil or some other value at the end of the command line. Is there any way to stop this?

AutoLISP automatically prints out the last value it has stored on the command line. The universal way to eliminate this action is to end your routine with the PRINC function. You will see the PRINC function at the end of almost all AutoLISP routines that you download. Putting (princ) at the end of a routine is called *exiting cleanly* or *quietly*. If you are using the DEFUN function, put the (princ) as the last function before the final closing parenthesis. Here you see the routine from the previous question with the (princ) added:

```
(defun c:pp ()
  (command "_chprop" "_all" "" "_c" "bylayer" "")
  (command "_-layer" "_s" "0" "_f" "approval" "")
  (princ)
)
```

Is there any way to avoid seeing all the commands on the command line as you use an AutoLISP routine? It looks messy.

The CMDECHO system variable determines whether you see prompts and input on the command line during the COMMAND function. By default, command echoing is on. To

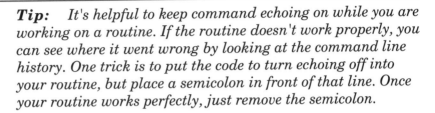

turn it off, set it to 0. You usually set CMDECHO to 0 at the beginning of a routine and turn it back on at the end.

Tip: *It's helpful to keep command echoing on while you are working on a routine. If the routine doesn't work properly, you can see where it went wrong by looking at the command line history. One trick is to put the code to turn echoing off into your routine, but place a semicolon in front of that line. Once your routine works perfectly, just remove the semicolon.*

Here you see the same routine used in the previous two questions, with the addition of two lines turning off command echoing at the beginning, and turning it off at the end of the routine. You use the SETVAR function in AutoLISP to set the value of system variables. This routine executes completely quietly, with no prompts.

```
(defun c:pp ()
  (setvar "cmdecho" 0)
  (command "_chprop" "_all" "" "_c" "bylayer" "")
  (command "_-layer" "_s" "0" "_f" "approval" "")
  (setvar "cmdecho" 1)
  (princ)
)
```

If I change system variable settings in my routine, how do I know I'm returning them to their original settings?

It's an excellent policy to make sure that you set variables back to their original settings. Here's how you do it:

● First create a variable equal to the current setting. You get the current setting using the GETVAR function.

● Then set the variable to whatever value you want. It doesn't make any difference if you are setting the system variable to its current value or changing it.

● At the end of the routine, use SETVAR again to set the system variable back to its original value, using the variable you created.

Here's how it works, using the example from the previous few questions:

```
(defun c:pp ()
  (setq echo (getvar "cmdecho"))
  (setvar "cmdecho" 0
  (command "_chprop" "_all" "" "_c" "bylayer" "")
  (command "_-layer" "_s" "0" "_f" "approval" "")
  (setvar "cmdecho" echo)
  (princ)
)
```

The second line of the routine creates a variable, *echo*, that is equal to the current value of CMDECHO. The GETVAR function gets the value, which is stored in the echo variable. The third line of the routine sets the value of CMDECHO to 0 so the routine can run quietly. After the two commands run, the SETVAR function sets the value of CMDECHO to the value of the echo variable, that is, back to its original setting.

When I use an AutoLISP expression to divide 3 by 2, I get 1 as the answer. How can I get the correct answer of 1.5?

You probably used the following expression:

```
(/ 3 2)
```

When you give AutoLISP integers, it returns integers. When you give AutoLISP numbers with decimals, called floating-point numbers, it returns numbers with decimals. Use the following expression to get the answer of 1.5:

```
(/ 3.0 2)
```

How can I get a number or some text from the person using my AutoLISP routine so that I can use it later in the routine?

There is a series of AutoLISP commands, all starting with GET, that allow you to get input from the user. Here is a list of some of the more common ones:

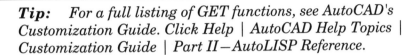

- GETINT gets an integer
- GETPOINT gets a point
- GETREAL gets a real number
- GETSTRING gets a text string

Tip: *For a full listing of GET functions, see AutoCAD's Customization Guide. Click Help | AutoCAD Help Topics | Customization Guide | Part II—AutoLISP Reference.*

Each of the GET functions lets you create a prompt that lets the user know what you are looking for.

In an earlier example, you saw a routine that created a command—REVLINE. (See the box "Putting AutoLISP Routines in the .MNL File," earlier in this chapter.) This command changed the current color to red, prompted the user for a line, and changed the color back to Bylayer. Suppose you had different levels of approval, and each person used a different color. Here's how you could modify that routine:

```
(defun c:revline ()
  (setq col (getstring "\nWhat color do you want to use? "))
  (command "color" col)
  (command "line" pause pause "")
  (command "color" "bylayer")
  (princ)
)
```

Here's how the second line of this routine works:

The GETSTRING function prompts the user, "What color do you want to use?" The \n simply places the prompt on a new line. Notice the space after the question mark. This creates a space between the prompt and the user's answer, making the answer easily distinguishable from the prompt. Then the SETQ function takes the user's response and saves it in the variable col.

Then, the third line of the routine uses the color command and sets it to the value of the variable col. Note that this will produce an error if the user types a nonexistent color.

What happens if I use the same variable in more than one routine?

Depending on how you manage variables, the value of variables may be available to other routines or restricted to one routine. You may want a variable to be limited to one routine so that you can use the same variable again in another routine without holding its previous value. Limiting a variable to one routine usually avoids confusion.

On the other hand, you may want to hold the variable's value for another routine that is run after the first routine. Careful management of variables will provide the results you want.

In the routine used in the previous example, the first line is as follows:

```
(defun c:revline ()
```

The two parentheses with nothing inside are a holding place for local variables. A *local variable* is stored only in its own routine and is not available for later use. This is often the desired result. By *declaring* the variables, that is, stating them explicitly at the beginning of the routine, you can restrict the variables to one routine.

The routine has only one variable, col. Here's how you would declare this variable:

```
(defun c:revline ( / col)
```

The space inside the parentheses actually has two purposes:

- Before the slash, you can place *arguments*. Arguments are required values that you must supply with the function. If you have only arguments, you don't need the slash.

- After the slash, you place local variables. If there are no arguments, you still need the slash.

To get a feel for how local variables work, try the following:

1. Open Notepad and type the following routine, taken from the answer to the previous question.

```
(defun c:revline ()
  (setq col (getstring "\nWhat color do you want
  to use? "))
  (command "color" col)
  (command "line" pause pause "")
  (command "color" "bylayer")
  (princ)
)
```

2. Save the file as REVLINE.LSP in AutoCAD's \Support folder or in a folder that you have placed in AutoCAD's support file search path. Don't close the file.

3. In AutoCAD, load the file by typing (**load "revline"**).

4. Type **revline** on the command line and follow the prompt to type a color and pick the line's start and end points.

5. Notice the current color in the Color Control drop-down box. It should be changed back to Bylayer.

6. On the command line, type **color** and press ENTER. At the prompt, type **!col**.

7. Check the Color Control drop-down box. AutoCAD changes the current color to the color you typed in the REVLINE command, because the variable's value is still available.

8. Return to REVLINE.LSP. This time change the first line as shown below (and as explained earlier in this answer), declaring the variable after the DEFUN statement.

```
(defun c:revline ( / col)
```

9. Save REVLINE.LSP.

10. In AutoCAD, reload REVLINE.LSP. Run the routine again.

11. On the command line, type **color** and press ENTER. At the prompt, type **!col**. This time, AutoCAD does not change the color, because the variable was restricted to the original routine.

USING VBA

 How do I get started with VBA?

VBA is Visual Basic for Applications, and to use it, the first step is to install it. If you have AutoCAD Release 14 (as opposed to Release 14.01), you have the preview version of VBA, which means that you have to install it separately.

At the time of this book's writing, AutoCAD Release 14.01 was already available, which installs VBA automatically along with AutoCAD.

 Note: *Windows NT3.51 requires Service Pack 5 to run AutoCAD VBA. Autodesk "highly" recommends you to have Service Pack 2 for Windows NT 4.0 installed before installing VBA. These service packs are available free of charge from Microsoft. The easiest way to get them is from Microsoft's Web site at www.microsoft.com.*

For more information about ActiveX Automation and VBA, see the following box.

What's the Difference Between ActiveX Automation and VBA?

ActiveX Automation is a Microsoft facility to make objects in one application available for use in other applications.

VBA is a programming language included in AutoCAD and many Microsoft applications.

In order to use ActiveX Automation, you need a programming language, but it doesn't have to be VBA—other options include C++ and Delphi. But since AutoCAD includes VBA, you already have the tools you need to create programs that access objects in other applications.

Installing VBA

To install VBA in Release 14, put the AutoCAD CD-ROM in your CD-ROM drive. Run SETUP.EXE from the \Vbainst folder. (In Windows 95 and NT 4.0, choose Start | Run and type **d:\vabinst\setup** where *d* is your CD-ROM drive.) The next time you start AutoCAD, you will have a new pull-down menu, called VBA, shown here:

The VBA environment has only four commands that you can use within AutoCAD, listed here:

Command	Use
VBAIDE	Opens the VBA integrated development environment (IDE), where you can create dialog boxes and write code.
VBALOAD	Loads an existing VBA routine into the VBA IDE.
VBAUNLOAD	Unloads a VBA routine.
VBARUN	Runs a VBA routine. Type **-vbarun** to avoid the dialog box.

Starting a VBA Routine

To start a new routine or edit one you've already written, choose VBA | Show VBA IDE. In Release 14.01, you start using VBA on the command line—type **vbaide**. (IDE stands for integrated development environment.)

In either release, you see the VBA environment. It is a new window with its own button on the Windows taskbar. To start a new project, choose Insert | Module from the pull-down menu. AutoCAD opens a text editor window. Figure 8-2 shows the VBA IDE with a new, blank module window.

Where is AutoCAD? Go down to the taskbar and click the AutoCAD button to return to your drawing. You can also press ALT+F11, choose View | AutoCAD from the menu, or

Menu →
Toolbar →

Project window →

Properties window →

Module text editor →

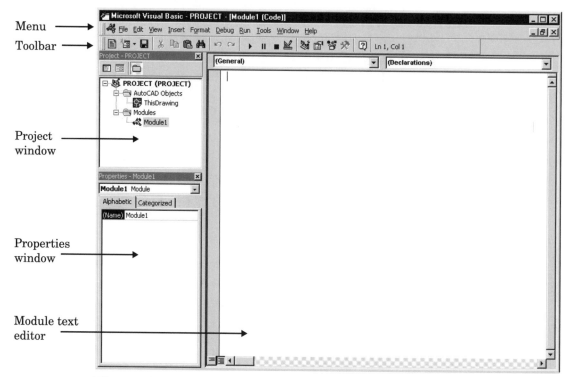

Figure 8-2 The VBA environment contains all the tools you need to start working with VBA

click View AutoCAD, the first button on the Standard toolbar of the VBA IDE.

Getting Help

Because VBA is applicable to many applications, AutoCAD provides several types of help, but all the options can be confusing. VBA is an object-oriented language, which means that the main focus is on objects. You can find lists of objects that apply not only to AutoCAD, but to Windows, Excel, Word, and so on.

A good point for getting started is to look at the Object Browser, a list of objects. Click the Object Browser button on the toolbar or choose View | Object Browser. At the top of the Object Browser list is a drop-down list that by default says All Libraries. Click this list to see the available libraries. To start working with AutoCAD objects, choose AutoCAD from the drop-down list. You see the list shown in Figure 8-3.

Objects are often combined into collections of objects, so that you can manipulate the collections as a whole. Objects have properties and methods. Some properties that would apply to a circle, for example, are color, area, and center. You use methods to perform actions on objects. For example, you can copy, erase, or move a circle. Most objects also have their own Add method, such as AddCircle, that you use to create that object. From the Object Browser you can explore the lists of objects and find out what methods and properties apply to specific objects. For example, click |AcadCircle, as shown in Figure 8-3. The right window, Members of '|AcadCircle', lists the methods and properties of a circle.

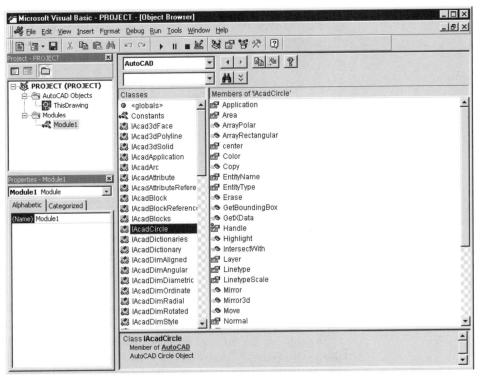

Figure 8-3 The AutoCAD library of the Object Browser lists AutoCAD objects that you can use for VBA programming

To get information on the |AcadCircle object, click it in the Object Browser and click the Help button in the Object Browser window. (Don't click the Help button on the Standard toolbar, because that brings you to Microsoft VBA Help, which is generic to all applications that support VBA.) AutoCAD opens its AutoCAD Automation Reference on the Circle Object page. Here you get a description of the circle object and a list of all the properties and methods that apply to that object. You can click any item to jump to that item's description.

If you choose Color, for example, you see the Help page for the color property, as shown in Figure 8-4.

Notice the link to Example at the top of the page in Figure 8-4. Here is the real treasure. Click Example to find sample code that you can use or modify for your own purposes, as shown in Figure 8-5.

All in all, there are three manuals:

● The AutoCAD Automation User's Guide (ACAD_AG.HLP) covers ActiveX Automation concepts and techniques.

● The AutoCAD Automation Reference (ACADAUTO.HLP) describes every object, method, and property.

● The VBA online manual (ACADVBA.HLP) provides information on the VBA environment. To access this help, choose Help from the VBA IDE menu, or click the question mark on the VBA IDE toolbar.

The first two manuals are accessible from within AutoCAD.

Understanding the Hierarchy Model

Objects come in a hierarchy. To see this structure, choose any object from the Object Browser and click Help from the Object Browser's toolbar. On the resulting page, choose Objects | Object Model. You will see the diagram shown in Figure 8-6.

To access an object, method, or property, you lay out the hierarchy in your code, separating each item by periods. For

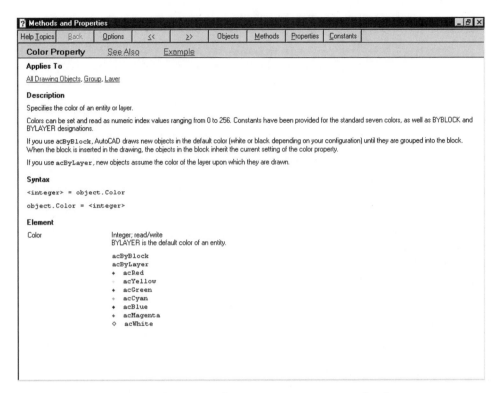

Figure 8-4 You can find Help for any property or method

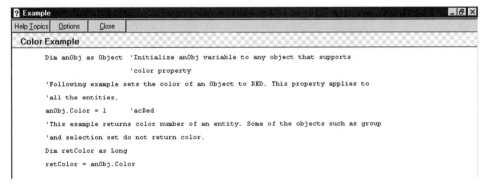

Figure 8-5 Every method and property has sample code—a great learning tool

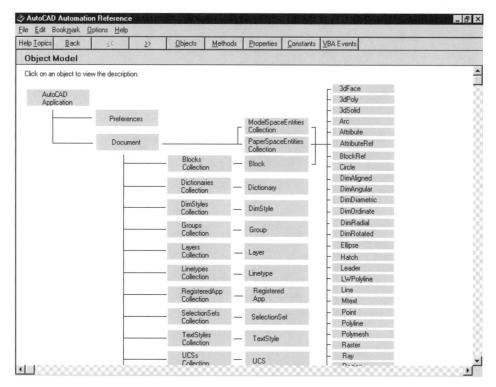

Figure 8-6   VBA objects are structured in a hierarchy

example, here is some code taken from one of AutoCAD's sample VBA routines.

```
Set AcadObj = GetObject(, "AutoCAD.Application")
Set aline = AcadObj.ActiveDocument.ModelSpace.AddLine
(startPoint, endPoint)
```

In this code, you create the variable AcadObj to get the object "AutoCAD.Application." Then you create a variable, *aline*, to create the line. The start and end points must already have been specified. Here you can see that:

● ActiveDocument is an object of AutoCAD.Application

● ModelSpace is an object of ActiveDocument

● AddLine is a method of ActiveDocument

For a short tutorial to create your first VBA routine, see the following question.

 Tip: *These two books on Visual Basic, which is the starting point for VBA, will help you get started programming:* Visual Basic from the Ground Up, *by Gary Cornell, and* Visual Basic Programmer's Reference, *by Dan Rahmel. Both are published by Osborne/McGraw-Hill.*

How can I draw a circle with VBA?

To create an entire routine with VBA, you generally create a dialog box and then attach code to the dialog box buttons. Finally, you display the dialog box. The following routine draws a circle whose center is 5,5 and whose radius is 2. Of course, it would be a lot faster to just use the CIRCLE command to draw the circle, but by creating an entire routine from scratch, you will get an overview of the process required to create more useful routines.

Follow these steps:

1. Choose VBA | Show VBA IDE or type **vbaide** on the command line.

2. Right-click the space in the Project window and choose Project Name. In the dialog box, type **DrCircle** and click OK.

3. From the Standard toolbar of the VBA IDE, choose Insert UserForm. The user form will become a dialog box. If necessary, drag the Toolbox so it doesn't cover the Project Window. Your screen should look like Figure 8-7.

4. Notice that the Properties box now lists UserForm1 and all its properties. Find the Name property at the top of the list. In the right column, change the name to **formCircle**.

5. Find the Caption property. Double-click the right column, which now says UserForm1, and type **Draw a Circle**. The caption in the user form dynamically changes as you type.

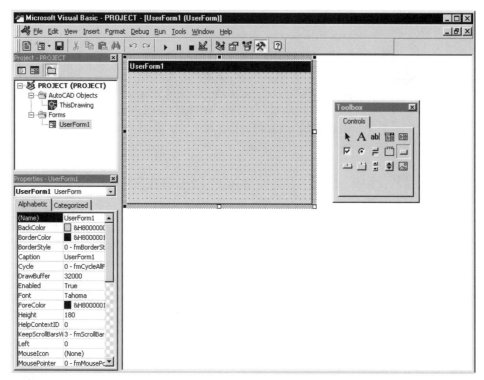

Figure 8-7 The VBA IDE after inserting a user form

 Note: *If the Toolbox disappears, click any blank area of your screen.*

6. Click the CommandButton button on the Toolbox window. (It's at the end of the second row of controls.) Move the cursor to the user form and drag to create a large button across the center of the user form.

7. Click the CommandButton button on the Toolbox window again, and drag a smaller button below the first one. Your user form should look something like Figure 8-8.

8. Click the big button once. Notice that its properties now appear in the Properties box. Change its caption to **Draw Circle**.

9. Click the smaller button and change its caption to **Escape**.

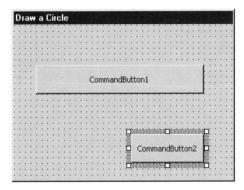

Figure 8-8 A user form with two buttons

10. To create the code attached to the big button, double-click it. The text editor opens with the first part of your code already created for you.

11. Now that you've gotten this far, you should save your project. Choose Save from the Standard toolbar of the VBA IDE. In the Save VBA Project As dialog box, you may notice that installing VBA has added a folder, \Vbasamp. (You may also have a backup folder, \Vbabkup.) Double-click the \Vbasamp folder to add your project to that folder, which contains some VBA samples (or place the project in another folder in AutoCAD's support file search path). Name the project **DrCircle** in the File name text box. Notice that VBA projects have the extension .DVB.

At the cursor, type the following:

```
'Define Variables & Data Types
Dim cen(0 To 2) As Double
Dim radius As Double
Dim dcircle As Object
Dim acadObj As Object

'Specify Data
cen(0) = 5#
cen(1) = 5#
cen(2) = 0#
```

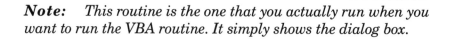

```
    radius = 2

'Object Calls
  Set acadObj = GetObject(, "AutoCAD.Application")
  Set dcircle = acadObj.ActiveDocument.ModelSpace.
    AddCircle(cen, radius)
    Unload Me
```

✳ **Note:**   *The text editor provides some assistance as you type, and color-codes the text.*

> This code defines the variables, sets the center point and radius of the circle, gets the AutoCAD application, and adds a circle with the specified center and radius. When defining variables, it is advisable to declare the data type. To easily determine the best data type for a radius, for example (which is Double), open the Object Browser, choose |AcadCircle from the AutoCAD library, choose Radius, and then click Help.

12. You could return to the form by double-clicking it in the Project window and then double-clicking the second button, but there's an easier way. At the top of the text editor, click the left drop-down list that says CommandButton1 and choose CommandButton2. VBA starts a routine for the second button for you.

13. In the blank line already provided by the text editor between the beginning and the end of the second routine, type **Unload Me**.

14. From the VBA IDE menu, choose Insert | Module. You will see a new text editor. Type the following. (Again, the text editor will help you out.)

```
Sub DrCircle()
    formCircle.Show
End Sub
```

✳ **Note:**   *This routine is the one that you actually run when you want to run the VBA routine. It simply shows the dialog box.*

15. In the Project window, change the module's name to **modCircle**.

16. Click Save on the Standard toolbar and save the .DVB file again. Note that there is no quick save, although the current name appears as the default in the dialog box. You have to replace the file explicitly each time you save.

17. To run the routine, return to AutoCAD by clicking the View AutoCAD button at the left of the Standard toolbar. Since the routine draws a circle whose center is at 5,5,0, make sure that this coordinate is visible on your screen. Choose VBA | Run Macro, or type **vbarun**. Choose modCircle and click Run. The dialog box appears.

18. Click the Draw Circle button. The VBA routine draws the circle and the dialog box disappears.

Congratulations! You've created a VBA routine. Now it's simply a matter of doing some reading and lots of practicing, and soon you'll be able to create routines that save you time and increase your efficiency.

How do I use a VBA program that I find on the Internet or in a magazine?

If the program is already in .DVB format, you can copy it to any folder in AutoCAD's support file search path, load it with VBARUN, and run it. However, often what you see are snippets of code that need to be completed. In that case, you need to create a project using the code and save it before you can run it.

Can I get a VBA program to automatically run when I open AutoCAD?

If you write VBA code and save it as ACAD.DVB, AutoCAD will automatically load it when you open AutoCAD.

However, VBA itself only runs when you use a VBA command. To run VBA and the VBA program, follow these steps:

1. If you have an existing VBA project, open it and save it as ACAD.DVB. Remember the name of the routine.

2. Make sure ACAD.DVB is in AutoCAD's support file search path. In Release 14, AutoCAD adds a folder \Vbasamp, but does not automatically add it to the search path.

3. Add the following code to ACAD.LSP. If you already have some code under S::STARTUP, just add the second line of the following code to the end of the existing code (before the final closing parenthesis).

```
(defun S::STARTUP ()
  (COMMAND "-VBARUN" "drawcircle")
)
```

In this example, *drawcircle* is the name of the Sub, as in the example in the earlier question, "How can I draw a circle with VBA?" AutoCAD automatically loads and runs drawcircle. You use the command-line form of VBARUN to avoid opening a dialog box.

 Note: *If the VBA project runs by displaying a dialog box and requires you to click a button, you will still have to click the button to run the routine.*

 ## How do you modify an object?

While a complete discussion of this topic is not possible in this book, here you see some code that draws a line. It is very similar to the code in the earlier question, "How can I draw a circle with VBA?," except that it draws a line instead of a circle. After drawing the line, it changes the line's color to red. The first line refers to a button in a dialog box that the user clicks to run the program and draw the line.

```
Private Sub DrawRevLine_Click()
'Define Variables & Data Types
 Dim startpt(0 To 2) As Double
 Dim endpt(0 To 2) As Double
 Dim line As Object
 Dim acadObj As Object

 'Specify Data
 startpt(0) = 5#
```

```
startpt(1) = 5#
startpt(2) = 0#
endpt(0) = 8#
endpt(1) = 8#
endpt(2) = 0#

'Object Calls
Set acadObj = GetObject(, "AutoCAD.Application")
Set line = acadObj.ActiveDocument.ModelSpace.AddLine
(startpt, endpt)
line.Color = 1 'acRed
line.Update
Unload Me
End Sub
```

How do I create variables in VBA?

You usually create variables by declaring them at the beginning of a routine, using the DIM statement. You usually state the type of variable as well.

Here's a declaration statement that creates a variable named Radius. The variable type is Double. The variable types are listed below.

```
Dim Radius As Double
```

You can create different levels of variables:

● If you place the declaration within a procedure, the variable can be used only in that procedure.

● If you place the declaration at the top of a module, in the Declarations section, the variable is a module-level variable and can be used in all procedures in the module.

● If you use the Public statement, the variable is available to all procedures in the project, as in the following example.

```
Public Radius As Double
```

You are not required to declare your variables in advance; you can declare them *implicitly* by just using them in a statement. However, implicitly declared variables are of the variable type *variant,* which uses more memory. Another reason to explicitly declare a variable is that VBA checks the

variable's spelling as you use it later, reducing the chance for spelling errors.

Variable names can't be longer than 255 characters and must start with an alphabetic character. You can't use the same variable name more than once within the variable's level.

Variables can be of the following types:

- **Boolean**   Can have only two values, True or False
- **Byte**   Can hold positive integers from 0 to 255
- **Integer**   Can hold integers from –32,768 to +32,768
- **Long**   Can hold integers from –2,147,483,648 to +2,147,483,648
- **Currency**   Can hold values in the following range: –922,337,203,685,477.5808 to +922,337,203,685,477.5807. Used for currency and when accuracy to several decimals is important.
- **Single**   Stores single-precision floating-point variables. Single variables use less memory than double variables but are more limited in their values.
- **Double**   Stores double-precision floating-point variables. Most numbers that do not need to be integers are double data types. Coordinates are created by using three doubles for the x, y, and z values.
- **Date**   Stores dates and times as real numbers. The number to the left of the decimal point represents the date and the number to the right of the decimal point represents the time.
- **String (for variable-length strings)**   Stores text strings. Can include letters, numbers, spaces, and punctuation. Can be both fixed length and variable length.
- **Object**   Stores objects such as an application, a drawing, or an object in a drawing
- **Variant**   The default variable type. Can contain numbers, dates, or strings. Any variable for which you do not declare a type becomes a variant variable, which takes up more resources.

Is there any way to integrate VBA and AutoLISP?

You cannot completely integrate VBA and AutoLISP. These two programming languages are very different systems of customizing AutoCAD. However, you can run a VBA routine from an AutoLISP routine, using the VBARUN function. For example,

```
(command "_-vbarun" "drawcircle")
```

You need both the underscore and the hyphen before the VBARUN function.

Can I put a VBA program on a menu or a toolbar button?

By using the VBARUN function, you can use an AutoLISP routine to run a VBA routine. You can then put that AutoLISP routine on a menu or attach it as a toolbar button macro.

Glossary

ADI An acronym for AutoCAD Device Interface, an Autodesk standard for drivers for printers, video display, plotters, etc. An ADI lets AutoCAD communicate with peripheral devices on your computer.

ADS An acronym for AutoCAD Development System, a programming tool that lets you create programs that work directly with AutoCAD. ADS has been generally superseded by ARX in Release 14.

Aerial View A window allowing you to instantly view and pan.

alias A shortened version of an AutoCAD command name. You can customize the ACAD.PGP file or use the Alias Editor to create your own aliases.

annotation Text, dimensions, tolerances, attributes, or notes in a drawing.

API An acronym for *application programming interface*, which means any programming environment that works directly with an application, in this case AutoCAD. ARX and ADS are examples of APIs.

ARX An acronym for AutoCAD Runtime Extension, a programming environment utilizing C++ that lets you develop your own standalone programs that work directly with AutoCAD.

ASE   An acronym for AutoCAD SQL Environment, a feature that enables you to access and modify external databases from within AutoCAD.

associative   Related to its applicable objects. Dimensions and hatches are associative, meaning that they are appropriately modified when you modify the objects to which they're related.

attribute   Text attached to a block. An attribute can be given a specific value each time you insert the block. The values can be extracted and turned into a database. Attributes are also used for precisely placing text in the same location multiple times, as in a title block.

audit   The AUDIT command examines the integrity of the current drawing and tries to correct errors. Use AUDIT to test for possible corruption of data in drawings that you can open.

AutoCAD SQL Environment   *See* ASE.

AutoLISP   An uncompiled programming language that you use to program AutoCAD.

B-spline   A curve defined by specified control points; also called a NURBS curve. *See* spline.

Bezier curve   A kind of B-spline curve.

bind   To turn an external reference (xref) into a block.

bitmap   A type of graphic consisting of dots or pixels.

blips   Marks on the screen that remain where you picked a point. REDRAW removes blips. BLIPMODE must be on (a value of 1) for blips to be displayed.

block   A named object consisting of one or more component objects.

Boolean operation The process of adding, subtracting, or overlapping 3-D solids or 2-D regions.

boundary A closed region or polyline.

bump map A 2-D image that uses changes in brightness to simulate bumps when placed on a 3-D object during rendering.

button A button can refer to the buttons on a mouse or puck or the tools on a toolbar. You can customize both types of buttons.

ByBlock An object property specifying that the object takes its color and linetype from the block that contains it.

ByLayer An object property specifying that the object takes its color and linetype from its layer definition.

calibration Used with a digitizer, the specification of an exact relationship between the digitizer's surface and the actual size of the objects in a drawing. Used to trace hard-copy drawings into AutoCAD to convert them to computerized drawings.

Cartesian coordinate system A system of defining coordinates using three perpendicular X, Y, and Z axes.

chamfer To bevel (cut at an angle) the edge or corner of an object.

chord A line connecting two points on a circle or arc.

clipping planes Front and back planes that cut off the view in a perspective or parallel view, created with the DVIEW command.

command line The mechanism for inputting AutoCAD commands, options, coordinates, or values from the keyboard.

control points Points that AutoCAD creates to define a spline curve.

coordinate filter *See* point filter.

crosshairs A cross-shaped cursor used to locate points and objects in a drawing.

cylindrical coordinates Coordinates in the format *distance<angle, distance* where the first distance is the units in the XY plane, the angle is the angle from the X axis in the XY plane, and the second distance is the units in the Z direction.

digitizer An electronic tablet that allows you to draw and execute commands. You use a puck, which is similar to a mouse but has the ability to provide exact point specification. While a digitizer is usually used for regular drawing and issuing commands, its special purpose is to let you digitize paper drawings—turning them into AutoCAD drawing files.

direct distance entry A way to enter a second point just by typing the distance. You indicate the direction by moving the cursor in the desired direction. For example, you can draw a horizontal line by specifying the first point, moving the cursor horizontally, and typing the line's length at the "To point:" prompt.

DWF An acronym for Drawing Web Format, a compressed file format that lets you display drawings on the Web without making available the actual drawing objects.

DXF An acronym for Drawing Interchange Format, a text file format that contains all the data in a drawing. You can use DXF files to import or export drawings between CAD programs.

elevation The current z coordinate at which all objects are drawn. By default, elevation is 0. You can set the current elevation (and thickness) using the ELEV command.

entity AutoCAD's original term for an object. You still see the term "entity" in programming environments. For example, the AutoLISP function ENTSEL lets the user select an object. It stands for *entity select*.

environment   The location of, and settings for, other files on which AutoCAD depends, such as ACAD.DWT (the drawing template). In the context of AutoCAD's SQL environment, an environment is the entire database system including the database management program and the actual databases.

explode   To break complex objects, such as blocks, into their component objects.

external reference (xref)   Another drawing file that is referenced in your file, creating a link between the two. You can see and snap to objects in the xref.

fence   A set of temporary lines that you use to select objects. AutoCAD selects all objects that cross the fence.

fillet   To round the edge or corner of an object.

fit points   Points that you specify to define a spline curve.

floating viewport   A border that displays various viewpoints and/or zoomed views of your drawing. Floating viewports are created in paper space with TILEMODE off. They are used to lay out a drawing for plotting and are especially useful for 3-D drawing. You can move, resize, and delete floating viewports; they are actual objects in your drawing. You can also freeze their layer to hide the viewport border.

flyout   A submenu for a toolbar. When you click the top toolbar button, the flyout appears, displaying more buttons.

freeze   To set a layer's mode so that the layer is not displayed, regenerated, or plotted.

grid   A rectangular grid of regularly spaced dots that cover the screen. The grid can help you judge the size of objects. You can set the spacing between the grid dots using the GRID command.

grips   Small square handles that appear on an object when you select it. Click the grip to make it hot. You can use the hot grip to move, scale, rotate, mirror, copy, or stretch objects.

group   A named set of objects that you can modify together.

hatch   A pattern of lines that fills a closed area. Its purpose is to indicate shading or texture. Release 14 introduced solid fills.

hide   To remove from display any surfaces that would be hidden from a certain 3-D viewpoint. Hiding creates a more realistic display and lets you visualize your 3-D model more clearly.

image   A raster or bitmap graphic. AutoCAD can import images in several file formats, including BMP, TIF, RLE, JPG, GIF, and TGA.

island   An enclosed area within a hatch area; for example, a small circle within a big circle. You can set AutoCAD to either hatch or not hatch these internal islands.

isolines   Lines that AutoCAD uses to show the edge of a surface from a certain point of view. You can set the number of isolines that AutoCAD uses with the ISOLINES system variable.

layer   A mechanism for organizing your drawing by color and linetype. Every layer has a name, and every object must be on a layer.

linetype   A type of line. The linetype specifies whether the line is continuous or formed of dots, dashes, and spaces. A linetype is one of the two important properties of a layer. (The other is color.)

mass properties   Properties of an object that has volume. You use the MASSPROP command to calculate these properties. Some of the properties are center of gravity, centroid, moments of inertia, products of inertia, and radii of gyration.

materials For rendering, properties attached to objects that give the objects color, reflection, transparency, roughness, and refraction. Materials make objects look realistic in the rendering process.

mesh A set of polygons that create faces representing a surface. You define the surface by specifying the vertices of the mesh.

method In Visual Basic for Applications (VBA) programming, an action that you can perform on an object, such as Copy or Move.

model A 2-D or 3-D representation of a real object (or potentially real object) in your drawing.

model space A three-dimensional coordinate space where you create models; the space where you draw models to real-world scale. *See also* paper space.

node A point. You use the Node object snap to snap to a point.

normal A line perpendicular to a plane or surface.

NURBS An acronym for *nonuniform rational B-spline*, a B-spline curve defined by a series of control points.

object Anything that is considered to be one element in your drawing, such as a line, a circle, or a line of text. An object is the same as an entity.

object snap A geometric point on an object that you can select; for example, endpoints, intersections, and circle quadrants. Also called an osnap.

OLE An acronym for Object Linking and Embedding, a way of inserting data from another application into your current application, in this case AutoCAD. Objects can be embedded with or without a link to the original file.

ortho mode A setting that restricts drawing to the horizontal and vertical directions.

orthogonal Having perpendicular intersections; being at a right angle to another object.

paper space A drawing mode used for laying out a drawing for plotting, with TILEMODE off. In paper space, you create floating viewports with different views of your drawing.

parallel view A way of viewing a 3-D object without showing perspective, using the DVIEW command.

partial menu A small, customized menu that you create and insert into the regular AutoCAD menu. It usually contains just one or two menu headings. You load a partial menu with the MENULOAD command.

perspective view A view of a 3-D model that shows perspective, so that parallel lines appear to merge in the distance.

pixel Short for picture element. Pixels are the dots that make up a picture on your computer screen. Certain graphics programs allow you to change objects by changing them pixel by pixel.

plan view The view of a model looking from above. Plan view is the only possible view for 2-D objects, but just one of many possible views for 3-D objects.

point filter A filter that locates a coordinate by filtering out X, Y, and Z coordinates from existing points in your drawing. Also called a coordinate filter.

polyline A group of lines and arcs that are one object. You can draw 2-D and 3-D polylines. 3-D polylines cannot contain arcs.

primitive A basic 3-D shape—a box, wedge, cone, cylinder, sphere, or torus. AutoCAD can draw both surface and solid primitives.

profile A profile is a set of user preferences that you can save and use when desired. A profile is also a display of only the edges and silhouettes of a solid's curved surface in the current view.

property   In Visual Basic for Applications (VBA) programming, an attribute of an object, such as Color or Layer.

purge   To delete from the drawing database all unused symbols, such as blocks, layers, linetypes, shapes, and text styles. Purging a drawing reduces the drawing's size.

raster image   A graphic image created by changing digital information into a series of dots. A bitmap.

ray   A construction line with one endpoint, and which extends infinitely in the opposite direction.

redraw   To refresh the screen, thereby getting rid of blip marks and stray remains of editing commands.

reflection   Highlights created by light on a surface when rendering.

region   A closed 2-D area.

render   To display a model in a photorealistic manner.

resolution   The number of pixels displayed on a computer screen, or the number of dots per inch printed by a printer. The higher the resolution, the clearer the image.

right-hand rule   A system to determine the direction of the positive Z axis. It is also used to determine the direction of positive rotation for certain commands. Place the back of your right hand near the screen and point your thumb in the direction of the positive X axis. Point your index finger up in the direction of the positive Y axis. The direction of your other fingers is the direction of the positive Z axis, or the direction of positive rotation.

ruled surface   A surface created between two curves, or between a point and a curve, using the RULESURF command.

running object snap An object snap that stays on until you turn it off. You set running object snaps using the DDOSNAP command. You can then use the OSNAP button on the status bar to turn all the running object snaps on and off as needed.

schema A set of database tables, used in accessing external databases.

script A set of commands that run one after the other automatically. Usually called a macro in other applications. A script file is a text file, with the filename extension .SCR, that contains the commands. You use the SCRIPT command to run a script from within AutoCAD. You can also run a script on a number of drawings by starting it from the command-line expression that you use to open AutoCAD.

selection set The group of selected objects.

shape An object that you define using special codes, used to create simple but repeatedly used shapes or fonts. Shapes are compiled and then loaded into a drawing before you can use them. You create the shape codes in a text file with the filename extension .SHP.

snap A drawing mode that restricts the cursor jumps to points on an invisible grid. You can set the spacing using the SNAP command.

solid A 3-D object that contains volume.

spherical coordinates A type of coordinate in the format *distance<angle<angle*. The distance is the total number of units from the origin or the last point. The first angle is the angle from the X axis in the XY plane. The second angle is the angle from the XY plane in the Z direction.

spline A smooth curve passing through, or near, fit points that you specify. AutoCAD uses a particular kind of spline called a NURBS (nonuniform rational B-spline) curve.

support file search path The folders that AutoCAD looks in for support files, such as fonts, hatch patterns, linetypes, AutoLISP files, etc. You can add folders to the support file search path using the Files tab of the Preferences dialog box.

surface A topological 2-D area defined in 3-D space. Surfaces don't have volume, but you can hide and render them.

system variable A setting that stores modes and values that affect the way AutoCAD functions. By changing system variables, you can change the way many commands and features function. Some system variables are read-only, which means that you cannot change their values.

tabulated surface A kind of ruled surface, defined by a curve and a line or polyline.

template A file with the filename extension .DWT that AutoCAD uses as a basis for opening a new drawing. You can save many of the usual drawing settings in a template to reduce the time spent setting up a drawing, such as unit type, limits, text styles, dimension styles, etc. A template can also be a file used to specify block attribute data for extraction.

temporary files AutoCAD creates temporary files during a drawing session. These files usually are closed when you exit, but if your system crashes, they may be left on your hard disk. After closing AutoCAD, you can delete them. By default they have a filename extension of .AC$ and are stored in the \Temp folder of your \Windows folder.

tessellation lines Lines used to help display a curved surface.

thickness An extrusion into the third dimension. Giving a 2-D object a thickness turns it into a surface in 3-D space.

tiled viewport A bordered view of a drawing created in model space. Tiled viewports divide up the screen completely. They are used for drawing and editing when you want to see more than one view of your drawing at one time.

ToolTip   The description of a toolbar button's command, which you see when you hold the cursor over the button for a couple of seconds.

tracking   A method of locating a point, based on the coordinates of existing points. Used in 2-D drawing only.

transparent command   A command that can be used within another command. If you are typing the command on the command line, place an apostrophe before the command name.

UCS   An acronym for *user coordinate system*, a coordinate system that you define by specifying where (relative to the world coordinate system) the origin is, as well as the direction of the X, Y, and Z axes.

unit   The distance used for measuring purposes. The unit is the basis of all coordinates. You can set the unit equal to inches or millimeters when you plot the drawing.

user coordinate system   *See* UCS.

VBA   An acronym for Visual Basic for Applications, a programming language supported by AutoCAD.

vector   An object with direction and length, such as a line.

viewpoint   A location in 3-D from which you view your drawing.

viewport   A rectangular boundary that contains all or part of your drawing. There are two kinds of viewports: floating and tiled. *See also* floating viewport; tiled viewport.

Visual Basic for Applications   *See* VBA.

WCS   An acronym for *world coordinate system*, the default coordinate system that is the basis for all other coordinate systems that you define.

WHIP! viewer   A program that lets you view DWF files on a Web site. With the WHIP! viewer you can zoom, pan, and print.

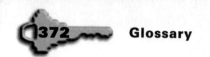

wireframe A representation of a 3-D object, using lines and arcs. A wireframe has no volume and cannot be hidden or rendered.

world coordinate system *See* WCS.

xline A construction line that extends infinitely in both directions.

xref *See* external reference.

Index

TECHNICAL SOFTWARE
Guaranteed Results.

Like what you've heard from the AutoCAD experts who wrote this book?

Well, keep reading...

Technical Software, Inc. is Ohio's premier provider of computer-aided engineering software, training, and consulting services. We're also one of Autodesk's oldest, largest, and most recognized dealers. But did you know we've actually been around longer than Autodesk itself? Here's the rest of the story:

In 1982, Greg Malkin was ready to launch his own business. Armed with a business plan based on a mail-order catalog of engineering software, Greg did his first customer demo on a desk in the corner of his bedroom. It was there that he met with many customers for the first time—customers who continue to work with us today.

Time went by; Autodesk appeared on the scene, and *Cadalyst* magazine was published for the first time. In 1986, **Technical Software, Inc.** moved out of the house and into a real office. TSI started hosting the Northeast Ohio AutoCAD User Group, which has continued to bring in new members each year. In 1988, AutoCAD Release 10 was on the market and business was beginning to boom. In 1990, TSI launched the national AutoCAD Helpline℠. From 1991–1997, the company received more awards than our offices could hold—so we moved again. We started writing *Cadalyst*'s popular "Dr. Debug" column, and we took our show on the road in a series of national training classes.

So, what's up with TSI today? We're still growing in the mechanical, AEC, GIS, and education markets. We're helping our customers achieve their goals with networking, document management, and strategic technology planning services, and we're always looking for talented people to join us. We offer big-company experience in a small-company setting, along with a fun and challenging work environment. If you'd like to learn more about TSI and help us write future chapters of the company's history, we'd like to hear from you.

Here's how to reach us:

Technical Software, Inc.
23550 Commerce Park
Cleveland, OH 44122
phone: 216/765-1133
fax: 216/765-1703
email: ellenm@techsoftware.com